Your John

THE CUTTING EDGE
Lesbian Life and Literature

THE CUTTING EDGE
Lesbian Life and Literature

Series Editor: Karla Jay

THE CUTTING EDGE
Lesbian Life and Literature

Series Editor: *Karla Jay*
Professor of English and Women's Studies
PACE UNIVERSITY

EDITORIAL BOARD

Ann Allen Shockley, Librarian
FISK UNIVERSITY

Elizabeth Wood
Musicologist and Writer
Committee on Theory and Culture
NEW YORK UNIVERSITY

Bonnie Zimmerman
Women's Studies
SAN DIEGO STATE UNIVERSITY

Your John

The Love Letters of Radclyffe Hall

EDITED AND WITH AN INTRODUCTION BY

Joanne Glasgow

NEW YORK UNIVERSITY PRESS
New York and London

NEW YORK UNIVERSITY PRESS
New York and London

Library of Cogress Cataloging-in-Publication Data
Hall, Radclyffe.
Your John : the love letters of Radclyffe Hall / edited by Joanne
Glasgow.
   p.   cm.—(The cutting edge)
Includes bibliographical references and index.
ISBN 0-8147-3092-2 (alk. pap.)
   1. Hall, Radclyffe—Correspondence.   2. Women authors,
English—20th century—Correspondence.   3. Lesbians—Great Britain—
Correspondence.   4. Love-letters.   5. Souline, Evguenia,
1904-1958?—Correspondence.   I. Grasgow, Joanne, 1943–
II. Title.   III. Series: Cutting edge (New York, N.Y.)
PR6015.A33Z494   1996
823'.912—dc20   96-35603
[B]   CIP

New York University Press books are printed on acid-free paper,
and their binding materials are chosen for strength and durability.

Manufactured in the United States of America

10   9   8   7   6   5   4   3   2   1

4698-48

Contents

All illustrations appear as a group after p. 116.

Acknowledgments

This edition of Radclyffe Hall's letters would not have been possible without the generous help and support of many people. For their professionalism, helpful suggestions, and wonderful humor, I wish to thank the librarians and staff of the Harry Ransom Humanities Research Center at the University of Texas at Austin, especially Catherine Henderson and Patricia Fox. I also wish to thank the library staff at Bergen Community College for their willingness to track down materials and odd pieces of information for me, and Giacomo Scarato for providing information on prewar Italy.

I owe special thanks for editorial support and advice to Niko Pfund of New York University Press and to Karla Jay, the editor of this series.

For their personal support, I am indebted to many people, most particularly Angela Ingram, whose enthusiasm for this project and overall generosity made my stay in Austin not only possible but delightful. Thanks too to Martha Evans, David Kievitt, and Jane Marcus, who kept me going when I was discouraged. And to Ann Costello my deepest thanks of all.

Introduction

The letters in this volume tell many stories—stories of fierce desire, of fulfilled and unfulfilled longings, of friendships, of struggles, of work and of the blank spaces between work. Too much has been written about "John" Radclyffe Hall as if the only reality of her writing—indeed of her very life—were restricted to the vision of inversion or lesbianism expressed in her most famous novel, *The Well of Loneliness*. These letters, then, are intended to supplement that single-lensed version, to expand it and to let the woman, not just the novelist, speak for herself.

In 1934, when these letters begin, John Radclyffe Hall was fifty-four years old. Since 1915 she had lived exclusively, almost completely monogamously, with Una, Lady Troubridge (married to, but estranged from, and then the widow of a British admiral), a woman who loved John devotedly, who believed in her genius, and who sacrificed her own youthful ambitions to further John's career. By 1934 that career had reached its pinnacle. *The Well of Loneliness* had been translated into many European languages, and, although banned in her native England, was selling a hundred thousand copies a year worldwide. She had received over ten thousand fan letters, and her latest novel was still selling briskly, though to disappointing reviews. In 1926 she had received both the James Tait Black prize and the Prix Femina for her best-selling novel *Adam's Breed*. She was a literary celebrity, and she and Una were regular figures at prominent opening nights during the London theater season and at literary parties. They also had a wide circle of friends in Paris (Natalie Barney, Romaine Brooks, Colette) and in Italy (Una's cousins the Tealdis and the patrician acquaintances from Una's youth). They lived in upper-crust Mayfair, were known at the most fashionable restaurants and clubs, and had recently bought an Elizabethan cottage in Rye, on the English Channel, a cottage they both dearly loved and renamed the Forecastle. It was in most respects a full and satisfying life.

But in 1934 everything changed. Between books, feeling blocked and unproductive, John had a recurrence of pain and weakness in her right leg, which had been injured in a fall from a horse thirty years before. At Una's urging, therefore, they went to Bagnoles-de l'Orne, a spa in Normandy where John had once been treated for the same injury. During the course of treatment, throughout which Una acted as facilitator, correspondent, indeed general manager, Una herself came down with severe gastroenteritis. Still hobbling, unwell, and feeling unhelpful, John sent to the American Hospital in Paris for a private nurse. That nurse was Evguenia Souline. Until the end of John's life nine years later, the three, John, Una, and Souline, were to form an imperfect, stormy triangle.

Two of the three legs of this triangle are well, if imperfectly, known. John is the subject of Una Troubridge's memoir, *The Life and Death of Radclyffe Hall* (1961), and of two biographies, Lovat Dickson's *Radclyffe Hall at the Well of Loneliness* (1975) and Michael Baker's *Our Three Selves* (1985). Una is the subject of Richard Ormrod's *Una Troubridge: The Friend of Radclyffe Hall* (1984). Evguenia Souline, however, is relatively unknown, except through the lenses of these three books. As far as we know, Una never read John's letters to Souline, but both Dickson and Baker did. Yet each very clearly "cut and pasted" from them to fit his own conclusions about the triangle participants and the triangle itself.

In a sense these biographers are correct.[1] Souline has posthumous importance for most readers only because John loved her. Still, I believe, her story, even filtered through John's eyes, is important because it was very important to John and because it still speaks to us at the end of the twentieth century about how we live life, how we experience passion, how we find love, and how all those experiences are lived in the context of our sociohistorical moment.

From her earliest memories, John had felt vulnerable. Unloved by her

---

1. It must be acknowledged that no facts are ever "objective." As a reader of these letters, I too have my own biases and beliefs. However, I have tried to be as scrupulous as possible in limiting my glosses on John's words. Zero-degree intervention is impossible; nevertheless I have tried to let John speak for herself and to let readers hear her words free of my intervention. This introduction will, however, let readers know as precisely as I can what my own interpretations are. I let them stand against those of John's biographers.

abandoned and almost mad mother, her very existence blamed for her mother's unhappiness, resented and neglected, John early on developed strong and lasting sympathies for the downtrodden—for abused animals, for waifs, for humble people unable to realize their dreams. As an adolescent, and after her mother's remarriage to the prominent music teacher Alberto Visetti, she felt even more vulnerable, aware of her sexual "difference" from other girls and her revulsion at her mother's expectations for her. She knew what it was to be misunderstood, to be unacceptable, to be lonely. When in 1934 she met Souline, all those feelings resurfaced, projected this time onto the "lonely" Russian nurse.

Indeed since late adolescence, Souline's life had been lonely in a profound sense. By one conventional standard, the term is misleading: Souline did have a wide circle of friends and acquaintances among the Russian exiles in Paris. But, like many of them, she was basically without family, without status, and without financial reserves. At seventeen she had been violently uprooted and was in many respects unprotected and vulnerable, all qualities that called forth John's deepest sympathies.

Most of the facts about Souline's life come to us from John's letters, particularly the long letter of July 21, 1937, and these appear to be a recapitulation of details and events Souline had recounted. She was born on January 5, 1904, but where or to whom we do not know for certain. We do not even know her birth name, since Souline is not a Russian name, no patronymic is ever given, nor is her father's name ever mentioned. Two recurring details give us some clues—the references to White Russians and to being a general's daughter. White Russia, usually known in the West as Byelorussia or now the Republic of Belarus, was once one of the Soviet Socialist Republics, and obviously part of the Russian Empire before 1917. It borders Poland, and in another reference in a 1939 letter John refers to Souline's birth in Poland, although it must be remembered that Polish borders have changed back and forth considerably in modern times, with much of it, particularly the eastern parts, belonging to Russia at one time or another. John also refers to Souline's upbringing in Smolna, but Smolna is clearly not a town or city. It appears on none of the many maps I have consulted, in no gazetteers, in no place-name indexes. I have concluded, therefore, that wherever Souline was born and then raised was probably the accidental result of her father's position as an army general.

Given Souline's dates, it is certain that her father would have been initially an officer in the Russian Imperial Army. Given also the facts of his exile and death, it is almost certain that he commanded troops fighting against the Bolsheviks in what has come to be known as the "White" Army, as opposed to the "Reds." In the letters John makes frequent use of the terms *cossack* and *Tartar* to refer to Souline's parentage. Whether her father was a Cossack general or not, we cannot know. But certainly the term *cossack* refers not to an ethnic/racial group, as *Tartar* does, but rather to a political and economic accommodation with the Tsars and Empire, resulting in a great measure of autonomy and strong group identification for the Cossacks (see Longworth). The repeated mention of Souline's "Asiatic" features, particularly her slanted eyes, might indicate Central Asian heritage, which would be compatible with Cossack lineage for many, though certainly not all, of the Cossack groups. Still, whether that Asiatic heritage came from her father or mother or both is unknown. About all that is certain, then, is that her father was a general and that she was therefore raised with wealth and aristocratic privilege.

When the White Russians, led by General Wrangel, were defeated finally in the Crimea in 1920, there was a massive evacuation, chaotic and hurried, in British and French ships from Sevastapol to Istanbul, across the Black Sea. From there, according to the masterly account of exile given by Mark Raeff in *Russia Abroad,* the defeated Russians hoped to regroup, rout the Red armies, and return home.

In the meantime, though, the exiles were now poor, ragged, and ill-housed, a drain on the resources of the Turkish state. Many suffered severe privation, even starvation. Sickness ran rampant through the refugee camps (a scene to be endlessly repeated throughout the twentieth century). Even with the few particulars we can know for certain, Souline's experience seems very typical for White Russian evacuees. There was genuine hunger in the camps; there was a desperate need to relocate away from the first port of refuge; there was a fierce scramble for employment. As a result, many White Russians left Istanbul for Europe. The largest numbers went first to the Kingdom of Serbs, Croats, and Slovenes, the next largest to Germany and to France. Conditions varied in each place, of course, but in every country of refuge the young and untrained were seriously disadvantaged.

In this Souline was woefully typical. She was only seventeen. She had been raised as an aristocrat's daughter, trained for nothing that could be useful in the harsh world of émigré life. Where could she go? What could she do to earn her own living?

Two nongovernmental organizations provided the bulk of the relief to Souline and other evacuees—the Red Cross and the YMCA. It was in the Kingdom of Serbs, Croats, and Slovenes that the Red Cross offered Souline training as a nurse. She seized the opportunity, not out of any aptitude for the profession, nor certainly for any love of the calling, but out of the most dire necessity. After her training, she went briefly to the United States, where she could not find work, and then in the early 1920s went to Paris, got the necessary working permit as a nurse, and settled into her Parisian life. In a few years she had saved enough to bring her ailing father from Serbo-Croatia to Paris, where her brother also joined them. She took work as a private duty nurse, lucrative when she could get it, and as a general floor nurse at the American Hospital in Neuilly when she could not.

While the letters make clear Souline's personal history, they do not, for obvious reasons, make clear the general social and political climate for Souline in those years between 1924 and 1934. One fact that is never explicitly stated, but was enormously critical to Souline's life, is the sheer size and shape of the White Russian émigré community in Paris. Estimates vary, but by the mid-1920s there were close to two hundred thousand of them living in Paris. They had established their own churches, schools, newspapers, employment networks, publishing houses, and small businesses. It was a viable community enclave.[2]

Most importantly, however, it remained politically separate from the larger Parisian and French worlds. Initially the retreating White Russian army planned a swift regrouping and reinvasion of the homeland from bases in the south of Europe. In this scenario, the Red Army would be defeated and the Bolshevik regime would collapse. Exile was thus temporary and short-lived. They saw themselves as evacuees, not expatriates. This early hope of 1921 had collapsed by 1923, at which time it seems certain that Souline was already in Paris. Nevertheless, the large émigré community sustained its faith in eventual return and manifested that faith by turning inward and isolating itself from full participation in Parisian life.

This inwardness had two important political consequences for Souline. In the first place it made her part of a huge stateless group without

---

2. All of the summaries of White Russian émigré life in Paris are distilled from Mark Raeff's splendid volume *Russia Abroad,* a book well worth reading for anyone interested in this period of European history.

official papers. The newly formed USSR would not, of course, recognize, document, or issue passports to those committed to its destruction. The League of Nations stepped into this chaotic situation, issuing identity documents named Nansens, after the Swedish head of its refugee committee. Participating League of Nations members, including France, agreed to honor these Nansen documents in lieu of passports. But Nansens were in some ways restricted. Issued by no recognized government, they were not backed by international treaties—or sanctions—that could be invoked in dealing with criminals, political agitators, or other undesirables. So each country honoring Nansens found it necessary to impose restraints congruent with its circumstances and the number and nature of the activities of its refugees. For Souline, living in France, the restraints were minimal as long as she remained within French borders and provided that she always had a valid work permit showing continuous paid employment. Hence, Souline, who had her work permit from the American Hospital, was relatively untroubled as long as she remained at the hospital.

This had been her situation for at least twelve years when John, with her English passport, relative wealth, and habit of European travel, suddenly appeared. An appreciation of the seriousness of this ambiguous status will help readers of these letters to understand Souline's very evident desire to maintain her working status even in the face of John's determination to provide her enough financial security to abandon it. John's commitment to Souline was sincere, but Souline's need to secure her own position was equally sincere. Unless John could—or would—provide the *personal* security (as might have been the case if she were not a lesbian but a man free to marry) that would release Souline from the restrictions of her Nansen status, Souline could not afford to abandon the only security she had known since age seventeen. When it was clear, as early as January 1935, that John would not abandon Una, Souline became determined to maintain her own status in a way that would ultimately throw all John's plans to the wind.

The second political factor that colors much of the material in these letters is linked to the first. As an insular and proud exile community, most White Russians in France (like most in Germany and in the Kingdom of Serbs, Croats, and Slovenes) refused to assimilate. However attenuated their original hopes of quick return might have become, many were still convinced that the Bolshevik regime would crumble fairly quickly. By 1923 even this hope had been dashed. The Communist regime, despite the inherent political strains and domestic turmoil following any revolution, showed no signs of collapse. The émigrés were thus left with a stark choice: become integrated into the host country, even seeking citizenship, or maintain full Russian identity and remain unassimilated exiles. This choice became even more pressing in 1924 when France officially recognized the USSR, thereby ending even the pretense that Lenin's government could be seen as illegitimate. There was to be no going back. Nevertheless, most of the White Russians in France chose to remain Russian, despite the hardships of alien status. Souline must have found strength in those numbers.

French naturalization would have provided some obvious benefits: far fewer travel restrictions, less surveillance, less monitoring of activities, acquaintances, and organizational memberships. But despite her father's former prominence, Souline seems, at least at first, to have been almost apolitical. When she was finally able to bring her father to Paris, he was destitute and almost broken physically. He died before John met Souline. The letters do mention briefly the continuing, but strained relations between Souline and her brother, who seems to have wanted Souline to use John's financial largesse to help him out. We also glimpse some of the strains between Souline and other displaced White Russians, her only real support group. It seems clear that the actual support they were able to give each other was minimal, probably only emotional and cultural, certainly not financial. Souline therefore was not someone who would have warranted close official monitoring. Her activities were personal, her time almost wholly devoted to survival and to apolitical socializing with a girlhood friend and with those Russian friends she had made in Paris. She thus felt little pressure to change her status in France.

John, however, found Souline's status intolerable. Souline could not easily join her and Una in England; indeed she could travel only minimally outside France. Worse, in John's eyes, as political events in Europe in the mid-1930s became increasingly entangled, even Souline's friends were to John a potential source of trouble and danger. French naturalization for Souline thus became one of John's obsessions.

Moreover, as political stability decreased and military interventions seemed increasingly likely, European governments scrambled to find alliances to shore up their national interests in the face of European/North Atlantic economic disaster and growing calls for reform, if not revolution. It was a time of bread lines, massive unemployment, and rampant unrest. Concerned about fascist states surrounding it (Spain,

Germany, and Italy), France in 1935 signed a nonaggression pact with the Soviet Union. One result of this accord was increased surveillance of the Russian émigré population, many of whom were indeed overtly political and committed to the overthrow of the Soviet government. It was a perilous time for White Russians.

John seems to have been far more alert to these perils than Souline was. When the Great War destroyed her comfortably secure Georgian English life, John had been thirty-four, older than Souline was when they met. That she often treated Souline as a child heedless of the pitfalls ahead is the result, at least partially, of this awareness.

Not that John was without her own political enthusiasms based on nationality and class, some of them merely naive, others far worse. Among the naive enthusiams, I count her and Una's fascination with fascism, especially as embodied in Mussolini, whom they cheered from their balcony in Florence. Like a good many independently wealthy Britons, she saw Mussolini not in terms of the disastrous military and political course he pursued, but rather in terms of class—the strong-minded leader bringing to heel, as she saw it, the unruly and heretofore unregulated and turbulent masses of the poor. By 1940 she and Una were disabused of this romanticized flirtation with tyranny masked as discipline. But more long-lasting and far worse was the anti-Semitism the letters convey. The letters reveal very ugly sentiments about Jews, no matter how much she exempted people like the Home Officie's Humbert Wolfe, who helped secure Souline's entry into England. Nothing in the events of the 1930s or 1940s would allow us, even without the benefit of hindsight, to dismiss the impact of such sentiments. It is possible to wonder, however, how much indulgence John gained in expressing such views, given Souline's rabid Russian anti-Semitism.

In addition, John believed that only great powers should rule. The "little countries," the Balkans, for instance, or colonially occupied lands, countries whose populations were "peasant," should not be allowed to exist autonomously, but rather only under rule of a larger power. Other-wise, peasant hatreds, tribal loyalties, she thought, would destroy any hope of world order. Yet she hated war and thought it the complete destruction of women and children. All these political passions and complexities are evident in the letters.

They are also important to our understanding of some of John's more obsessive commands and demands in the letters, and they help us to understand some of the emotional undertones as well. It was a troubled and troubling time. Its sense of déjà vu undid many Europeans who had lived through World War I (one thinks of Virginia Woolf, for instance). It was especially troublesome to John because she had fallen in love with a genuine outsider, a refugee truly without protection.

There is much more in these letters, though, than commentary on the enormous political and economic difficulties of the 1930s. In the early letters, because she saw Souline as innocent and ignorant sexually, John spent considerable effort trying to explain inversion. Almost invariably readers of *The Well of Loneliness* have read John's portrait of the protagonist Stephen Gordon either as autobiography (which it is not) or as John's last word on the nature of inversion (which it is also not).

John had read thoroughly and carefully almost all the material on homosexuality (or inversion) that was available to her in the first decades of the twentieth century. She read Richard von Krafft-Ebing, Iwan Bloch, Edward Carpenter, Magnus Hirschfeld, and another dozen less well known authors. She corresponded with scholars studying inversion and its "causes." Ultimately she found Havelock Ellis's analyses the most congruent with her own experiences—although she continued to have great hope that further scientific inquiry would reveal the definitive truths about the nature and causes of inversion.

One of the salient features of Ellis's description of inversion is its conflation of biology (including body shape and size) with gender. This was a conflation rather typical of late nineteenth-century thought, as even a cursory reading of the psychomedical texts reveals. One result of this blurring of biology and gender performance was the widespread interest in the phenomenon of "The Third Sex." Authors routinely discussed effeminate males and mannish females as though gender markers (clothing, gait, even careers and activities) were directly and uncomplicatedly an outgrowth of biology—and as though there were only a simple binary system of male/female and masculine/feminine.

Inversion, thus, was a "given" both of and in nature, an essential self, much in the way that later theorists have posited a gay or lesbian *identity*. Following Ellis, then, it is hardly a surprise that John portrayed Stephen Gordon as a morphological invert with broad shoulders, narrow hips, athletic limbs, etc. This was a calculated polemical choice. There should be no mistake for any of her readers about exactly who Stephen was.

There should also, however, be no mistake about who John was. She certainly did not model Stephen on herself. John was five-foot-four, weighed 120 pounds, and for the first forty years of her life had waist-length blond hair. She was slim, but round-hipped. Nor was her childhood at all like Stephen's, save for the loneliness she experienced because of her felt "difference," and particularly in adolescence the profound difference in her erotic desires.

As the letters reveal, it is precisely this difference in erotic desires that defines the invert in John's view—not "mannishness," certainly not dress or personal style or mannerisms or activities. She believed that sexual orientation was not determined by how one acts, but rather by whom one desires, an object-relations theory of inversion. Thus, she believed that most people were probably bisexual, Souline among them. The congenital invert, like herself, was one who had never had any erotic attraction to a member of the "opposite" sex. In this sense, Una, although married and a mother, was in John's view a congenital invert. In other words, insofar as a woman feels primarily same-sex erotic desires, in that sense she is an invert. This view has nothing to do with biological abnormalities or physical characteristics. Though she did not use the same terminology, John certainly did not confuse gender performance with inversion. In the final analysis, John's views on lesbian identity are primarily what we now term essentialist. She certainly believed she was born "that way." She also firmly believed that God made her that way and that she was good.

Beyond their value as a source for John's views on matters political and sexual, these letters will, I suspect, interest many readers because of the unfolding of the drama of a doomed love affair. The best impulses from any quarter could not evade that doom, given the hopes, dreams, ideals, and personalities of the three women involved. There are storms, scenes, tender moments, wild passions, and above all the conflicts of loyalty and honor.

Radclyffe Hall had always been a lover of women. As soon as she was old enough to claim her considerable inheritance (about ten million in today's dollars) and her independence, she turned her back on her mother's world and on the conventional life role her mother had tried so hard to cultivate in her. After several youthful affairs, she came to love a much older woman, Mabel Veronica Batten, always called Ladye. For eight years she lived at Cadogan Square, at first in a flat near Ladye's and then with Ladye, after Ladye's husband, George Batten, died. John was intensely loyal to Ladye emotionally, but she was not exclusively monogamous. The most serious of her affairs was a year long passionate romance with Phoebe Hoare in the year preceding the First World War. Though Ladye was troubled, saddened, and eventually jealous, the affair finally ended with the outbreak of war and Ladye and John lived contentedly for another year, until John met Ladye's cousin Una, Lady Troubridge. The ensuing affair was not short-lived. It was to become the foundation of John's mature life, a marriage in all but name that lasted from 1915 until John's death in 1943.

It began, however, in conflict, sorrow, and guilt, an emotional constellation that John tried desperately, though unsuccessfully, not to repeat eighteen years later when she fell in love with Souline. In 1915 John was thirty-five, Una twenty-seven, and Ladye fifty-eight. The physical desire the two younger women felt was intense, almost overpowering. They ran off to John's cottage in Malvern, where John had always summered with Ladye. On John's return to London, Ladye was distraught. They quarreled bitterly, and two days later Ladye was dead of a heart attack. John's guilt was enormous, as was Una's remorse. They did not make love again for many months. When they did reunite, they were always careful to honor Ladye's memory, seeking her forgiveness—and later her advice—through a spiritualist and medium, Mrs. Osborne Leonard. They joined the Society for Psychical Research to explore the phenomenon of what they always believed to be genuine communication with Ladye. There is a sense in which this original triangle was the pattern for the final one of Una, John, and Souline.

While an observer would be foolhardy to construct a paradigm that would apply to all love triangles, one can nevertheless note certain fairly common characteristics. In the stereotypical Western pattern, it is the husband who takes another lover, leaving wife and mistress in an antagonistic, but oddly parallel situation. This is the stereotypical pattern not because of any essential masculine polygamous drive or any essential feminine monogamy, but rather because in Western civilization women have not historically been allowed autonomous sexuality. Lesbian couplings, however, break this stereotype somewhat, in that all parties in the triangle are women and therefore, in most societies, must construct their autonomous desires as "outlaws." The result is that in a sense lesbian partners are freer than their legally married heterosexual sisters to determine their sexual courses of action.

At the same time, though, lesbian love and sexual desires strong enough to lead to commitment often act themselves out in many of the same ways that heterosexual desires do. Many commentators on Radclyffe Hall, most notably Michael Baker in his 1985 biography, have read John as the "husband" in this triangle. I believe that Baker is simply wrong, primarily because he believes John wanted to be and tried to "be" a man, which the letters show to be patent nonsense. John was a lesbian—not the same thing at all. Nevertheless in symbolic terms, Baker is right. If on the level of symbol and symbolic language (Lacan's "Law of the Father"), the one who can act on desire is the male, then indeed John was the "husband," married to Una but desiring and acting on desire for the "Other Woman," Souline.

I doubt, however, that the symbolic pattern explains anything very clearly. Far more critical, I believe, is an understanding of desire itself. However one chooses to act on it, most people it seems have indeed felt the intense power of desire. In literature, in biographies, in diaries, in conversations whispered over restaurant tables, people talk and have always talked about *wanting* another person. To be "head over heels" in love is common enough. There is no need to question the passionate intensity of John's desire for Souline as expressed in these letters—or, if we had letters from 1915, of her passionate desire for Una at that time. In that sense, the passion is a given, simply a phenomenon, without need of explanation. When such passion can be pursued without conflict, whether from within because of divided loyalties, or from without because not reciprocated, then few of us ever question it, however mad we may seem to outsiders.

John's situation was not, however, without conflict. She loved Una; they had lived together for eighteen years; Una had stood by her through her triumphs (prizes for her work) as well as through her trials (literally the obscenity trial over *The Well of Loneliness,* and the additional trial of their joint vilification in the press). Una's passionate desire for John had never lessened, though it had been tempered by her willing deferral to John's needs and habits, including the habit of writing through the night, as well as by Una's own physical ailments, especially her hysterectomy in 1932.

Despite some biographers' claims, John and Una were still sexually involved with each other in 1934. It was not the case, as Ormrod and Baker suggest, that John "needed" Souline for physical satisfaction. Moreover, desire is not a default mechanism; it is neither turned on or turned off by sexual satisfaction or its absence. John was consumed by desire for Souline for several months before that desire was satisfied. It was, it seems clear, simple and inexplicable desire.

It was, however, problematic desire. When she saw what was going on, Una was shocked, hurt, threatened. John felt almost ill with obsessive longing. And Souline seems to have been terrified. She was sexually inexperienced, probably a virgin, as John claims. She reacted to the violent outpourings of John's earliest letters with both fascination and fright. John was clearly the seducer.

Souline gradually gave in to John's importunings, both sexual and financial. Again and again John declared her passion and her concern for Souline's material well-being, making lavish gifts and begging Souline to accept financial security. Souline was finally overwhelmed. Her story is in some ways the classic story of the Other Woman. As she came to accept John's declarations and her passion, she also seems to have believed that she could persuade John to leave Una. John was, after all, telling her that she had not been in love with Una for many years, despite her altogether different reassurances to Una. John swore over and over that she could never be happy, indeed could hardly bear to live, without Souline's love. Although John had also made it clear from the very beginning that she would never leave Una, Souline's apparent desire for exclusivity seems natural, a reasonable wish, if not a reasonable expectation, in light of John's words to her.

There are some problems of interpretation inherent in the materials we have available. It is impossible, for instance, to know the exact nature of Souline's feelings from 1934 through 1937. There is no doubt that she resented Una and Una's hold on John. Nor is there any doubt that her responses swung wildly—from passion to tantrums to humor to quiet acceptance of the impossible situation. This spectrum of reactions seems perfectly understandable, especially if Souline were indeed struggling to reconcile what she wanted with what she knew she could have, a situation not unfamiliar to anyone who has ever found herself in the position of the Other Woman.

Though this interpretation of Souline's feelings seems plausible, even probable, we can do little more than speculate. The only surviving letter from Souline is dated 7 June 1939. In it she accuses John of willfully misunderstanding her, of overreacting, and of being alarmist and gloomy. This, however, was 1939, five years, many disappointments, and several major stormy scenes after the whirlwind passion of 1934. Whatever Souline had initially hoped for had long given way to simpler affection, acceptance of continued financial support, and a growing determination to hew to her own course in life. She refused John's continuing pleas for renewed sexual intimacy. And she steadfastly refused to give in to John's most ardent wish that all three live in proximity, if not together. John, it is clear, wanted Souline, but would not abandon Una. Souline, it is equally clear, would no longer be John's lover if John still lived her daily life with Una. Souline had read the situation as clearly as she could—impasse. And so she determined to get on with her own life, her own wishes, her own future. John was heartbroken.

But what of Una in all this? Here we are on surer ground. Una's daybooks do record her feelings, her reflections, her abiding thoughts along with many passing ones. Initially, as we know even from the letters, she was devastated by John's passion for Souline. She did try to nip that passion in the bud, invoking John's commitments, their mutual loyalty, her own health problems. When it became clear that John could not or would not free herself of this obsession, Una tried to compromise and bargained for the least unacceptable terms, evidently hoping that the passion would be short-lived. That hope failing, she determined to make the best of a heartbreaking loss.

Why did she stay? The most obvious answer seems also to be the truest: She loved John and believed in her, both as a woman and as a writer. She trusted the closeness of their union, she valued her own role in nurturing John's work, and she believed passionately in John's decency and honor. She also believed that Souline understood none of this and valued it even less. She saw Souline as vapid, woefully ignorant of and therefore impatient with John's writing commitments, intellectual life, and social and professional contacts. To Una, Souline was simply unworthy of John no matter how much John might lust after her. Una was not about to relinquish John and John's career to Souline.

Just as importantly, through it all Una retained a sense of her own worth; she believed in herself and in the quality of her love for John. This *amour propre* must have been extremely hard to hold on to in the face of John's lovesick mooning and distracted, possessive, often angry absorption in "securing" Souline when Una was not only "secured" but deeply devoted to John. Perhaps Una was wiser than either John or Souline ever knew. John certainly misread Una at this time, believing that Una sincerely accepted, even loved, Souline for John's sake and simply because Souline made John happy. Souline, however, knew better.

Una did send Souline gifts, wrote to officials on her behalf, and even wrote begging Souline to join them when John was disconsolate and unable to work. She could not be faulted either in her courtesy or in her outright actions. After the initial devastation and protestations, she never gave John any reason to question her behavior. But Una would not simply go, would not relinquish her claim on John's affections, loyalty, and sense of honor. And Souline knew all this, far better than John did. Eventually, as is clear from the letters, Una "won."

Was the victory worth the battle? Una believed so, as did John. In the end John did, through considerable efforts on Una's part, manage to protect Souline by giving her relative safety in rural England during World War II. But as John became more and more gravely ill, she turned to Una for comfort, for ease, for love. She died telling Una, "It was you. It was always you."

The careful reader of these letters might, however, question the absolute certainty of Una's victory. Triangles almost always wind up hurting all the parties involved. There are exceptions, of course. One thinks of Vita Sackville-West, of Natalie Barney, of Virginia Woolf. Usually, though, where triangles do no damage, it is because passionate intensity has already evolved into friendship or affection. People intensely "in love" do not go gently into triangles.

In the case of John, Una, and Souline, all parties were deeply hurt. To some observers, Baker and Ormrod particularly, Souline seemed to come out least damaged. She ultimately set the terms of her relationship with John in a manner that protected her own interests, including John's continued financial support, and that left her free to pursue her own future, including marriage and then after Souline's death the sale for profit of the letters in this volume. Such a view, though, does an injustice to what seems to have been Souline's genuine struggle with, for, and against John's love. She wanted it all; she got much of it, certainly the most sexually passionate aspects, but she was ultimately left high and dry by John's other and deeper passion—her commitment to decency and honor, and above all to loyal affection and love for Una.

Una was damaged too. According to her daybooks, she cried herself to sleep many nights when John was in Souline's arms. She was haunted by memories of her own nights of love with John and by her evolving understanding of the hurt those nights had caused Ladye many years before. She knew she struggled simply to endure John's faithlessness. Where was John's heart?

Ultimately, however, it was probably John herself who was most damaged. At the height of her writing powers, in midstride as an artist, she fell helplessly in love. Though she started two other novels, she completed only one more book after 1934, *The Sixth Beatitude*, a commercial failure. From 1934 through 1936 she found herself unable to concentrate on her writing whenever Souline was, from her point of view, being "difficult." As matters deteriorated in 1937 and 1938, she had nearly fatal bouts of bronchial and chest ailments. She had a nervous breakdown and was suicidal. From 1939 on, her entire body broke down, first her bones, then her eyes, then her teeth, finally her entire digestive system, consumed by an inoperable cancer.

I am not suggesting that the progression of physical illnesses was purely psychological or tied to the rupture with Souline. Pathology has never been that simple. Her physical maladies would have manifested themselves eventually in any event. Nevertheless, it is also probable (and often the case) that both resistance and resilience are directly correlated with psychological well-being. The best fighters of any disease or physical breakdown are those with the greatest will to go on. John had less and less of that will to fight and conquer.

On an intuitive level, John knew this about herself. She wrote to Souline about her despondency, her suicidal dreams. Later she wrote about her struggle against lung impairment, her battle against failing recuperative powers. Her letters by then were always factual, never accusatory. Still, the fierce fighting will seems to have gone out of her. The final letters are simply sad, elegiac, and resigned. In a sense she was the greatest loser of them all in this troubled triangle.

This collection of letters will, I hope, illustrate the themes I have highlighted here—the politics, the passion, the drama. In the end my greatest hope is that they will expand our knowledge of one of the truly influential writers of the twentieth century.

WORKS CITED

Baker, Michael. *Our Three Selves: The Life of Radclyffe Hall.* New York: Morrow, 1985.

Dickson, Lovat. *Radclyffe Hall at the Well of Loneliness: A Sapphic Chronicle.* London: Collins, 1975.

Glasgow, Joanne. "What's a Nice Lesbian Like You Doing in the Church of Torquemada?" In *Lesbian Texts and Contexts: Radical Revisions*, edited by

Karla Jay and Joanne Glasgow, 241–54. New York: New York University Press, 1990.

Longworth, Phillip. *The Cossacks: Five Centuries of Turbulent Life on the Russian Steppes.* New York: Holt, 1969.

Ormrod, Richard. *Una Troubridge: The Friend of Radclyffe Hall.* London: Cape, 1984.

Raeff, Marc. *Russia Abroad: A Cultural History of the Russian Emigration, 1919–1939.* New York: Oxford University Press, 1990.

Troubridge, Una. *The Life and Death of Radclyffe Hall.* London: Hammond, 1961.

Note on the Text

There are 576 items in the collection of correspondence from Radclyffe Hall to Souline, far too many for full inclusion in a single volume. As an editor, I was therefore faced with two choices: either present all the items by excerpting interesting or pertinent passages (a tempting choice), or omit even some I found very interesting, and present whole letters, whether long or short. I chose the latter option, realizing, of course, that I would inevitably be presenting some repetitious material and some very tangential passages. My reason for choosing this second option will, I hope, become clear to readers. Primarily I wanted to capture the intensity, the obsessiveness, and the preoccupations the letters convey. Excerpts cannot give the reader any sense of these qualities. On the matter of the inevitable repetitiveness, I used a very simple observation from my own life—namely that any long-term relationship contains more repetition than novelty. In the case of John and Souline, the repetitions are true to the nature of the relationship. I also wish to assure readers that I have not omitted any letters which contain material not dealt with in those that I have selected.

A second matter of editorial choice concerns spelling and punctuation. John was a notoriously bad speller. Even Souline, for whom English was her *third* language, mentioned this to John. I have kept John's spelling, correcting with brackets only when the meaning would otherwise be unclear or ungrammatical. There are, however, a few instances when even spelling is not the issue, but rather idiosyncratic usage. For instance, *thoroughly* is always *througherly*. *Huge* is always *hugh*.

I have, however, silently added necessary punctuation, most often missed periods, but also on occasion missed commas. Many of these letters were written in either great haste or great passion. Under both circumstances, punctuation is the first thing to go. There is no discernible benefit to the reader in intrusive editorial brackets for punctuation. I want instead to have the letters read smoothly so as not to distract from the content.

Finally, I have bracketed at the beginning of each letter the place from which John wrote it, as the issues of separation, distance, and travel are central concerns of many of the letters.

Your John:
The Love Letters of Radclyffe Hall

July–September 1934

This section contains representative letters from the earliest and most critical part of the nine-year correspondence. John wrote at first in letter/ response intervals, then increasingly frequently, every two days, then daily, occasionally more than once a day. The initial physical attraction that had begun at Bagnoles gained more and more control of John's hyperactive imagination. The first forty letters are in effect an ardent seduction, carried out by means of the postal systems of two countries. Hence, getting and sending mail preoccupied John's mind. Since Souline's letters have not survived, except one from 1939, we can only speculate about her responses to the increasingly fervent outpouring from John. Two reactions seem to alternate—flattered interest and terror.

The letters selected here are the first in the long correspondence between John and Souline. Souline had returned to Paris and her nursing work at the American Hospital in Neuilly. John and Una remained another week at Bagnoles to complete the treatment on John's leg. There were three more letters, one from Bagnoles and two from Paris, before John and Una traveled to Italy. All four reveal the increasing power of John's erotic obsession with Souline, an obsession that had been fueled by a few stolen kisses and embraces. The letter of July 27 is a long outpouring of frustration and unhappiness. Invariably when John was upset, she wrote at great length, but hastily, as her carelessness about spelling and punctuation indicates.

Hotel des Thermes
Bagnole de l'Orne
Orne, Normandy[1]

July 17, 1934

My dear. As I tried to tell you yesterday on that perfectly damnable long distance telephone, (quite the worst line I have ever spoken on, at all events at my end) we expect to leave here for Paris on 24th. I shared in a bath on Sunday in order to hurry the treatment along. I shall only be in Paris a short time on my way to Italy, and please may I come and see you in the Francisque Sarcey.[2] Let it be at 2.45, about, on the afternoon of the 26th if you will. I say the 26th instead of the 25th in case I am held up here a day longer for some unforseen reason—one never knows. Don't ask anyone to meet me, you know by now that I am shy of people, also there are things that I want to say to you—not frightening things— I don't know why I always have a feeling that you are scared of me, but so it is, and I don't want you to be scared. Anyhow I don't think you will refuse to see me. Knowing at least a tiny corner of your mind, I hear you thinking a very ridiculous thought about your room being just one room and not an enormous apartment off the Bois[3]—but one room is large enough for me if it is not for you! I am really a very humble person. The letter you promised to write when I shouted at you in an agitated voice yesterday, has not arrived. The post-card turned up late yesterday afternoon. I waited until the morning post came in before venturing a long-distance call which I hate; however it was worth the fuss and strain of trying to hear your fading voice only to know that all was well with you. I heard myself shouting: 'Don't do away Soulina' did that make you laugh? I was in the hot little telephone box in the front hall with the door tightly shut, so no one heard my undignified appeal but you. Somehow I expected a letter today, felt I had a right to a letter today, and because it has not come I am enormously down-hearted. Also I wanted to ask you this morning whether you thought my white collar

1. Bagnoles-de l'Orne was a small village in Normandy with a population under six hundred. It was noted for its thermal springs and spa, but particularly for its carbonic acid bath treatment. John had visited it once before in July 1922.

2. A tiny street off rue de la Tour in the sixteenth arrondissement near Passy Cemetery.

3. A reference to the famous (and posh) Bois de Boulogne. John's next comments indicate that Souline was sensitive to the disparity in their lifestyles.

was clean enough to wear a second time and what stock[4] I should put on, the blue with white spots or a black one—then there were my cuffs. Never mind, you must write now in answer to this telling me to come on 26th and if you can please write by return. If the 26th won't do then will you suggest any other day. I leave for Italy on 30th, so any day before that.

Yours—John

P.S I shall get any letters you write myself—and open them myself and—are you surprised? Answer them myself![5]

Hotel des Thermes
Bagnoles de l'Orne

July 20 1934

My very dear. Your darling stiff little letter came yesterday. I wish that I could write French as well as you write English—Only in one place did your English go wrong: in my country one would not—in the circumstances—have begun: 'My dear Miss Hall.'! Try to get it into your head that never again can I be 'Miss Hall' to you. Call me anything or nothing, as you will, but not that except when you are speaking of me to strangers.

And now about our plans for the 26th. I want to change them. What I want you to do on that day is this: meet me at Lapeyrouse [La Pérousse] (you know, Quai des Grands Augustins)[1] at 12.30 and we will lunch there alone together, just you and I. After lunch we will go back to my hotel where I shall have a sitting room and there (if you are willing) we will spend the afternoon. We shall be quite alone and able to talk undisturbed. It will be better so; I will explain when we meet. Meanwhile write to me here by return telling me that you agree to the

---

4. What Americans would call a tie; defined by the *Oxford English Dictionary* as a stiff neckcloth.

5. John is here alluding to the customary practice of Una's dealing with much of John's correspondence, a practice that Souline would probably have observed as nurse to John. Una, in her self-chosen role of helper, manager, and companion had become to uncomprehending eyes what an American newspaper correspondent could only describe as "Miss Hall's secretary."

1. La Pérousse is still a famous and expensive restaurant in Paris. It is located on the Left Bank, almost directly across from Ile de la Cite, a few minutes' walk from John's hotel.

change of plans. And just in case your letter should get delayed on the way and thus miss me here, drop me a line to the Paris Hotel: Hotel Pont Royal—Rue du Bac,[2] where I shall have arrived by next Tuesday afternoon all being well—we leave here by the 11.48 train that morning.

Take care of yourself and know that I am counting on this meeting in Paris as I have counted on few things in my life.

Yours
John

Pont Royal Hotel, Paris

July 24th 1934

Darling. Thank you for your little note of welcome. Yes, I am here in Paris, and it seems so strange that only a few weeks ago I did not know that Paris meant you. I want to come to you—its red hell to be here and not be able to see you until the day after tomorrow and then only for a few hours. But I cannot come nor am I going to ring you up, even though I long to hear your voice speaking to me in your darling broken English. Please, Soulina, never learn to speak English quite properly, will you? No, you can't do anything for me except to think of me a very great deal until we meet on Thursday, yes, and often. One other thing you can do also, and that is to take a taxi on Thursday. I insist upon this, and you will pocket your pride & let me pay for the taxi too. I am not going to rush forward and pay the man myself when you arrive as that would look too obvious. You will pay him and I will pay you later—that is how it will be done, says John.

Bless you. There is so much I want to say but my pen won't write it.

Yours, John

Pont-Royal Hotel, Paris

July 27th 1934

My dearest. After you left me last evening I was too done in to feel very much. It was as though you had taken my strength away with you, leaving an empty shell behind, and last night I slept from shere exhaus-

---

2. The Pont Royal was a category four (luxury) hotel on the Left Bank in the seventeenth arrondissement.

tion. I slept, Soulina, as once before in my life I slept as the result of a fearful grief[1]—nature knows when we have endured to the uttermost, and when the point has been reached she steps in and saves us for her own purposes, though God alone knows what they may be, they are always hidden from us at the moment.

But now I am awake, very terribly awake. I woke up almost before it was light with those last words of yours hammering on my heart. 'I can't believe that this is the last time I shall see you.' And this is going to be a day of deep pain, and I am tormented because of you, and this torment is now only partly of the senses—but is now an even more enduring thing and more impossible to cure—my sweet, because it is a torment of tenderness, of yearning over you, of longing to help you—of longing to take you into my arms and comfort you innocently and most gently as I would comfort a little child, whispering to you all sorts of foolish words of love that has nothing to do with the body. And then I would want you to fall asleep with your head on my breast for a while, Soulina, and then I would want you to wake up again and feel glad because I was lying beside you, and because you were touching this flesh of mine that is so consumed by reason of your flesh, yet so subjugated and curbed by my pity, that the whole of me would gladly melt into tears, becomming as a cup of cold water for your drinking. And if this is wrong then there is no God, but only some cruel and hateful fiend who creates such a one as I am for the pleasure that he will gain from my ultimate destruction. But there is a God, make no mistake, and I have a rightful place in His creation, and if you are as I am you share that place, and our God is more merciful than the world, and since he made us, is understanding; and He knows very well what the end will be, seeing what you & I cannot see, knowing why you & I have been forced to meet, and why this great trouble has come upon us. Soulina, I implore you to cling to this belief, because without faith our souls will be undone at this time of all but unendurable suffering.

I am haunted by the thought of your loneliness, by the knowledge that I am leaving you alone, by my terror that you may fret and get ill, or perhaps do something reckless and most foolish, for to me you seem

---

1. While we cannot know for certain what grief John writes of here, it seems likely that the reference is to the death of Mabel Veronica Batten (Ladye), which occurred when John was in the first throes of her passion for Una, a passion very similar to that John was now feeling for Souline. The irony, of course, is that Ladye was grieved by that passion, just as Una was now grieved.

even younger than your age,[2] and then you have no one to whom you can talk or go to for advice and help in your need, and this thought makes me feel that I must go mad. But I shall not go mad, but will keep very sane for your sake, so that I can always help you.

Oh, I know what you are enduring this day—every mile of the road I am close beside you, and your hand is in mine, and your heart is in mine, and your pain is my pain, and your need is my need, and I cannot, no, I cannot see the light but just stumble along beside you in the darkness, and yet I know the light exsists, and this is Faith, to realize the light even if only painfully and dimly, and I—poor unworthy sinner that I am, so hampered and tormented by my body that desires you, I have got to make you also realize the light is no less bright because I may fail to submerge the flesh entirely in the spirit.

Soulina, for my sake don't fret yourself ill. Oh, my God, Soulina do take care of yourself. While we are both in the world there is hope— and surely, surely we shall meet again.

As I am writing your letter has come, and it is a beautiful letter. It is as though I had struck the rock with the staff of my love and at last—at last the spring has gushed out, out of your heart into mine, beloved. But our paths are not seperated—this is not good bye. Something tells me that all this was meant to happen, that we shall meet again, that our love will last, that our mutual desire the one for the other is only the physical expression of a thing that is infinately more enduring than our bodies. Surely Soulina, you must feel this too? Otherwise why did I let you go from me even as you came—I, who needed you so and who could have made you incapable of resisting, could have made you no longer want to resist? For you are not a woman of ice and this I well know, my little virgin, and I agonized to take your virginity and to bind you to me with the chains of the flesh, because I had & have so vast a need that my wretched body has become my torment—but through it all my spirit cries out to you, Soulina, and it tells you that love is never a sin, that the flesh may be weak but the spirit is strong—yesterday it was my spirit that saved you. Must I always save you? I do not know. I cannot see far beyond this pain—this pain that I feared would come with the morning.

This is a very terrible day, for we are so near, and I long to come to

---

2. There is some confusion in the letters that follow. At one time in 1934, John gives Souline's age as thirty, but in another as thirty-two. Souline was thirty.

you and make you forget everything but me—God help me, I aught not to write like this for our time is not yet, if it ever comes our time is not yet. But I love you, I love you.

If you also love me you will not fail to write, will take care of yourself in every way, and will not quite shut me out of your life—that would break me completely, utterly, and I do not feel that you ought to break me. But you will not Soulina, because you love me.

Lady Troubridge has been very wonderful, she sends you her love and asks me to tell you that she will write to you from Sirmione.[3]

I cannot, I dare not write any more, and since you have your living to earn and I am a marked woman, as I told you, I beg you to lock up this letter of mine together with all my other letters. Soulina, I do love you too terribly.

John

From July 31 to September 19 John and Una stayed at the Albergo Catullo in Sirmione. John wrote forty-one letters during that period, most of them extremely important not only because they describe her inflamed feelings for Souline, but also because they explain many of her views about "inversion," Catholicism, literature, life, and love. Una was alarmed at the growing obsession for Souline, which John could hardly conceal. Una extracted a promise that John would not have a sexual relationship with Souline, a promise ultimately broken. John's torrid letters frightened Souline, who contemplated leaving for the United States with a friend, Mrs. Baker, whom she had nursed. At this suggestion John became distraught and hurried back to Paris two weeks earlier than she had planned, lest Souline leave before they could meet.

[Sirmione]

Tuesday, July 31st 1934

My beloved. I do not know how I have the strength to write what must be written—it is this: I cannot see you in Paris on my way back to England. I had been counting on this—I had thought I shall see her once more before I go back and take up the burden of my everyday life—

---

3. Sirmione, where John's friend Mickie Jacobs had a villa, was a popular health resort on Lake Garda, with a population at the time of about six hundred.

perhaps I shall see her several times even; it was something that Una said
that made me dare to hope. And then in Paris she seemed so merciful.
You remember that she sent you her love and said that she would write
to you, then yesterday she did actually write to you. Last evening I got
your letter in answer to mine written on Friday before I left for Italy,
and your letter made me long so much to see you and touch you and
hear you speak if only once again, and I said: 'I shall try to see Soulina
on my way home, I shall go and see her.' And somehow, God knows
why, I thought Una would consent, for she knows how it is with me,
with us, and she knows too something that I have not told you: she
knows that I am ill with misery—not seriously ill, nothing for you to
worry about, but all is not very well with me, which in the circumstances
is natural. Then I found that she means to keep us apart. I dare not
blame her, I do not blame her. She and I have been together for 18 years.
When all the world seemed to be against me at the time of the 'Well of
Loneliness' persecution,[1] Una stood shoulder to shoulder with me, fighting every inch of that terrific battle. She has given me all of her interest
and indeed of her life ever since we made common cause, therefore she
has the right to do what she is doing and she will not ceed that right,
but insists on it with all the strength which lies—as she well knows—in
her physical weakness. It has been very terrible, she has reminded me of
her operation,[2] of every illness she had through the years. She has told
me that she is very ill now, that Fouts[3] warned her to avoid all emotion,
that if I do see you everything will happen between us, and that then she
could never be happy again but would fret herself until she died. She
says that she will not tolerate our meeting. When I said that I would
control myself if only I could see you again, she would not believe me,
and this morning, after a scene which lasted all night, she suddenly
hurled herself onto the floor and looked as though she were going

---

1. *The Well of Loneliness,* which portrays female inversion sympathetically, was published by Jonathan Cape in 1928. Although it received favorable reviews in the more
respected papers and journals, the novel became the subject of a vicious journalistic attack
and was officially declared obscene in a trial that became a literary cause célèbre. See Vera
Brittain's *Radclyffe Hall: A Case of Obscenity?* (New York: A. S. Barnes, 1969) for a full
discussion of the case. Although John herself was not on trial, both she and Una endured
scathing press attacks, cartoons, and caricatures.
2. Una had a hysterectomy on July 5, 1932, to remove fibroids and relieve excessive
menstrual bleeding.
3. One of Una's doctors. She had many over the years.

demented. I think that it may very well be that her operation has made her more excitable—women are like that after that operation. Then she has reminded me over & over again until I have nearly gone mad, that I have always stood for fidelity in the case of inverted unions, that the eyes of the inverted all over the world are turned towards me, that they look up to me, in a word, that for years now they have respected me because my own union has been faithful and open. And when she says this I can find no answer, because she is only telling the truth—I have tried to help my poor kind by setting an example, especially of courage, and thousands have turned to me for help and found it, if I may believe their letters, and she says that I want to betray my inverts who look upon me almost as their leader. Oh, but whats the use of telling you any more of the hell that I went through last night & this morning—I have a debt of honour to pay, I am under terrific obligation, and can I shirk the intolerable load? It is less whether I can shirk my load than whether I have the strength to bear it. But one small comfort would Una conceed, she agrees that we shall write to each other—I think she knows that there comes a stage when human nature can no longer endure, and that I simply cannot endure never hearing from you—that would kill me, I should die, Soulina. The thought, the knowledge, that you are in the world, & might be suffering, in trouble, in poverty, even ill perhaps and so terribly alone, having neither parents nor country, and you so small somehow—well, I just could not bear it. As it is I remember that you were once ill, seriously ill[4] and so little money—and sometimes I cannot sleep at night because you do not take care of yourself, and because I cannot take care of you. And I think of a thousand worrying things, I think: 'Has she got two pairs of glasses—does she keep an extra pair in her bag in case she breaks her frames in the street—if she does not do this, keep an extra pair, she is so very blind that one day she may get run over.' Then I think: 'Is she careful not to catch cold—will she be careful this coming winter? Does she get terribly over tired? Does she eat enough good & nourishing food?' These are the kinds of thoughts that will come when I lie awake thinking about you. Therefore if you love me as I love you you will write to me, Soulina. You will let me know any change of address, you will let me know what you are doing—you will let me know whether you are well or ill—prosperous or in need of

---

4. Souline had twice had tuberculosis.

help—and this you will do out of your compassion. And I will write to you also. And if you refuse to write, Soulina—then God help me, I don't think that I can go on, for I am almost too desolate as it is, to go on living. Its so strange and rather terrible to be as I have been since I met you—I feel that I am no longer myself—I am nothing at all but one great ache—I think I have told you this already. And I cannot remember that I have a career, that I am quite a well know[n] writer—that all seems like a dream—and as vague as a dream; and I cannot seem to associate myself with my friends and my home in England anymore. Like you, I am homeless & I have no country. In your letter of the 28th you ask me if love can be only spiritual—why surely there can be a love of the spirit, and this love I think I must have for you as well as a love of the body. But oh, my God, I am so terribly unhappy—haunted too by an unendurable fear that I have made you unhappy. I who would lay down my life for you have only made you suffer through me. Why did we have to meet, we two? What do we mean you & I to each other? And listen, my beloved, what have we done that you & I must punish each other? I don't think that I shall ever write another book—I think that something in me has gone out—I think that in parting with you I am finished.

And now I am going to ask a great favour which of your charity you will grant me. I know that just now you are hard pressed for money, you must be in present conditions in France,[5] & if you write & tell me that this is not so I shall simply not believe you, Soulina. I want to send you £100.[6] I want you to spend a little on me in stamps for those letters that you will write me—for the rest I want you to buy yourself small comforts. It is not for the others, the white refugees,[7] it is only for the one that I love. I insist that you spend it all on yourself—that is what I want you to do to please me. But put a few pounds aside, if you will, just in case you wanted to send me a cable—you might want more help—one

---

5. John is referring to the effects of what is known in the United States as the Great Depression. Economic conditions in France were particularly bad, and Souline depended almost exclusively on her low wages as a floor duty nurse and the bonuses she sometimes received from grateful patients whom she nursed in private duty cases.

6. This sum would be roughly equivalent to $2100 in today's dollars, a generous offer.

7. References in other letters indicate that the White Russian refugee community in Paris was, like many such communities, tightly knit and supportive of each other. Souline's own family seems to have been quite destitute. Her father, a former general, died so poor that there was no money even for a headstone.

never knows, and perhaps you might even want my help quickly. I am going to write today to my Bank and find out how they can let you have the money, explaining that you cannot cash a crossed cheque.[8] I expect they will send you a Bankers Draft or something. It maybe a week before I hear, but as soon as I do hear I shall instruct them and let you know what I have arranged. And this is the only drop of comfort I have, that I can send you a small sum of money. When you answer this letter let me know how long you will be working at the hospital—& do you sleep there or at your own place? I feel that I want to know where you are sleeping. And write to me quickly if only a few lines. I am longing to get away from here though now I shall wait for your letter of course, & for my banks answer to my letter. For some reason, Una wants to stay on, but I do not—it is too beautiful—I cannot endure its beauty just now—always my heart cries out for you to share it. I think I had better go back to England, but Una does not feel well enough, she says, and if this is so I must not force her. God bless you and keep you heart of my heart—my joy & my unbelievable grief, for that is what you have become to me, Soulina.

John

[Sirmione]

August 1st 1934

My little beloved. Blessed be God I shall see you on my return from here before I go to England. It was during lunch yesterday that Una became kind & reasonable again and suddenly withdrew her opposition, not, however, without insisting that I give her my word of honour not to be unfaithful to her in the fullest and ultimate meaning of the word. She said that if I would consent to do this she would not oppose my seeing you in your appartment or anywhere else—and because my need to see you is so great, just to see you and touch you and hear your voice, and also because it seemed to me that I had no choice but to accept her

---

8. This was a common banking device to protect checks from being cashed by unintended parties. There was a double line in the middle of the check, from top to bottom, the "cross" John refers to. Banks would not cash such checks, but would instead route funds internally to the proper accounts. This provided additional security for travelers, as lost or stolen checks could not be cashed.

conditions, I promised, and when I return from here I shall come to your appartment if I may, for I want very much to see that room, and the bed on which you sleep so that when the time comes I may have the picture of it all in my heart to look at when the sea is between us. Thinking that today you will get the long letter that I wrote last Tuesday telling you that Una would not consent to our meeting, and that you would be terribly distressed, I wrote you the following telegram this morning: 'Find I can see you in Paris on my way home, this telegram contradicts last Tuesdays letter, writing. John.' I can only hope you will get my last Tuesday's letter and the telegram about the same time and thus be spared unnecessary worry; anyhow I have done my best to spare you. Beloved this letter will have to be brief because your John is very, very tired—the effort to write that letter on Tuesday, and the utter misery and desolation that came on me after I had posted that letter, these things cannot be endured without battering ones soul and I still feel as though my body & soul had been put on the rack and tortured. I could neither sleep nor eat, I could only think of not seeing you again. And this happening has made me realize, as nothing else perhaps could have done, that my love of you goes far beyond the body, for now as I write this it seems to me that nothing matters, nothing at all except that I shall see you again and for a few hours have you near me. When we shall actually leave here is uncertain, now that Una has given in thus far I am not going to drag her away all in a moment as the sun & air seem to be doing her much good, and I am sure you will say that I am right, recognizing the duty that I have towards her. Meanwhile I anxious[ly] await your reply to a letter I wrote you yesterday, asking how long you will continue to work at the hospital—that is very important, I feel, I must know your plans before making my own so I hope you will answer that question. Be of good heart my very dear one, and try to think as I do that all will be well in the end. I am so intensely happy at the thought that we two can meet in peace without let or hindrance that for the moment that seems enough, the relief is so intense after the storm that just passed over. I kiss you many times in my heart, and my arms are very tightly around you now and always, Soulina.

Your John

P.S. One thing you need never fear, you need not fear that your letters will not reach me safely.

August 7th 1934

My beloved Soulina.

Know this my beloved, that I received your letter of August 5th early this morning, and that I would not give way to my impulse to answer it instantly because I wanted to think and above all to be calm before writing to you—this much I owe to you and to myself because our situation is no light thing, it is rather a terribly momentous thing that has come upon us from God knows where and certainly God alone knows why—the point that has got to be faced and met as best we can is that it is upon us.

First I am going to deal with your earlier letter in answer to mine (the outrageously inconsiderate letter that I sat down & wrote off to you on impulse last Tuesday [July 31] when I felt very near desperation) that letter of mine should never have been written in such utterly selfish terms of violence, my excuse is that the thought of never seeing you again was more than I could bear, is more than I can bear, but now I am going to write about it calmly, because you also have got to be calm & give this thing deep consideration.

But for the moment about your letter of August 2nd. There are just two things that hurt me more than anything else in it, and the first was the last—that p c. [postcard] of yours which said that you hoped that I destroyed your letters and that no one else would read them. Think that over, heart of my heart—Do you think that I am the kind of hound who would not protect your letters with my life, who would let any other eyes but mine see the precious & to me sacred words you have written? You cannot have meant that p.c. my beloved, because if you really thought such a thing then you being you could not possibly love me. No, Soulina, your letters are safe—they are locked away in my dressing case of which, my dear, there is only one key and that key is on a chain round my neck, and just one or two are in my note case for comforts sake, but this also is safe as the note case never leaves me by day and is not handed over to any one, nor does it ever leave me by night—so now I hope that you are contented. The second point—that about the money: you say that my suggestion was "foolish." Is it foolish to wish to help someone one loves, someone whom one cannot really protect from hardship and strain and the buffets of the world because one is not free to protect them? Is it foolish to lie awake many nights remembering that the creature one loves more than life was once threatened with a serious illness, having neither money nor country nor home, and that here was this John in the world all the time who could, at least, have made the cross lighter—a little lighter to bear, perhaps? Is it foolish that out of my comparative plenty[1] I should wish to ease a most unhappy heart that must go with me every step of my way until I could tear it out of my body—should wish to ease it so innocently, by making it feel that through my small gift the woman I love could buy little comforts, could pay little bills and have small pleasures? If all this is foolish then I am your Fool and as such you will have to take me, Soulina. But you also say that you "love me too much." That is utterly false, you don't love me enough—perfect love knows neither doubting nor pride, it knows only that while it would give all things it would gladly accept all things, my Soulina. It does not say: "I am poor—she is not, I can neither repay nor give back in kind and because I love her I must hold my head high, and because I have lost my unhappy country I must not be one whit the less proud in case she should suddenly not respect me"—no, the perfect love says none of these things and why? Because it is unable to think them. It says: "We two love and that is enough—I give all, she gives all and the count is equal. Even with the same happiness that she gives do I accept the gift that she gives, and by my acceptance I, also, am giving; and if I feel gratitude (a most lovely virtue) then I greatly rejoice to feel gratitude because my acceptance has made her so grateful." These are the thoughts of a perfect love, and I beg you to let your dear love for me think them and thus become free from the smallest blemish. Accept the miserable £100 and by doing so make me eternally your debtor.

And now another point in the letter of the 2nd. You say that you will not even write unless I insist that you shall do so. I do insist. Let there be no mistake. I insist upon this in shere self-preservation. If I loose sight of you utterly & entirely as I must do if you will not write to me, then I shall most surely loose sight of myself—I shall loose myself in a wilderness of doubt, anxiety and complete desolation. Is it for this that you came into my life, in order that you might destroy my life? Destroy what is left of my inspiration? Make me unable to work again because my mind is perpetually tortured? Make me unable to face the years? Is it for

---

1. Currencies fluctuated considerably during the years of John's financial support of Souline. But even a very conservative estimate of John's net worth at this time would indicate that her assets totalled well over ten million in today's dollars.

this? I don't think so, Soulina. When I do think so then I have no god, and your hand will have killed my God for me, will have put out that poor little flickering light that is being so blown about, my faith, do not plunge me into the outer darkness—you dare not plunge me into that darkness. And then Una is so willing that we should write, and in this she sees straighter far than you do. Are we to think her devoid of all heart—a hard, cruel woman without any compassion? To do so would be unjust to Una. Nor do I think that ever again will the scene of the other day be repeated—it was very, very unlike her indeed. And remember that I have made the promise that she seems to cling to above all else—the promise that has been very hard to make—harder than you can possibly know because I think you are still innocent. But adoring you as I do I could make it—for the physical aspect is so much less than the other and finer side of my love—I suppose you would call it: 'the love of the spirit.' Rather than never see you again I would torture my flesh, would scourge it with whips—so now you know how much I love you, Soulina.

But this letter of yours that came early this morning, and for which I have been waiting & longing; watching every post, not sleeping at night, getting up and facing another day as though I were facing my execution, going down stairs and asking always the same question: "Has the post arrived yet? Is there any letter for me?" And when there has been no letter for me, and I have thought: "She has cut herself off—Soulina has either stopped loving me or else she is so mad as to try to do this thing, to cut us apart & leave me bleeding." Truly, my dear, I should bleed to death. It is easier sometimes to bleed to death than to live when one has been desperately wounded. Then your letter came. So you will not see me in Paris on my way home to England? You think it better that we should not meet but you give me no reason for there can be no reason. Yes, and only the other day you wrote: "When shall I see you?" Do you remember? I tell you that you are aching to see me, just to hear my voice & to see my face that has grown very thin these last days for your sake—A thin, ugly face I know but your own—such as it is, it is yours beloved. What I am feeling you also must feel. And you feel as I do that the great denial duty & honour impose upon us is terrible as all such denials must be; but less terrible, oh, but less terrible far than what you have decreed—complete separation. Listen, Soulina, I will <u>not</u> endure it, I will not allow you to do this thing, to send me away over seas to my country without first having seen you again & heard your voice, and said all the things that I have to say—the endless, gentle, brave and kind things that all lovers, even those who are not free, have a right divine to say to each other—the things that come welling up from the soul and have nothing to do with the turbulant body. I want to discuss your future plans, to see for myself whether you look well; a thousand things I want to discuss. And you shall say where I must sit while I discuss them, beside you or on the other side of the room. If you wish it I will not even touch you—in every thing I shall obey your wishes. Only one wish I refuse to obey: I will not consent not to see you in Paris. Don't you know oh, my foolish but very dear child that afterwards you would go mad with regret?, would think: "I could have seen my John's face, and heard her speak words of comfort to me, and we could have talked of small, intimate things, and I should have seen that she was alive, should have seen with my own eyes that she was alive and the same living, breathing creature that loves me. And John would have been in this room of mine and have touched my things, and the memory of her would have remained and been with me here—but now it is not here & perhaps never will be." And then will come the intolerable regret, so that I tell you you will cry out for me. This is what I would save us both from my most dear one.

Una knows that you have refused to see me and she offered to write & ask you to do so, but this I will not allow her to do—why should she when I can speak for myself? Honestly, she is willing that I should see you as she wants to spare me unhappiness, and I have told her that I will honourably keep my promise. She well knows that we could not help this thing and that she still has from me a real devotion. But my love for you is stronger than life or death. It has nothing to do with my devotion to Una. Does this seem to you strange? But so it is and I am speaking Gods absolute truth—it has nothing to do with my devotion to Una.

Are you truly my: 'Obedient Servant,' are you? Then I say to you, see me in Paris. If I can command you in anything, then I command you to see me in Paris. See me as a friend, or even as a stranger if that is what you want, but for Gods sake see me. And as I am only a human being and none too certain that you are my servant, and as the shock of your refusal has gone deep and my anxiety is burning me up like a white-hot iron thrust into my body, I beg you to cable me: Yes—or no. Just one word & your name & let the word be "yes" if you have any compassion, Soulina. As for your plans, I will fit mine to yours. If you are called away on a case you won't be kept on the case forever, and I will see you when you come back. You say that life seems vague, but it must not—Vagueness is dangerous for those who like ourselves are so often very near to despairing. I most earnestly intreat you not to be vague, plans we can & will make for our meeting. At the risk of offending that pride of yours I enclose 100 francs[2] for the cable—It won't cost that but I have no smaller bills, and for all I know you may not have received the 200 francs I sent you for postage. Are you really going to shut your door in my face? Soulina, are you going to shut your door in my face? somehow I simply cannot believe it.

Your John

P.S. I did not send this letter off yesterday but kept it back in order that I might re-read it this morning. I have just re-read it and find that I have nothing to add to or to take from it—You see, it is such a vital letter that I wanted to be careful.

[Sirmione]

August 11th 1934

My beloved. Your cable came at 9.00 this morning. Oh, bless you! bless you! bless you! And listen, darling; I think it will be possible for us to meet more than just once in Paris on my way home—I am almost sure it will. Of course I shall fit my times in to suit yours as just now you are working, and I am not, but all that we will arrange later on, only I wanted you to share my joy; it will mean that we shall not only meet to say goodbye as you & I had to do last time. As I told you in my recent letter I expect to be in Paris by the end of September. Your letter 8th speaks of two days having passed with no letter from me, but didn't you get two letters together? The posts are amazingly uncertain. And how could you think that I would feel angry with you and want to punish you? Only one thing would make your John angry & that is if you did not keep me posted regarding any change of address—if, in fact, you tried to escape from my love, from our love, that I would not permit for a moment, my need of you is too pressing, Soulina. And I will not let you be "bitter" any more. How can we either of us feel bitter now that at last we have found each other? Sad, desperately sad we may feel but not bitter. Someday you shall lie quietly in my arms and tell me all about

2. Roughly $34 in 1988 dollar value.

it, sweetheart—all about the things that are so hard to speak of, but which will seem less hard once they have been told. My love tells me that there are many such things—remember that now they belong to me also—that your pain has become my pain and that therefore I have a right to share it. But won't you try to get comfort from my love, from the fact that I am alive in this world even if I can't always be near you? Feel warmly wrapped up in my love of you, darling, and remember that where ever I may be I shall always come to you if you really need me. I told you this in Bagnoles when I gave you those English addresses. About your letters my dearest dear, I know well that you must often feel tired and unable to write after working all day, and when this happens just send me a post card. I wont have you straining yourself to write when you are worn out, if I felt otherwise it would certainly be a queer way to love you; but a post card yes, please, just to let me feel that I am in your thoughts as you are in mine every moment of the day and often most of the night, and when it is not too great an effort then a letter telling me how much you love me, telling me that you love me more & more, that never have you loved anyone so much, that if it were possible, if I were free, released from the promise of which you know, you would give yourself to me body & soul—that is what I am waiting to hear from you, Soulina, that is what I am longing to hear from you—but never let me hear it unless you mean it because it is far too grave a thing for you to say just in order to console me. Darling, if I had you here this moment my love would surely not make you feel afraid as you tell me it does sometimes in my letters. Love is capable of being almost cruell to the loved one—because sometimes it is past all endurance—love is a kind of agony—haven't you learnt that yet, Soulina? Perhaps you have not, you are only half awake, and timid, you are, of waking up fully— yes, I feel that you are still timid of love. But this I swear, I would be very gentle—at least I would try to be very gentle—Oh, but I would be, because I love you with so much more than my body. Therefore you need never feel afraid of me, darling, unless it must always be a cause for fear when one creature loves another so utterly. Perhaps that is always a cause for fear, but if so it is also a thing in which to glory.

I want to write more but I cannot today having somehow managed to catch a slight chill; or else it is that I am indulging in a slight (very slight) attack of malaria—I told you that I had it once badly in Rome, and since then it has hung about me a little. Now don't get the wind up, I am not really ill; and moreover things are getting so peaceful with Una that I feel very nearly happy by comparison. By the way, Una asks me to ask you whether you can remember how many of those little belladonna pills you used to melt in a glass of water for her to take in the morning— they were homeopathic—very little white things—she has lost the prescription giving directions.[1]

God bless you, and do take care of yourself. I was glad to hear about the party, but try not to get too over-tired. Anything that gives you pleasure makes me glad so long as you don't forget me.

Your John.

P.S. About your cloths. Don't laugh, but I often think about your cloths. As far as possible you should always wear collars like the one on the black coat you had at Bagnoles—an upright collar, even higher than that one—and I liked the silver clasp, it was right. You see you look so unlike other people, that you aught to dress to your type. And overcoats aught to have high collars too—fur collars like the one on that grey coat of mine that Una has adopted. That was a standup double collar. I don't want you to look like the Russian ballet, but unless you remember your type you look wrong. How I do adore to have the dressing of you. Darling, we can't get away from the fact that you do look a little like a darling Russian-Chink,[2] thats what I love about your face—its not like any other face in the world. The next time you are getting yourself new cloths remember what I say and dress to your type, it should not cost any more money to do so. I can shut my eyes and see your darling face, but when I do this I want to kiss it. J.

Sirmione

August 13th 1934

Darling. Yesterday so long a letter went to you that this one has every intention of being briefer, otherwise I can imagine your getting bored, or, worse still, allowing a patient to die while you read all the never ending things that I have to say to you. Darling I am almost quite well again—you see I am grown so conceited since you have loved me that I

---

1. At Bagnoles, Una had a severe attack of gastroenteritis, for which the belladonna had been prescribed.

2. It is obvious from the way that John was to develop this as a term of endearment that she did not intend any racial slur, even though such terminology seems utterly distasteful to late-twentieth-century ears.

tell myself you must want to know how much better I am, that you're probably worried, and so I hasten to reassure you. There have been many great storms in this place, and probably the constant thunder upset me, although it has never done so before—anyhow today the air is clear and light and everyone hoping that these are at an end, I suppose that they can't go on forever. So you are fond of music; this I have learnt from what you told me about the nurse who played well & who made you feel sentimental so that you wanted me at your side. You ask me what was I doing at that moment? What am I ever doing these days but thinking about you and longing to be near you? Whatever the outward me was doing my thoughts were very far away—in Paris. But how strange it is how little I know about the woman I have come to love and how little that woman knows about me—We know that we love each other intensely and that is all that matters, my Soulina; and yet, just because I do love you so much there are thousands of less important things that I am longing to know about you, and this is not curiosity but the need I feel to creep very close, to creep into your everyday life and thoughts—even foolish and trivial things become dear when they are a part of the creature one loves—Don't you feel this about me too? Yes you must; and letters are so unsatisfactory—though without them where should I be these days? Which means that you've just got to go on writing even if you've only time to send me a post-card. Well, now, what do I know about you, Sweetheart?

I know a name—Eugenie Soulina; perhaps it is your true name perhaps not—but to me you will never be anything but Soulina, because by that name I first loved you—I know that you are afraid of life—that I think I knew the moment I met you—I told you that you were afraid of life at Bagnoles. I know that you are a little afraid of love though now even fear cannot help you; love you must, so better make friends with love. I know that you have suffered very deeply, so deeply that you have become very silent and reserved, have put on a kind of armour, defending yourself against the world, or is it perhaps against yourself? I am not yet quite sure, but one day you will tell me. I know that you brood, you brood a great deal—remembering things that I can only guess at, but I think they are things that cause you regret, that sometimes make you hate your present position, and not only hate it, Soulina, but resent it with everything in you—very bitterly indeed I feel that you resent your position. And one other thing I feel that I know—someone once gave you an emmotional shock—who was it, I wonder—a man or a woman?[1] And did you love them as much as you love me? I don't want to think too much about this because I am now so far away, and I can't hear your voice, or see your dear face, or feel your arms round me—Did you love them as much? Listen, they can't have loved you as much as I do—I know from my soul that they can't. I love you more than you have ever been loved or ever will be as long as you live—so forget about them in me, Soulina. And remember this oh, you beloved of my heart: the circumstances that have made you what you are— lonely & homeless and none too rich, are the circumstances that have brought us together. But for all that has happened we might never have met, for you might well have still been in Russia. Could you have done without meeting me? I say that now you have met me, you could not— and so it all had to be as it was, the resentment, the pain, the years of suffering all because I was waiting for you in the world—I, who have so little to offer as I realize with my own bitterness, for the bitterness is not all yours, beloved, but I who can I do offer you my love, the love of my body, my mind & my spirit. Where ever you go that love will be with you, and I do believe what I wrote in: "The Master . . . ." "There is neither time, seperation nor distance." "It is all here & now, it has always been here; there is neither time, seperation nor distance."[2] But because we are human I want to protect you, to do for you little simple humble things—put you to bed early when you feel tired, take care of you whose whole life is spent in taking such care of other people. I want [to] discuss what cloths you buy, and to find out what is your favourite sweet, even what things you like to eat! And then I want to order those things and sit and watch you while you eat them! I want your bathroom to be very nice, your bedroom to be very large & sunny, I want you to have everything on this earth that I can possibly afford to buy you. This is my particular bitterness, that your life must be made apart from mine. But at least my devotion is mine to give, and at least you can let me help you a little—that I demand in return for my love—that you let me help you, my obedient servant.

I am wondering whether you are going away; but of course you will

1. Souline had once been engaged to a photographer. From later letters we can surmise that he lived in Paris, perhaps a member of the White Russian émigré community.

2. A refrain John would continue to use when writing to Souline. It is taken from a passage in her novel *The Master of the House,* describing the feelings of the "Christlike" protagonist Christophe for his cousin when the demands of adulthood and war first separated them physically.

let me know in good time. Meanwhile remember that the world is not so large and that we are going to meet in Paris.

Your John

Sirmione

August 17th 1934

My little Beloved. Yesterday I sent you a few hasty lines only because, as I told you, I had to <u>make</u> myself answer certain members of my reading public who had written me encouraging and rather beautiful letters. I have always made a point of answering such letters personally, and occasionally it takes up a lot of my time. All that I really wanted to do was to sit here and write many pages to you, but the other letters were an absolute duty.

Your letter of the 12<u>th</u>. I will answer that first. You want to know why I: 'like you so much' I think you mean: why I love you so much, and I answer that I do not know, my Souline. The most mysterious thing in the world is why two people meet and fall in love. Why did you fall in love with me? And why was this thing so strong between us that we dared not remain alone together at Bagnoles?, or if we did find ourselves alone, then we would move away from each other because each was so terribly conscious of the impulse that we had to come close, very close together. And that day in your bedroom when I tried to pay the Hospital fees—do you remember? I wanted to take you into my arms, which in the circumstances, as they then were, would have been little short of outrageous. But because I was near you I could not think clearly, and because you were near me you could not think either—and what a queer bill we finally made out! I can only hope that after you left you made out a saner bill for the matron, otherwise she must have thought that you'd gone mad. And you ask me to explain the greatest mystery in life—the mystery of physical and spiritual attraction—beloved of my heart, it cannot be explained—not even by an experienced writer! The future. We will talk of that when we meet—let it take care of itself for the present, and I absolutely forbid you to worry. Do you hear? I mean this—I forbid you to worry. The next thing will be that you'll be getting ill, and if you do that what in God's name shall I do if you've worried your beloved self ill because of me? Try very hard to be good and obey me. Meanwhile, do as I am doing and that is to concentrate on our meetings in September; but I see that you are trying to do this from your letter. You say that you find sweetness in obeying me, and that is a very lovely sentance, you find sweetness in it, you say, because you love me.

And then you ask me if this is right? My heart, my very, very little lonely child who has been so mishandled and so buffeted by life, who has seen too much misery and too little joy—it must be for me, John, to make it right that you should not only obey me but trust me. And believe me—oh, believe me you are more than right in feeling that I am indeed your friend—love without friendship is not love but lust. I cannot help desiring you, Sweetheart, because I am very terribly in love, because I love your body as a lover—but I also love so much more than that, and this being God's truth I want you to know that you can always count on my friendship. And well did I know that you, being you, would do anything to make me happy. That is the only way you can love—you can only love generously and entirely, and this is the only way worthy of Love, and this is the way that I also love—I would do anything to make you happy—If I could, were it possible (but this you must know) I would have you with me always, my beloved; and if you asked me to leave you as you are, innocent of the full meaning of passion—if I were convinced that you really meant that, then I swear that I would try to obey you, to respect the thing you would not want to give, even if I knew that you would give it in the end because you thought that it would make me happy. Can any poor devil say more than this to prove that they are friend as well as lover? I am not very certain regarding your plans. In your letter of 12th you say that you think you are coming to the end of 'general duty' about the end of this week. I have worked it out that you may be off general duty tomorrow the 18th. Then you say that you are going to take two days rest. But you also speak of 'the case.' Now I think you must mean that you may get a case, after which (if you do happen to get a case) you will go to Cannes or Menton[1] for a fortnight.

But suppose that you should fail to get a private case, will you go South at once, do you think? Anyhow I have your Paris address, but if you can, try to make all this more clear, and when you do decide to go South let me know—write to me before you leave telling me exactly

1. Resort towns on the French Riviera. Cannes, with a population then of 36,647 is sixteen miles southwest of Nice, and Menton (population 11,079) thirteen miles east northeast of Nice on the French and Italian border.

when you are going, and where I am to send my letters. If they are still to be sent to your apartment while you are away, then don't forget to leave the concierge (I cant spell her this morning) money for postage, and please give her a tip—you will naturally know how much to give—but give something, it will make her more careful to forward. And now about that £100. as I told you yesterday I have written to my bank instructing them to pay it to their Paris agents: Lloyds and National Provincial Foreign Bank. 43. Boulevard des Capucines. The agents will notify you when they have the money. You will need no identification beyond your PassPort. This I have taken some trouble to arrange as I don't want other people mixed up in our business. I am sending you back the letter from my Bank. I have written a few words to the manager in Paris on the back of the London letter. When you go to the Paris branch, show that letter and ask to see the manager—this should make it all simple for you. And please let me know that he has seen you and taken trouble in the matter. <u>And don't keep £100 in your room</u>—I wrote you yesterday about this. And don't be a little fool, my dearest, talking about not being able to repay me except by love & devotion. If you said that you had suddenly discovered that you had never loved me at all, that would not alter my love for you and I should still insist on your taking the money—so now you know that I have a strong will! Know also that the generosity is yours and not mine—that the gift is not mine but yours, for by accepting this money from me you have given me a little peace of mind, and for that I do very humbly thank you.

Your letter of August 13th. In this you are worrying yourself again because I asked that you would tell me if—Suppose I were ever released from my promise—you would live with me as your lover. I asked if you would give yourself to me. You say that you are not yet 'sure'; at least, my heart, I think thats what you mean me to understand by what you say. And you want to be near me just because you not quite sure, but at the same time you are frightened; and you say: 'Of course there is no question about anything now, is there?' Be at peace my very dearly loved coward, there is no question about anything now—no question at all—does that content you? Oh, you who know so much "in theory" as you once told me very proudly—you know less than nothing, but nothing at all! And God only knows what you have learnt "in theory." I tremble to think what you have learnt—I tremble to think what you may have been reading, surely something about very freakish things indeed, otherwise why this fear?[2] Darling, listen, I am John—your John—the John that you say you love; what do you think I should want to do to you? What horror do you think that I have in mind? No, my sweet, you know less than nothing at all. But don't worry so much for that makes me worry. Only, my darling, I am not such a freak that the thought of the love of my body need scare you. You ask me if I am happy as we are—meaning: am I happy though I cannot have you in the fullest and most perfect meaning of those words. And I answer: better half a loaf than nothing. Rather than not see you ever again I would go through hell. It is you that matter whether you desire me physically or not. Were I free to do so I could make you desire me—there, I have said it again, I could make you. And now be at peace—love is very sweet and let it go at that; only you must not fear me.

What do you mean about sleeping in your room unless 'we have no work at all'? Are you proposing to sleep in the street? What is the rent of your room, you must tell me. Do you think I am going to allow you to starve? There are things that we must discuss when we meet—the money I am sending may help for the moment. Oh, you funny, adorable, innocent woman, and you thirty years old! How you make me want to cry, and how you do manage to make me love you.

Your John

PS This snapshot was taken in Mickie's garden. The spots on my arm are not a fell disease, they are frightful mosquito bites painted with iodine—They are all gone now. Also I am well again.

Sirmione

Sunday. August 19th 1934

My Beloved. Your little letter of August 15th, telling me that you are no longer on floor duty, I got yesterday. Dont apologize for not having sent a post-card. Sweetheart, I don't long for post-cards! It was only my fear that while you were working hard it was a strain to have to write a letter to me sometimes—that was and that is all, darling. I do wish that you

---

2. John appears here to assume that Souline's knowledge of homosexuality would have come from her medical training and not from personal exposure to homosexuals. Most medical discussions at that time would have derived from the Krafft-Ebing model of physical and psychological abnormality and seen same-sex attraction as perversion.

could go off down South, the sun would do you worlds of good and I feel that you are tired? Am I right? The trouble is that as you were so dear but so foolish about that damned money, that you may not be able to go as soon as you could have had you let me have my own way days ago—I mean that you have delayed the business. I wrote to the Bank in London last Thursday and I fear that they won't get my letter until tomorrow, Monday. As soon as they do get my letter they will take immediate steps to pay over the £100 to their Paris Agents, but some days of delay there are bound to be.

Your letter of 17th has just arrived, and thank you for answering all my questions, my dear. Your resentment at the position in which you find yourself is obvious to me because my love for you has sharpened my wits—I do not think that it would be obvious to other people. You feel that you have missed something in life, something that you want and need and have—like all human creatures—a right to. What in God's name can I say to you? When I read those words my heart turned over, because I know, I know what you have missed; and far better than you can I know what we are missing, but even were I free to give you this thing that you have a right to, that I long to give you with a longing so intense that I also am worn out—even were I free you would think it wrong. You have written: "It is emotionally wrong." That is your conviction, you said this in Paris—our fulfillment would seem to you emotionally wrong. I cannot pretend that I understand you—no, I cannot, but I am not the least angry; and I like you to be perfectly frank with me, darling, I like you to tell me your doubts and fears, even if I can't always understand and share them. "Emotionally wrong"—but my dearest child it is not emotionally wrong for your John. I have never felt an impulse towards a man in all my life, this because I am a congenital invert.[1] For me to sleep with a man would be "wrong" because it would be an outrage against nature. Can't you try to understand, to believe that we exsist—we people who are not of the so called normal? Where's your medical knowledge?—we do exsist and believe me you must not

1. John is here using the terminology she learned from her study of Havelock Ellis in 1926–27. A congenital invert in Ellis's schema was one constituted by nature to have exclusively "homosexual" attractions. In contrast to what Ellis called "pseudo-inverts," such people had physical, emotional, and mental attributes of the opposite sex, attributes that are now generally seen as aspects of gender construction. John seems not to have adopted Ellis's psychological and biological ideas wholesale, but she was clearly deeply influenced by his studies and, as all these letters reveal, believed in innate homosexuality.

think us <u>perverted</u>. I am not perverted my very dearest heart, nor am I in any way a devil & evil. I have done my share of good, hard work in life as many another invert is doing—Do try, for my sake and for your own, to look upon inversion as a part of nature. Is it not enough that we are seperated and that this in itself must make us both suffer? Why add this other and unnecessary torment? Why sit thinking: "My love for John is <u>wrong</u>. I can't help loving John but its terribly wrong." Listen, I forbid you to think it wrong. You are being entirely childish and ab-surde, Souline, and I simply wont have it, darling. Another thing: you are insulting our love—you, who love me, are soiling our love by these thoughts, and thats why you've got to stop them, to stop them for your own sake as well as for mine. When we meet in Paris you shall tell me all about it, and I will listen with infinate patience. You shall tell me every doubt, every fear, whether you can explain them or not—and whatever you say I shall not get angry—this I promise, dearest, I won't get angry. But meanwhile, as I can't come to you at once which is what everything in me is crying out to do, meanwhile don't add this torment to yourself—You say at the end of your letter, my darling: "I am all worn out as it is, my John." And, I don't know know what I can say to this, because of course you are all worn out with this added tormenting of yourself day & night—this added torment of thinking your love wrong. I don't know whether I want to kiss you or shake you! Now, listen, my dear—I don't know much about you, but perhaps this is your first deep emotional experience and as such has come upon you as a shock. Believe me, that will pass, I don't mean the emotion itself but the shock, the shock of it will pass. You and I have just got to have some long talks together and get many things cleared up. I intend to be a week or 10 days in Paris—I shall come to your apartment where we can have peace and get to know more about each other. You want our love to be "pure" and yet "vital." You shall try hard to tell me what you mean by that. I don't think that you really know what you do mean—you are all "balled up" as the Yankees say. And I notice that you ignore one thing in my letter—I maintain that I feel that at some time in your life there has been some other emotional shock—even if this falling in love with me has been your first deep experience of love, even if the other experi-ence was less shattering. The other thing may have been a man—why not? That would not surprise me in the least. Have you never heard of bi-sexuality? Don't you know that an enormous number of people are bi-sexual, capable of falling in love equally with a man or a woman?

You may be bisexual, and if so what of it? That also is a very common fact in Nature. It is neither good nor bad, above all it is nothing to fear, is merely a very common fact in nature. Nature, my darling, is not limited by the views of . . . lets . . . say . . . a hospital matron. Nature has such vast ideas of her own, and its useless & foolish to kick against them. If you don't like her ideas it cant be helped, you've just got to make the best of it, and try to believe that everything is meant, that nothing in natures scheme is ever waisted. Bi-sexual people outnumber the inverted—I cannot at the moment remember statistics. We inverts are about 20 per 1000, the bi-sexuals are many, many more than this. I helped a young doctor a little while ago to prepair his paper for his final medical degree at Cambridge; he maintains that the bi-sexual is the true normal. No one fainted at Cambridge, no one even turned a hair, and I am glad to say that he took his degree! Someday I shall send you a copy of his paper.[2] Well, dearest, I think I have written enough. This letter is not about Sirmione, but about Souline—both begin with an S—and so does Silly oh, heart of mine. I am glad & proud & thankful that you love me—Do you hear? I am proud. Yes, and you must be proud that you love me and that I love you, that your love for me is not all onesided, but is given back with both hands, my dearest. And courage, courage, all will be well—I don't know how, but all will be well; and you are not a morbid unnatural creature who has fallen deeply in love with a devil. There is nothing morbid about your love, it is perfectly in accordance with nature. And trust me. Love without trust is not love; and believe in me, love without belief is not love. If I am the "giver" then take what I give—love and deep, deep friendship, and take it without misgiving. If I am the "Master" then obey me in this: don't worry yourself ill by your doubts and fears. Look the thing straight in the face and say: 'I have fallen very much in love with an invert, and thank God, she has fallen in love with me. There is nothing to make me feel lonely & bitter. And all true, unselfish love is the same thing, the same joy the same torment—it is all the same thing—whether the love is between woman & man, or man and man, or woman & woman."

I think we can hold our heads high, my Souline.

Your John

---

2. Most probably Douglas Bryan, MRCS, LRCP. His paper on bisexuality was delivered to the British Sexological Society on April 11, 1933.

September 6th 1934

I am sending this letter express post, my beloved, as I want you to get it quickly. The reason is that I am not sure you're not right in telling everyone that your going to be out of Paris for our ten days. Yesterday I made a milder suggestion; I suggested that you should say you might be out of Paris, but on second thoughts it has occurred to me that you may be thinking of Mrs Baker.[1] I can envisage her ringing you up every five minutes to do her shopping, to pack her slippers, to cash her cheques, to see about her manicure, or worse still to come and hold her hand. Darling, that simply must not be—I'm sorry if she's a very sick woman, but I'm not going to have you anyone's slave. If your anyone's slave your going to be mine, only I'd hate to have you my slave—I prefer to have that the other way round. Well, dearest, do what you know to be best to ensure perfect peace while I'm in Paris. I think I was stupid to make any suggestion, after all you know your own circumstances much better than I do, and again, after all, if you're seen anywhere you have only to say that your plans for going away fell through, and yet again—its nobody's business! I feel like saying : to Hell with all the world for those ten days when we're going to be together. Last night I simply could not sleep—I went off to bed feeling fairly sleepy after an evening at Mario's caffee, but the moment my head touched the pillow I woke up and began to think about you—always you. And then I remembered very vividly that last meeting of ours in my hotel in Paris, and something you said kept hammering on my brain. You said suddenly: "Do you want to kiss my mouth?" I had kissed your mouth many times already, but you suddenly said: "Do you want to kiss my mouth?" And I wanted to answer something that I did not, or perhaps that I dared not—I don't know which, and so I think that I answered nothing. Perhaps you forgot this, and perhaps you remember. Anyhow those words kept me awake all night, for I saw how you looked, my beloved, when you said them. In my mind I could see you amazingly clearly. When I dropped off to sleep at long last, I had a very preposterous dream. It was this: You had written a long letter to Una, and in it you said that you were married, had been married some time and had left your husband, but that now

---

1. The American woman Souline had nursed during the summer of 1934. Her proposal to take Souline back to the United States in October had thrown John into the panic that her late August and early September letters reveal.

you were going back to him again. You said: "Will you please break this to John—I can't." My darling I woke up sweating! I think I love you too much, far too much. Shall I try to love you less, my Souline? How you'd really hate me to love you less, how dull life would seem if I loved you less—You observe that I am growing conceited. Yesterday came a telegram from Romain Brooks[2] saying that she is motoring to Sirmione. She arrives this evening I don't know for how long. I am based here & I have begun working and will have to give some of my time to her. You see she is really a very great artist, and then at one time she was fond of your John for a while, though your John did not respond, and this latter I tell you in strict confidence because one does not talk about women in that sense, one forgets about those things, except that one always feels slightly grateful. But to you I want to say every thing that comes into my head, as you will to me—moreover I know that I can trust you. And then, you see, its not you who are in question; I would never let anyone interfere with you unless I were absolutely powerless to help it, so don't think from this that I've changed my mind about Mrs. Baker or anyone else during our short ten days in Paris. Romain is older now, and for love she has very courteously accepted my friendship. Darling, I am rather desolate today—I am wanting you terribly badly today. It comes over me like this sometimes, and it hurts. It hurts me so much that I want to cry out—to beat my head against the wall—only one does not do those things, one just endures it as best one can. I am starving for you, that's God's truth, Souline. Be kind to me in Paris my little child—please take me in your arms and be very kind, please tell me that you want me as I want you, and then kiss me they [the] way I taught you to kiss, even though you were a backward pupil!

Your John

Sirmione

September 7th 1934

My Beloved. Your darling letter of September 5th came this morning. No, you won't be frightened when you see me—I hope you will be too

---

2. Romaine Brooks (1874–1970) was an American painter whom John met in 1917 at a party given by a mutual friend, Barbara "Toupie" Lowther. Brooks, an heiress, had been married briefly. She had a fifty-year relationship with Natalie Clifford Barney, another friend of John's. Brooks is the model for the painter in Hall's novel *The Forge*.

happy to think, and when one can't think one can't be frightened, for fear is the result of immagination. But you don't know quite what you feel, do you Sweetheart. Once you wrote that you feared me when I was not there, but that when you saw me you would not fear me—never mind, afraid or not afraid you can't escape from our love any more, our love's just happened and thats all about it. No, one cant forget that one is in love, not for a moment can one forget it, and as you say it changes all life—it makes life more real and yet less real. I think that being deeply in love is the greatest pain & the greatest joy, and that these together make for beauty, there is so much beauty in being in love, in giving oneself completely to another as I have given myself to you, so that I have no real life at all except the life I am living through you, and now all that I see I seem to see through you—its difficult to put this into words, I can only say that you're everywhere, that apart from you nothing has any meaning.

But what were those words that I wrote to you and that you won't tell me? Please, please tell me darling—write them back to me when you answer this letter, write them back as from you to me, my darling, because all my words apply to us both—that is if you love me, Souline. I have written so many things to you, so many things that I could not speak because of the awful distance between us, so many things that I just had to write or go mad, because I'm so crazy about you; but what were those particular words? Do they make you feel too shy to write them? Thats foolish, sweetheart; and another thing, I should never think that your efforts were childish—nor would I laugh. I might want to cry because you are still so innocent somehow, and that touches all that is pitiful in me; so that I am torn in half—one side of me longs to destroy your innocence and put a more vital state in its place, one side of me clamours to make a woman of you, so that whatever happens in your life you will at least have known the meaning of passion—not in "theory" but in practice, beloved, and believe me a mighty big gulf lies between them; the other side longs to take you in my arms and let you sleep quietly like a baby. Oh, you my torment, my most cruel desire— for surely you must know that desire is cruel? Surely you feel this urge for me; don't you feel it? You must know, your instinct must tell you. When the thing happens every woman knows however innocent she is— I think you knew that afternoon in Paris—I <u>know</u> that you knew that afternoon in Paris. Souline, I love you—I love you entirely—I love you so much that I cannot sleep. You have lighted a fire in me, beloved, and its burning me up. What am I to do who am being so bitterly tormented by love? But quite soon I shall hold you close up against me, and then I shall kiss you until you ask for mercy, until you begin to cry in my arms, not from fear, oh, no, but because you love me, and because love can be so wonderful, Souline. And your room—I think about it so often. To me it will be a beautiful room because you have slept there night after night. Darling, if that room were a bare little attic it would still seem beautiful to me. Surely, oh, surely you can understand this? I'm glad that you've got a case you like, I'm glad of anything that keeps you happy. Yes sweetheart, at times I am happy too, but not calmly—that is too much to ask! If you really want your John to be calm, well then I can only suggest that you dope me!

Your John

Sirmione

September 8th 1934

My darling. I have your second letter written on Sept. 5th late at night. Dearest; I had only really decided not to see you in Paris because I thought that you were going to leave me high & dry & go off to America with someone else—but no more of that—its all past, thank God. Yes, I would like you to go south after I leave Paris, especially as you have a Russian friend to go to, but we will talk of that when we meet. Thank Heaven Romain Brooks departed early this morning—she wanted us to return with her to her villa at Santa Margherita,[1] but of course, nothing doing. And the fussing—nothing good enough here in Sirmione, everything too primitive for her & so on. Also she has let herself go to pieces. Last night we all dined at St. Vigilio again, that wonderful place that I told you about and sent you p-cs of. I think that it was more wonderful than ever, a little misty because of the heat, and a sunset that made my heart ache quite badly. Shall we ever be there together, Beloved? I always think of us there together more than at any other place. Because I love you beauty becomes sad if I am forced to see it without you. Our meeting—can you believe it our meeting. A serious one you think and fear. Yes, you are right, a serious one, because all deep love is a serious thing, and entering into such a love is serious. Are you really afraid my

---

1. A town with a population of sixty-five hundred on the Italian Riviera fifteen miles southeast of Genoa.

little child? Are you really truly afraid of John? Sweetheart then I am afraid of you—yes thats God's truth I'm afraid of you, for such fear is often a part of loving. Only—and perhaps you think that this will be the difference—once you are in my arms I shall not be afraid—something stronger than fear will take hold of me, darling. And you? Do you really think that you'll still be afraid? Oh, foolish and pathetic creature that you are. I tell you that you will not be afraid—not afraid of love, not afraid of me and not even afraid of yourself, my Souline. Sweetheart, you want to be in my arms—you want to feel me close, very close, and you want to feel my kisses, beloved. If you told me that this was not so—if you swore it, I simply should not believe you. Souline, oh, my dearest, my very dearest—I can't write the things that are in me at this moment—all the longing and the love that I have for you. No, its no good, I simply can't write them.

But you know them already, you know the ache of body and mind & spirit when one loves, you know the terrible longing for nearness—and other things I think you must know, don't you, Sweetheart? For they also are a part of love, and you are in love with me—don't deny it. Yes, and you want me just as I want you. And never before in all your life have you wanted anyone as you now want me; and if when we meet I kiss your hand and sit down very quietly & gently beside you, what will you do? Do you think you'll be happy? Perhaps I'll just kiss your darling hand then see what happens. Shall I, Souline? Dearest, I must stop. When I write like this it makes me feel too much and thats rotten bad for one.

You know what I mean—your so far away and the longing for you gets so intense. Oh, yes, you're up against it, my Darling—I'm terribly in love. Now don't be scared—I can feel you getting scared as you read. Your not the only woman who has been desired in this world and you certainly wont be the last, but no woman can possibly have been more desired than you are. And there's nothing to be scared about, and don't run away, because that won't help you—I'd only follow & bring you back—thats what I'd do, so don't run away. But if when we meet you find you don't love me, don't want me—then its I who will go away. But please, please don't send me away if you can help it—

Your John

Darling—I love you—I want to write this at least a thousand times!

September 11th 1935 [4]

My very dear. Your letter of the 7th has come and somehow I particularly love it. Yes, dearest, forget whether my love for you "is wrong or
not wrong." Remember only that real and profound love cannot be
wrong; try also to remember that the good God knows his own business,
and that since He made me as I am and gave me the capacity to love
very deeply, He can hardly expect me not to do so. As for you—who
knows how He made you? Anyhow one thing is perfectly clear, He made
you able to respond to my love—now let this be sufficient for your dear
comfort. Yes, I also was thinking how strange it is that you should have
a mother as a patient. The other day when you wrote me about it, I
thought: 'Would Souline like to have a child?" Dearest I cant give you
that I'm afraid—no I can never give you a child—I can only love you
and love you and love you. And now if I tell you something very secret
you musn't laugh at me, my Souline. I suddenly saw you with a child,
and the child was our child and we were very happy. Would you love me
even more if I were a man? In some ways I should probably love you
less. I'm not trying to lessen the obvious importance of normal love
between men and women—and this love can of course be terribly
strong—only I think that the other love is stronger. Not always, but
when it is st[r]ong [it] is very strong—Dont you feel this yourself? I
think you must feel it. My sweetheart, this is going to be a little letter
because I am writing it from my bed. My ankle has been punished by a
mosquito of evil habits and is very swollen. What happened is this:
Yesterday morning I woke up uncomfortably wanting Souline. I thought
that I'd better get down to work and try to get a spot of peace that way.
I put Ponds[1] on my ankle and too tight a bandage, then I put a shoe on
and buckled that too tightly, then I worked for over 12 hours at my
book in tropical heat with my foot hanging down. At 12.30 p.m.[2] I was
conscious of pain—I undressed my poor ankle and the result was the
fattest ankle I have ever seen—a disgusting sight—I'm so glad you didnt
see it. This morning comes the little Italian doctor who orders bed,
fomentations and ointment and promises that Ill be O.K tomorrow.
Now no pain anymore except when I walk which I dont attempt unless

---

1. Ponds is still in use as a cold cream today. It is unclear if John was using a special
preparation with other medicinal properties.
2. Obviously 12:30 a.m.

I can't help it. Much less swelling also and less inflamation. This summer the mosquitos have been venomous here—this is the third bad bight I've had. I generally get slightly poisoned by the beasts but not so badly as I've been this summer. I attribute this entirely to Bagnoles. Once after Bagnole I had an awful boil or something very like a boil on my face— It brings one out in spots & blains—I hope I shall escape this—I don't want to arrive with dressings & plaster to see you in Paris! My love— my love . . . . I like writing those words, they relieve me and so I will write a line of them: my love, my love, my love, my love, my love—I do love you and want you so intensely.

Now listen. I want you to buy a present for me & give it to someone called Souline. I want you to go out and buy some flowers—any flows[- ers] that you think such a woman would like—no matter what they cost—and put them in her room on the 23rd of September. I will pay you for this when we meet, my dearest.

Now please listen again, and this is urgent. I want you to go & get your photograph taken—without a hat of course—go as soon as you can so that I can see the proofs in Paris immediately on my arrival. I am bring[ing] my photograph along when I meet you—But I'm not going back to England, my sweet without yours, so kindly do as I tell you.

Go and get your photograph taken at once.

I've just looked at my ankle and its ever so much better.

Your John

This is not such a little letter after all—

Sirmione

September 11th 1934

I see from your letter of the 8th my darling, that on the 8th you got no letter from me. I have written to you every day, so probably you'll get two letters together—this is what happens to me sometimes, a day passes without a letter from you; I am instantly down in the depths of gloom then I get two letters the following morning. You will know by now that Romain Brooks stayed only two nights & these were two too many, so fussy and unreasonable has she become—but I have written you already about her. And now I am going back to your letter of 7th. Dearest love, I want you just as you are, inexperienced and simple in matters of love—or rather in regard to certain sides of love. If you're really in love with me thats enough—think back on that afternoon in Paris and what you felt then, for you did feel, Souline. I was not the only one who felt physical desire, and this you well know if you are honest with yourself, even if you were telling me the truth when you said that you did not know to kiss me! Sweetheart, am I wrong? I can't think I am in view of that letter you wrote me after. I cant think that you're cold—some women are I believe, though I've only known one such woman. But I do think your frightened and terribly shy. You'r so shy that its like making love to a school girl—not that I've ever done such a thing! But it might be like that my beloved, Souline. However, I want you just as you are, and when we meet this time you will feel less shy. I think I was too uncontrolled that day in Paris—I rather lost my head and that scared you to death. But this, as a woman, you will easily forgive knowing that it was because of you—that I lost my head because of your nearness. And now please stop thinking this sort of thing: "Will John find me a bore because I know nothing?" "Suppose, after all, I am really cold—how awful. Suppose I feel nothing at all—what would John do then—very probably hate me." "What aught I to feel—what aught I to do—what is that John expects me to do?" My dear and very scared little child—there is such a thing as primitive instinct when we love, and in any case there is John. Peace, peace—don't torment yourself needlessly, and above all don't wish that you were different—whatever you are, responsive or cold, your the woman I love. When I fell in love with you I didn't stop to ask whether you were a passionate woman—I never thought of that—I had no time to think, I knew only that I utterly loved—that was enough & that still is enough—and let it be enough for you also. Last evening I felt terribly tender towards you. The feeling came over me in a wave. I think that this infinate tenderness can be even more painful when we are apart than moods of passion—I'm sure that it can, though God knows the others are hard to endure. But this tenderness seems to come from the spirit. The pain of it is less abrupt but very real—to me its a kind of desperate yearning, a kind of desperate spiritual need that is aching to find a physical expression, but not an expression connected with the senses. It must be, I suppose, that I love you in all ways—with my spirit and mind as well as with my body. Your letter of 8th Darling, what is there to explain in my sentance? I suppose I was still a little afraid that your tiresom American would interfere— but you give me the sentence without its contex[t] so that I don't know what led up to the words. Anyhow it is not important as I know you won't let her interfere. At least I feel that I know this now—at one time, my dearest, I did <u>not</u> know it. Are you terribly innocent or terribly blasee? Neither, my sweet, just a darling woman who has never until now come up against the real thing, and who therefore is feeling rather surprised, rather anxious and, as I have said, very shy. I am not very brown but I shall be smiling—at least I think so, though this meeting of ours is grave, as you yourself feel, beloved. How shall you kiss me? Exactly as you wish—I know very well indeed how I will kiss you, and when I have done with kissing your mouth you can kiss me on the cheek if you feel like it—but if you do feel like kissing my cheek then I must have forgotten how to be a lover. I wish your little Russian Princess very well—

Bless you, my own little Russian.

Your John

My ankle goes on well—it is now said to have been a horse-fly.

This is the only letter that John wrote during her stay in Paris from September 22 to October 1. As becomes obvious from the letters that succeed this one, all written after John had returned to England, the "solemn promise" made to Una had been broken. This letter, however, reveals John's desperate longing, Souline's continued resistance, and the crisis moment which their relationship had reached.

[Pont-Royal-Hotel stationery, 27 Rue du Bac, 7 Rue Montalembert, Paris]

September 22nd 1934

Telephoning is so cold and unsatisfactory—one speaks of commonplace things of necessity, placed as we two are. But your darling voice was there, and I so terribly glad to hear it—Oh, but so incredibly glad. I love your voice. Were you glad to hear my voice speaking from Paris to you? I wonder—my dear, my very dear, what can I say; except that I long to be with you at this moment, consoling, trying to make you more happy, letting you cry your eyes out in my arms if thats what you want. I do understand, though you are the only woman, my beloved, who has ever been frightened of me. It is bitter to me that I can't do right—that my letters bring you nothing but terror. I aught to be angry, but I love you too much—Soulina, be at peace—I'm not going to force you to do anything that you don't want to do. Dearest, one does not <u>force</u> a woman's love. You are your own to give or to withhold. I could never accept an unwilling gift. Can't you try to understand how revolting that would be—how utterly beastly, my little Soulina? Sweetheart, I'm John, not a drunken tramp. Don't beg for mercy—don't say 'I emplore you.' There is no need at all for you to emplore—and, Soulina, I shall not emplore either. No, dearest—if you feel as you seem to feel, terrified and revolted at the thought of this thing—then remain as you are. Damn it all, I don't want it—or if I do want it I'd rather kill myself than live with a frightened and unwilling woman. And remember, you are free, there is no obligation of any kind on your part towards me. Perhaps you would rather we met as friends? This need not prevent us meeting every day during this stay of mine in Paris, and it need not prevent my doing my best to keep an eye on you when I go back to England. You know that I love you so why should I repeat it? Meanwhile—I am full of deep sympathy, and I beg you to forgive any letter of mine that may have made you unhappy & disturbed. I am not quite as you are—perhaps its that. Or perhaps it is that you don't understand because you have never, and will never feel passion—thats not your fault, dearest, though its my misfortune. You see, I'm not angry—only shocked & grieved that you thought it necessary to write as you have done. When I read those words they struck me in the face—it was like a blow in my face, Soulina. Therefore be tired if you must, but be at peace—I love you intensely, and so I desire you more than you can ever hope to understand; but Soulina, remember, I am not going to beg. Is that pride? Perhaps.

God bless you my darling—my poor, poor child—Now, stop being scared—I insist upon that, because by being so scared you insult me.

Your friend
John

October–December 1934

John wrote to Souline daily from October 3 to November 3, 1934.
Many of the letters were written from London, where John and Una had
a flat, 17 Talbot House, in St. Martin's Lane. Others were written from
the Forecastle, an Elizabethan cottage John bought in Una's name,
which overlooked Romney Marsh in Rye. The two residences proved
useful for John as she sought to establish privacy for herself and Souline
while still living with Una. On November 3, John met Souline at Folke-
stone for a "honeymoon" that was always to remain a highlight in
John's memory. The letters during this month reveal some of the details
about their first lovemaking, but deal far more urgently with John's
growing concern about Souline's lack of citizenship or homeland. John,
enlisting the invaluable help of Una, kept pursuing schemes to enable
Souline to become a naturalized French citizen and thus more perma-
nently welcome in England.

[John's Talbot House stationery]
October 3rd 1934, 10. p.m.

Yes, and may God bless you also my darling love.

As though you divined what must be my desolation at this awful home-coming after leaving you in Paris—you sent me that cable my best beloved, and I found it awaiting me on my arrival. I sent you a wireless from the boat and a cable as soon as we got to Dover—the latter I left with the wireless operator who promised [to] send it as soon as he landed, this because I knew that I'd not have time to send it myself—there are Customs at Dover as well as the Customs in London—And always this sense of desolation—from the moment I left you this morning I have had it—its like a dull ache that flares up into pain—really

65

terrible, unendurable pain—then subsides again but never leaves me. Desolation—the feeling that somehow I am lost—that I can't find my way anymore without you—and strange, I feel that everything around me is strange, that I am a stranger in my own country—that nothing is real—this city is'nt real, the life I've come back to is'nt real anymore, my friends are'nt real, my career is'nt real—nothing is real but those ten days in Paris when I held you in my arms and taught you to love, when your heart beat close against my heart, and your mouth was on mine, and our arms were round each other straining our bodies closer & more close, until there was an agony in our loving—when we lay there together hour after hour and did not notice the passing of time, because you & I had got beyond time—there was reality, but this is a dream. Oh, Soulina, oh, beloved, oh, my terrible desire of body mind & Spirit— I am crying out for you. How darling it was of you to send me that cable and how it has really brought me comfort—the only drop of comfort since we parted. Oh, my dearest, never let me feel out of touch—keep me close, very close as I will keep you, otherwise I shall die of this seperation. I am dropping with tiredness and misery—but I did want to write to you tonight, just to let you know how intensely I love you. For your John's sake take care of yourself—Soulina.

Your John

Please oh <u>please</u> do take the tonic I bought you—you are going to be run down if you dont—please take it with you to Menton.

17. Talbot House

October 10th 1934

My greatly loved—Yesterday I wrote you a disgraceful letter and what is even worse, I sent it. It was one big, selfish, inexcusable wail because my body was crying out for you—and my wretched body is strong as you know, and Sweetheart, as you also know, it loves you. But I aught not to send you those kind of letters, because perhaps your dear body loves me and longs for me as I so often long for you, and I here in England and you in Mentone! This physical need can be all red hell, but we have so much more than the physical need and because of this we can cling to each other over the miles, we can cling with our minds: 'There is neither time, seperation nor distance.' Darling, darling you can't resent that letter because you are the cause of these turbulent feelings, and surely you could not have me feel less? Were I to feel less it would be an insult. Well, my darling love now to other things. Life here is growing always more crowded—people and more people it seems to me—nice people though, old friends for the most part. Then my boot-maker and my talier to see because now, more than ever, I don't want to get shabby—I say to myself that I dress for you, and this childish thought very often consoles me. Then I shall soon have to go to the Bank and see how I had best arrange for you[r] rent to be paid in a way that will give you the least trouble—and that consoles me most of all—it makes me feel that you <u>belong</u> to me—Thank you for letting me help you, my beloved, it is so understanding & generous of you.

Another thing. You have no warm coat—the fur coat you say is so grand that it bores you. I am going to try to send you a warm coat from England if I can find a suitable one—it will be good enough just for the time being. I have a man I know who thinks he can manage to send the coat to you having first paid the duty, so that I shall have saved you the trouble of paying the duty & then telling me what it was so that I could pay you back—but I must'nt send the coat until you are home once more in Paris. But this I do beg—when you get back north be careful—its the change from the South that's so dangerous—how I wish that you had a proper over-coat. I must have been quite mad not to buy you one in Paris. I think what fits me will be all right for you, because we both have rather wide shoulders. An old friend of mine I.A.R. Wylie the writer, has just returned from Russia. She was sent there by 'The Satur-day Evening Post.'[1] She is a very fine journalist and will write a series of articles on Russia. She went there with a perfectly open mind—if she had a bias it was tending to be Red—she has come back <u>whiter</u> than the driven snow. She says the conditions are perfectly frightful, (and mark you, they all did their best to impress her—the Reds know the great importance of The Saturday Evening Post). She says that the filfth is past all belief—where ever she went she found lice and bed-bugs, filthy steamboats and even more filthy trains—and in the hotels foul accomo-dation. Food of a kind and quality that made it impossible to swallow—

---

1. Ida Alexa Ross Wylie (1885–1959) was a poet, novelist, journalist, and woman of letters. Born in Melbourne, Australia, she had lived in England and traveled widely. In 1934 she spent six weeks touring the Soviet Union. Her observations were crystallized in an article "Soviet Sidelights: Reality and Illusion," published in *The Saturday Evening Post* (5 January 1935, pp. 12–13). She spent the final third of her life in the United States, living primarily in Princeton, New Jersey, with her lover, Dr. Louise Pearce.

and poverty, poverty everywhere—the greatest privation among the people. But what struck her most was the <u>sameness</u> of the people—everyone of exactly the same pattern—all their faces exactly alike, she says, a kind of dreary standardisation—no individuality left, of course; and no visible trace of our class left, nothing but what I suppose they call 'The Workers.'

This, she told me, made her feel very lonely and as if she had been dumped into quite a new world—a world that was mad and extremely unlovely. While there she became rather seriously ill with dysentery—there was no castor-oil, or indeed any medicines the doctor wanted—the German Doctor merely spread out his hands and said: 'I can't get what is needed for you, there are scarcely any medicines in the country—& that was in Moscow—Finally she made a mighty effort & got up, so mad keen was she to get out of that hell. She told me that if it had killed her outright she'd have crawled, if need be, over the frontier. Before leaving she lost her rather hot temper & told a Red journalist what she thought of the lies that she was told about conditions—I am greatly surprised that she left the country—that some unforseen accident didn't happen! Well, my darling, that is what I.A.R. told me—and <u>never</u>, <u>never</u>, <u>never</u> do you go back to Russia. Homesick you may be but not for that country—Be homesick for me—you who are homeless—let me be your lover, your home and your country. Beloved—please adopt my heart as your country.

I could go on writing to you all day, but I know I've got to get down to work. By the way, if there's war over this assisination of the King of Serbia[2]—I shall bring you to England if I think there is any real danger for you. Do you mind belonging to John, my Soulina?

Yours always—always
John

17 Talbot House

October 12th 1934

My own beloved. Your two letters have reached me this morning—they are the first to come from Mentone, telling of your safe arrival, and

---

2. On October 9, 1934, while on a visit to France, King Alexander of Serbia and the French foreign minister, Jean Louis Barthou, were assassinated at Marseilles by a Macedonian terrorist.

because of them I have been feeling almost happy—not perfectly happy, this because we are parted for the time being, but much happier. I am glad, glad, glad that you are in the sunshine, and especially glad to hear that you have a room in the same house as your friends—you remember that I wanted you to get a room there if possible. Be a bit careful of the bathing though, wont you? Its late in the year for bathing even down South, as I have warned you already.

My darling, your dream is also mine—if you only knew how much I long to be with you doing all the happy things you have thought of, and getting better and more rested every minute—for you and your love do rest me, Soulina. And now I will tell you yet again a curious fact that I told you in Paris—not every physical union is successful—some never give the complete sense of peace—of rested nerves and appeasement of body that I get when I have lived with you, on the contrary, some make one uneasy and restless—this is also true of normal unions. I don't understand it, for the union may be complete in the purely physical sense, and yet it will set one's nerves on edge—one won't feel calm and fit as one should do. The entering into a physical union is always a bit of a toss up, I suppose, and blessed am I in you, my Soulina—and blessed I do pray that you may be in me now that at last you have passed the barrier—may I bring you peace to both mind and body. And this I do want to say to you, my darling—now that the barrier has been passed, have no fear that it will not be passed again & [a]gain; don't go thinking that there's going to be any more trouble. The trouble that there was, was <u>entirely nerves</u>. No woman in your desperately nervous state could have hoped to get a normal reaction—remember how you fought me, my darling!

Just put the thing right out of your head so far as any apprehensions go—just say to yourself: 'I'm a normal woman, and when my John loves me my response is normal—my body loves John and John gives it joy—and will give it that joy many, many times.' Then think of our longed for meeting in England. When I know the date of that meeting I can rest more contentedly than I can do at the moment—you will let me know about your course[3] as soon as you can—as soon as you return to Paris, won't you darling? Maybe you will have to come before the course—and then again after the course, I don't know—I am waiting

---

3. Over the years Souline had several schemes intended to enable her to change occupations. Presumably John is referring to the plan to enroll in a typing course.

until I hear your definate plans, but Soulina, I do want you terribly badly. About Madame Makalinsky[4]—I'm so glad that she should know that we love each other—for of course you did not only tell her that you loved me—you surely told her how much I love you; if you didn't, then I want her to know how much I love you—please don't let her be in any doubt about that—you may tell her that I'm off my head about you. I'm so glad that she's not one of those people who talk about the physical facts in detail—I hate that, it makes me feel rather sick—though lots of married women do this I know. But now I have told you the facts of life—all the facts of life I believe I have told you—some good & some bad, for I thought the time had come when you aught to know all that there was to know of the sexual relations that exsist between people. There are one or two lesser things that I will tell you when you and I are together again—things that concern us and our way of loving—they are unimportant except in as much as they give more or less pleasure as the case may be—But I'd rather tell you about this when we're together. For the rest you now know all the essential facts, and the right and proper person to tell you was John, your deeply adoring lover.

About translating 'The Well . . . .' into Russian. Of course I'll allow the nice Lysa to do this.[5] She is a friend of yours and that's enough. I'd like her to make some money by it—As for my terms they need not be considered, though the deal would have to go through my Agent. As Lyza is such a kind & good friend to you, I'd wave the question of money in her case altogether—though the publishers and not she would pay me. Nor is this quite so noble as it sounds—the Reds pirate every foreign book they want—they steal books, and one can't do a single thing as we none of us want a law suit in Russia which would always be given against us.[6] Tell Lysa to go ahead if she wants to—she has my full permission and my blessing—if on the other hand she decides not to do it—then she equally has my blessing.

This day I have ordered you a warm coat—it will fit me & so I hope

4. One of Souline's circle of White Russian émigrés. She and Souline had known each other as school girls.

5. Lysa Nicolsky, one of Souline's closest friends in Paris. In the end Lysa did not translate *The Well of Loneliness* into Russian. Two computer searches of worldwide translations turned up no Russian edition during John's lifetime.

6. International copyright laws, always rather scrupulously adhered to in North America and Western Europe, were notoriously disregarded through all the Stalinist and much of the post-Stalinist Soviet rule.

it will fit you—size 38 it will be (English measure)[7] Its of the same stuff as a faun coat that Una had out in Bagnoles with her—I think this one of yours will be very smart—Una was going to get one like it had she wanted another warm coat, which she does'nt. Its not only warm but will keep the rain out a little because the surface is fuzzy. I'm not surprised to hear that Lyza caught cold—and thats precisely what I fear for you. And now listen, Soulina, and kindly obey me! The moment you get back from the South, you're to get that damned fur coat out of storage and <u>wear it</u> until my coat arrives, but while you're waiting for delivery from storage of the fur coat (a matter of several days) you're to wear a wooly[8] under your green coat—I don't care if the effect is unbecomming, I don't care if you feel uncomfortable, I care only that you shall keep in good health and not catch a cold at the beginning of the winter. Its awfully dangerous when one comes from the South, & this you know quite as well as I do. Soulina, my darling, I spoil you to death—but I mean what I say and I'll be very angry if you don't do precisely what I tell you about this. I can't send the coat till I know you'r back in Paris, and even then it may not reach you for some time as the Agents there will have to get it through the Customs so that they and not you will pay the duty—in any case their doing this will save you much trouble. My beloved, I send you all my heart—all my thoughts and all my desire. I kiss your beloved hands & your feet—I kneel down and worship you my most blessed woman—you who for my sake became a woman.

Your John

<u>P.S</u> You speak of having received <u>one</u> letter from me in Mentone. Well, I began writing to you there last Friday—& have written every day I think. Hope my letters will come to hand—I had not the address of the street you have now given me.

[Rye]

October 21st 1934

My dearest love. This is Sunday and it finds me at the Rye cottage. We came down yesterday and shall return to London either tomorrow or

---

7. American size 13–14 for outerwear.
8. A sweater, in U.S. terminology.

Tuesday morning. Meanwhile any letters or telegrams from you will be forwarded at once to me here—You see I never get out of touch with you and until I give you a definate notification that I am moving to Rye for a long stay you must please go on writing to me at the flat.

My dearest—I have not written for two days though I sent you a telegram yesterday morning about your not taking on that baby,—(you asked my advise & so I gave it) Also about your obtaining your visa either in Zuerich or Paris. As I said in my wire, if there is a delay because of your visa, it can't be helped. I would like you to come over as soon as you can, but as long as you come during November I shall have to be content. I can't think, my dear, that the visa can take more than two or three weeks, especially as Una has written to the Under Secretary of State on your behalf, as you will have learnt by now from her letter. She is really very anxious that you should come—and this is God's truth, for she knows very well that our seperation is praying upon me. Therefore, as soon as you get your visa come to me, either on the first or after—that is, Soulina, if you feel that you still love me.

My dear one, do you know why I have not written to you for two days? I will try to tell you. It was that first letter of yours that you wrote on the 14th of October. I got it by the evening post on the 18th, and somehow it was like a blow on my heart, following as it did on your cold little wire about the difficulty of getting your visa because you were now in Zurich. In your letter you expressed no happiness, no joy at the prospect of our meeting—only difficulties seemed uppermost in the mind of the woman who thinks she loves me. The Princess[1] who must not be inconvenienced—her baby who <u>might</u> become ill and need you—the Princesse's husband who has confidence in you—<u>their</u> plans (not mine) but theirs, my beloved, plans that while being rediculously vague were none the less going to be binding on you, so that I and my love could go hang if these people so much as held up a finger. And your work, yet not one word really in explaination of what the exact situation is in regard to the Princess. Is her job unpaid? From your post card from Monton I naturally thought that you were going to her as a nurse, were taking a job, but now I am not certain—perhaps you are staying with her as a friend? But if so why all this talk about work? If you are

---

1. Souline had upset John considerably by hastily joining one of the Russian émigrés as nurse and traveling with her to Zurich immediately after returning from the Menton holiday.

prepared to spend weeks with her earning nothing (and your first letter of the 14th told me clearly that you might be going to do just this) then why so much talk about work when its John who has begged you to come to England for a fortnight? These are some of the questions I've been asking myself and to which only you can give me the answers. You see, my dear, I had thought that your coming would fill you with happiness—was I wrong?

Moreover I have done many foolish little things, the things that are done very often by lovers. I have sent my sitting room curtains to be cleaned, have ordered a new suit and some new shirts, have been planning about having flowers in the flat and also in our appartment at Folkestone—have been thinking about what wine you would like the first night at dinner, and telling myself that on that first night there must be no love-making because you would feel tired after the journey and the crossing. I have been finding out what good plays are on now, so that I could amuse you while you are in London; and then I have been planning certain jaunts out of London, to such places as Hampton Court Palace[2] for instance, if the weather is fine. In fact, my dear, I have thought of little else than your coming. Then came the first letter of the 17th. Even now I simply can't understand it. My beloved—I am feeling deeply discouraged—on the night before I received that damnable letter I got the letter you wrote on your arrival—a letter so full of love and longing. How can it be possible for your mood to chang[e] so quickly and apparently so completely? Are you changeable, do you think, my Soulina? My love for you simply cannot believe it. This Russian Princess—do you find her so attractive that her plans mean more to you than our meeting? If so I beg you to tell me quite frankly, because, somehow, even your second letter written at a m on the 18th, makes me feel a little uneasy and doubtful. I seem to be reading between the lines that that letter was forced—I don't know why, and if I am wrong then I beg you to forgive me.

Soulina, I am giving you all I have to give of love and desire and thought and care. I am giving you so much more than my body—I am giving you my mind and my spirit, Soulina. I have not played my cards with precaution and skill as I have often done in the past—as many a

---

2. A magnificent palace in Twickenham, given to Cardinal Wolsey, advisor to Henry VIII. Fourteen miles west of London, it has become a major tourist attraction, famous for its Clock Court.

man will do with a woman; no, I have let you see into my heart, I have let you see just how much you mean to me. I might have tried to make you feel jealous by telling you this or that about other women—by playing this or that woman off against you. I might have treated you with more indifference, been less considerate and less patient, Soulina. I might have played upon my career—tried to impress you with my own importance—but my dear, your John has done none of these things, and why? Because loving you as I do they seem to me to be entirely unworthy. I want to be loved as plain John by Soulina. But do you love me? Do you—do you? How much I love you, you know—alas—already. If you love me you will come to me in England, your coming or not coming will be your answer.

You say that my asking you to come was so sudden—that is true and the reason is very simple. Suddenly I felt that I must see you again, that I could not sleep or work unless I saw you, unless I could feel your arms around me. And I knew that even if when you came you did not want the physical side—if you chose to deprive me of that means to peace and ease of body—I should still want you. For the sake of hearing your beloved voice and seeing you—knowing that you were there near me, I knew that I would keep out of your room—whatever it might cost I would leave you alone. Can I say more than this, Soulina? Sometimes since that letter of yours from Zurich I have had a very horrible thought: I have thought that you did certain things against your will, that you gave yourself to me in order to please me. I have thought that you turned like a poor trapped creature first this way then that, when suddenly confronted by having to come & be with me in England, and that this is why your letter was full of such pitifully trivial worries about nothing—the Princess, her husband, their plans and their baby—all of which have less than no importance unless you choose to give them importance—you are not these peoples bond slave, my dear, but a free woman if you wish to be so.

And now listen, and this I write without anger and with all respect for your will to freedom, as far as I, your lover, am concerned, I must be all to you or nothing. I agree that after your visit to me you must get back to work—I want you to do so, <u>but I will not agree that you do not come</u>—Unless you tell me that you no longer love me. If because of our bitter enforced seperation you feel that you do not love me as much as you thought you did when we were in Paris, if there is anyone else in your life, some new love, or even some overwhelming interest, if the difficulties attendant on our meetings (though God knows I do my best to ease them) seem more important than the meetings themselves—then Soulina I demand that you shall tell me. No woman has a right to torture slowly—no woman has a right to crush body, soul and talant. Soulina, I am not the weakling you may think me—Rather than not be sure of your love I would tear you completely out of my life—I would never see you again in this world—I would turn to my work and pray Almighty God that you had not killed my inspiration. Do you want me to do this—do you, my darling? Soulina, if you should refuse to come to England I don't think I should find it easy to forgive, because I should know that your arguments were false—there would be but one argument worthy of attention and that would be that you did not love me. You may have conceived that you have many duties—to Mrs. Baker & now to this Russian and God knows, there may be others as well—but if you love me they are all lesser duties. I, your John, am become your first duty. If they need you, (and you're always saying to me that this or that one has need of you,) if they need you then so do I need you, Soulina—I need you more than these lesser people. Have their needs more claim upon you than have mine? If this is so then you do not love me as I have a right to be love[d] by you—I who have given you all myself. I will not accept half a loaf from you—give me whole loaf as I give it to you, love me utterly or leave me, Soulina.

You say that I am a sensitive person, yes I am, & that makes me intuitive—Against my will I am forced to feel your moods—and since you left Menton your moods have distressed me. If I am wrong then once again I beg your forgivness, pleading my love which perhaps has grown sore through our seperation.

I am not over well because I am so worried and so unhappy and oh, so doubtful—nor can I work. But this is not pleading. I never plead with a woman, Soulina. But this I say to you—Come to England, let nothing stand in the way of that if, as I hope & pray, you really love me. Soulina, I am waiting for you here in England—if money is short I will send you money, for I totally ignore your cruel & false pride. Love admits of no pride and no self-respect when love is sincere—it accepts willingly knowing that in doing so it confers a privilage. But what love cannot stand & must not stand is less than all on the part of the loved one.

I don't care how long the visa takes to get so long as you will promise me to come when you have got it. Of course you will get your visa in the end, of that there surely can be no question—your hospital can help you; you are not destitute & likely to be a charge on my country! Una has done her best to help us by writing to the Under Secretary of State, & I hope you will abide by her instructions—I was with her when she went to the Passport office & what she has written you is what you must do—I vouch for its being what the man in charge told us. Oh, my dearest—come to me, I need you so much. Come—I am calling you day and night—is it possible that you can no longer hear me?

And now if I have misjudge[d] anything, overlook it—yet again I beg for forgivness. I am still all yours. I still love you & need you—I have not changed, I am still all yours. But I say to you: come. Something tells me that you must if we are to keep our love intact—I <u>know</u> that you must not refuse to come to England unless you have ceased to love me. For Gods sake don't spoil this very perfect thing—our love—by considering foolish trifles. Don't spoil it—love is so easily wounded & sometimes it may even bleed to death. I ask you in the name of our love to come, Soulina.

<u>Your John</u>

[Talbot House stationery]

October 24th 1934

My beloved and moja radost.[1] By now you will know that I have written again and why I did not write for three days—I simply dared not write, heart of my being. This letter will not be a very long one, but I wrote yesterday before leaving Rye, though the post will not reach you so soon from the country. And now I am not going to write about love—at all events not 'till I have written other things. <u>First of all</u>, then, about the all important visa. This morning Una got on to the office of the Under Secretary of State. She was told that her letter had been received and that now they were waiting for the application from the British Consul in Zurich, that the moment the application reached them the matter would have immediate attention, and moreover that they thought there would [be] no trouble about your getting your visa. It now appears to rest with the British Consul to hurry up and send the application, and as he may be slow in so doing, Una and I both think you will be wise if you

---

1. A Russian term of endearment suggesting "greatly cherished."

go & see him when you get this letter—merely say that you have called to enquire when he thinks he is likely to hear about your visa—or, ask if he has heard anything as yet; in any case make an excuse to see him in case he should go to sleep on the matter. I am enclosing a letter to you from Una, and this you are to show the Consul—that in itself will provide an excuse for your visit to him, and will bring to his notice the fact that your obtaining the visa is important—I consider it urgent that you show him Una's letter, so don't fail to do as I tell you, please darling.

Secondly. If you leave Zurich, or rather when you leave Zurich, you must let me know at once as you promise to do in your letter of Oct 22nd. But do not telephone, the risk is too great of missing your message as the time is different, I think in Switzerland that you are an hour later than we are in England. There is also the question of your having to wait for some time before getting through to me, so that one way and another we might be muddled. What I want you to do is to telegraph to me and please don't spare money, make your telegram a long one and a clear one, for the love of God make it clear—you must not be vague any more my darling.

Thirdly. I understand from you that you will only leave Zurich to return to Paris unless (as I suppose is just possible) you decide to go straight to Boulogne from Zurich—this you will naturally let me know in your wire—and that is why I say make the wire long & clear, please.

Forthly. Our destination in Folkestone is The Grand Hotel. And this I want you to make a note of in your diary or somewhere. My reason is that if I should miss you at the boat you are to go straight to The Grand Hotel and ask for Miss Radclyffe Hall's rooms and wait for me there until I join you. I don't see how I could miss you at the boat, but I have the kind of methodical mind that provides against all eventualities, that is if my heart and my mind join forces!

Fifthly. You must let me know by wire the exact day and time of your arrival in Folkestone—as I told you in a previous letter the times I gave you were only approximate—Cooks[2] in London thought the times might be changed in November. All this you could find out from Cooks in Zurich (I should thing[k] that they have an office in Zurich) unless you decide to stop off in Paris, in which case the Paris Cooks can tell

---

2. London's largest and most prestigious travel firm, founded by Thomas Cook in 1865.

you. There is also, of course, the American Express,[3] very excellent people from whom to get tickets.

Sixthly. In no circumstances, my beloved, will you follow your mad Russian Princess to some new place—if she leaves Zurich, you return to Paris. This you have faithfully promised in your letter and I earnestly beg that you will keep that promise. For one thing I do not want you to go with her to some new place, & for another it will certainly muddle the getting of your visa. To return to Paris would be all right if you notify the Council at Zurich, also Una; if you go back to Paris before the visa arrives. In that case take the matter up with the Consul in Paris as Una told you in her letter. Whatever you do, my dearest love, don't let the Princess get the better of you—don't go anywhere with her if she should leave Zurich, and this is the command of John who adores you and who simply can't wait until you come, so urgent is my great need to see you.

The snapshots you sent me: not too good, but they will get better and better with practice, dont as yet give up hope and return to a Brownie![4] Your letters from Mentone. I think I've received them all—only at first was there a little delay.

My work and why is it that the poeple I write of are so very often lonely people? Are they? I think that perhaps you may be right. I greatly feel the loneliness of the soul—nearly every soul is more or less lonely. Then again: I have been called the writer of "misfits." And it may be that being myself a "misfit," for as you know, beloved, I am a born invert, it may be that I am a writer of "misfits" in one form or another— I think I understand them—their joys & their sorrows, indeed I know I do, and all the misfits of this world are lonely, being conscious that they differ from the rank and file. When we meet you & I will talk of my work and you shall be my critic, my darling. If you wish to you shall be very rude—but I do hope you like your John's work just a little. I want you to like my work, Soulina.

Darling—I wonder if you realize how much I am counting on your coming to England, how much it means to me—it means all the world,

3. A major U.S. travel company, similar at the time to Cooks. It had evolved from an express service in the nineteenth century to a provider of money orders, later travelers' checks, then in 1902 to ticket agents, and in 1907 to providers of tours and itineraries. At the time of Hall's letters it was not yet in the charge card business.
4. An inexpensive camera made by Kodak.

and indeed my body shall be all, all yours, as yours will be all, all mine, beloved. And we two will lie close in each others arms, close, close, always trying to lie even closer, and I will kiss your mouth and your eyes and your breasts—I will kiss your body all over—And you shall kiss me back again many times as you kissed me when we were in Paris. And nothing will matter but just we two, we two longing loves at last come together. I wake up in the night & think of these things & then I can't sleep for my longing, Soulina. This is love—make no mistake about it—love has come to you—you are loved and loved. No one whom you meet is more loved than you are—no one in the whole world can be more loved. When you look at people you can say to yourself in your heart—"I also has [sic] got a lover—I am loved until the love is as pain, as a scourge of whips on my lover's back, as a fire that torments and consumes my lover." Blessed is this love that torments day and night, night & day, for it also illumines and sustains when the loved one is kind—be kind, then, my Soulina.

Your John

P.T.O.[5] Enclosed find another Frs 100 for your telegrams.

On November 4, Souline arrived at Folkestone, where she and John spent three days. They joined Una very briefly at the Talbot House flat. Una then went down to the cottage in Rye, only to be asked to switch again when John wanted to spend time with Souline at the cottage. Souline returned to France on November 20.

[Rye]

November 26th 1934

Beloved. I have seen our guest off to London and thus missed the morning post. She is a nice woman—Anne Elsner by name,[1] and she writes very pretty, tame & harmless little travel books all about Arabs and Brigands! After she went I walked across the marsh to Lesam Hill,

---

5. Please turn over (the page).

1. Anne Elsner had once rented the cottage (then called Journey's End) that John and Una renamed the Forecastle when they bought it in 1934.

and up Lesam Hill & home by the road that leads through the old Land Gate. And the mists had cleared away in the night, and the marsh at the foot of Lesam was lovely: emerald green with the little "dicks"[2] that drain it looking like liquid silver; and t[w]o miles across the marsh was the sea that lies between us, the sea you crossed, and that also was shining like liquid silver. Over everything was an English blue sky, very pale and pure, and that queer strong light that one only seems to get on Romney Marsh[3]—a kind of other-worldly light, strong & yet soft, & so beautiful, Soulina—but its beauty, indeed all beauty these days, is almost too painful to be endured when you are not near to share it with me. And so I walked on full of thoughts of you—full of regrets that you could not have see[n] the loveliness that I saw this morning, but full also of the determination that you shall see it, my beloved. No letter from you today as yet—that is because there has been a Sunday—I am growing to dread the week ends. I hope you will tell me all about the party; also whether you gave Liza the handkerchiefs and gloves and whether—if you did so—they pleased her. It seems so strange & so terribly wrong not to be able to talk to you, not to be able to discuss things together—and I miss your voice too terribly darling. Last night I had one of my fits of the glooms. When the weight of life lay heavey upon me, when everything seemed dust and ashes in my mouth, when I felt that I had not made good at all, that I never would make good being what I am—that the scales were too heavily weighted against me—I get like that sometimes & have done for years—it is the melancholy of the inverted. I tell you this because it is God's truth that you can lift me right out of such moods, that when I am lying in your arms & you in mine such moods cannot touch me, that you, Soulina, can make me forget the great weariness of spirit, mind & body that I feel sometimes—I feel battle-weary, and you are my rest, my joy and my ultimate justification. When I am with you I am younger than you are, I am young and carefree and irresponsible in nearly all things save your happiness; I am back where I was many years ago with only one difference—I know that I am kinder & more considerate & understanding. Oh, well, it may be that I should be glad that life has knocked me about a bit if because of this it has made of John a more worthy & steadfast lover for Soulina. Dearest I must stop. I have to write an appreciation of

---

2. "Ditch" in Kentish dialect.
3. One of three marshes that extend for miles east of Rye on the coastland.

Margaret L. Woods[4]—her novels etc. for her to use, she has asked me to do this for her, and after that I must get to work. God bless you my rest, my joy and my hope. As the man of the stone-age says to his mate in: "Miss Ogilvy"[5] so I say to you: "Hut of peace for a man after battle."

Your John

[Rye]

November 27th 1934

My dearest love. I got a letter from you yesterday (Monday) after all; it came by the latest post and I was so thankful. This morning there has come a letter of thanks from Liza. Darling don't quarrell with her, don't I implore you! I can quite understand your being disappointed that she did not come to your party, and I could slap her for having caused you a moments annoyance, but if her friend had just arrived from England I do feel that there was some excuse. She may have wanted a quiet evening with him—Put yourself in her place; if I had just arrived & had asked you to spend a quiet evening with me I hope that you would have chucked a party, even Liza's. Anyhow the thought of your long friendship with her is a certain consolation to me, so please make up your quarrell, if you've had one.

Beloved, I did not mean that I thought there was a chance of war coming now. I meant, & I mean, that if there should be a military alliance between France & Russia it might make trouble for you White Russians who are domiciled in France,[1] and I did not want you to go off the deep end and do anything without first consulting me. But now it would appear that no such two nation alliance is contemplated, and in any case I have your faithful promise to take no steps without consulting me first. I do not believe that war is coming—at all events just yet.

---

4. Margaret L. Bradley Woods (1856–1945), poet and novelist. Through her father she had been befriended by the poet Alfred Lord Tennyson. Her writing career spanned forty years, from 1887 to 1927.

5. A short story written by Hall in 1926 featuring another "misfit," whose finest hour is her service as leader of an ambulance corps in France.

1. In 1934 there was considerable tension over fascism in France. The Soviet regime in Moscow was encourging communists in the West to align with liberal/moderate socialist groups in their home countries. By 1935 the USSR had concluded a military alliance with France and Czechoslovakia.

Really if the nations engineered yet another such outrage I should feel inclined to take you and Una to some neutral country—I cannot think that I should have any patience left, or any hope in humanity, also I am not sure that I should even think it right to help in any way—no, I am not sure—however: "Sufficient unto the day is the evil thereof."

Oh, Sweetheart, I am so terribly sorry that you feel that your party was not a success, but I expect it was a success really. You were too tired to see straight about it; another time we'll get the sandwiches made instead of you slaving to make them. As I wrote you, I was dreadfully depressed that evening—and longing too terribly for your presence, but I tried not to call you—I tried with all my strength, but the longing and the heart-ach[e] were too strong, it seems, they must have reached you across the Channel. Or was it that you were calling to me? Soulina, what is this strange bond between us, this terrific thing that has come into our lives, so that when ever we are torn apart each of us must all but bleed to death for the other? Were it only a powerful physical impulse it would not be so bad, but its more than that, its so dreadfully, so painfully tender. Oh, yes, I desire you—I feel crazy sometimes, remembering our days & nights at Folkestone, but at other times I know very well that if I could never live with you again I should want to be near you, always near you, always able to hear your voice & touch your hand and wrap you round & round in my love—always able to protect you, Soulina. Do you feel this towards me? I think you do—you greatly desire me but you also love me. It may be that we two have met before— I think I believe in re-incarnation.

Soulina, you are not a beautiful woman, I suppose I was right when I thought you were ugly—but while I thought this I fell madly in love, and now I can see no face but yours, no face seems beautiful to me but yours—your queer little ugley, alian Chink Face. And no voice seems beautiful to me but yours—your queer, alian voice speaking broken English; and I ache to hear you speak my name which sounds different somehow when you speak it—when you say: "John" the name has more meaning.

So you went to church for my sake. I'm glad—if God doesn't understand then he can't be God. I pray hard for you and so please pray for me—Pray that somehow, without causing pain to others, we may be brought more & more together, that our burden of seperation may be lightened, or if, for some reason, it must not be lightened, that we two may be helped to bare it. Oh, my darling you will never know how much I love you. I am only half alive when we are apart, I am only alive in order to suffer. But in January I am coming beloved—God willing—I am coming to hold you in my arms and to make you forget everything but love. I can't write any more, I want you too much, my poor, exasperated physical body is too tormented. After all God made me and made me as I am, He who made you as you are, a passionately loving woman.

Your <u>John</u>

<u>P.S</u> Am sending you by this post some photographs (two) taken at the same time as the one I first gave you. I think you may like to have them.

[Talbot House]

December 4th 1934

My beloved. I am here in my flat again—this is the first time I have been at the flat since you left me, and its pretty grim I can tell you. How I miss you—I miss you too fearfully—thank Heaven I've got endless things to do while I am up in London. But when I arrived late yesterday afternoon your darling letter was on the sideboard and this helped—it helped me so much, you darling.

When we are together we will talk & talk of: 'We three' as you call it—that is if you wish to. My beloved what do you mean by being 'privileged'? I am not, and I have not been for years, the least in love with Una. I feel a deep gratitude towards her, a deep respect and a very deep affection—also an enormously strong sense of duty, all this for reasons that I have told you. For you I feel what? A consuming need that is not the need of our bodies only, and this you well know, or if you don't, well, if circumstance made it impossible that we should be lovers (which Heaven forbid!) I would be prepared to provide this to you. I feel for you the strong, vital love—the combative love, the protective love, the anxious yearning, restless love—and very very often the selfless love of the very young. As I wrote to you once—my love for you is more like: 'First love'—that is the only way I can describe it. I respect you for the courage you have shown towards life, I honour and adore you for the innocence that I found in you when I first came to you, I honour and adore you now for the passion that equals in its completeness your erstwhile innocence, and I feel an overwhelming desire to be with you day and night, both in moments of passion and in moments of rest that come after passion, and in moments of that simple companionship that we two are able to enjoy so much together. Also, dearest, I will never let you go so long as you love me—never, never. You belong to me and I to you—I am yours to love, and I hope to respect, you are mine to love, to respect and care for, even though we can't always be together. But let us rather talk of this when we meet—it is all too profound to express in writing. I have a letter from my solicitor and apparently his opposite number in Paris M. Hollander, can undertake the business of your French naturalization. I have ascertained what Hollander's fee will be, also the fee to the French government (apparently France require[s] a tip!) but this part of the business will not consern you—I shall attend to the financial side. I am going to see my solicitor on Wednesday, tomorrow, in order to get fuller details. You will please do nothing until I come to Paris. First I shall go & see Hollander without you, then I shall take you to him myself and introduce you—in this way, beloved, I shall hope to get you his best attention, his most careful and personal attention.

Your letter of Dec 2nd just arrived. My violent spell of work has subsided for the moment, should it come on again I can work here, for up here as well as down in Rye I can get an excellent typist. That is how I work, in fits and starts, in Rye or up here in London. But in any case I have to see to many things—not the least of which is your naturalization—indeed that is really my principal reason for coming up to London. I am terribly glad that you went to the dance and that you enjoyed it, bless you. I wish so much that I could have been there—but if people had stared I'd have felt very shy, because really I am rather shy, my Soulina. Darling most Chink-Faced little Tartar I must stop—I must dress and take poor Una to the dentist—she is scared to death about her eye-tooth which she broke but which will really be all right, thanks to this excellent American dentist. I am more disposed to go on writing to you—but you can't complain that this letter is a short one.

Feel loved and protected and "priviledged" my own—Surely sitting beside the fire in my heart is a priviledge, isn't it beloved?

Your John

[Talbot House]

December 5th 1934

My dearest love. Your letter of the 4th came by this afternoons post. Darling I am trying not to be depressed and to please you I will go on trying. After all we are much luckier than many other lovers in our position, this I know, but I am greedy for your nearness I suppose. If you were here you could surely kiss away my tiredness. Our child is sleeping for the moment; its trouble lies in the cutting of its third tooth. In other words while I have re-written that Chapter III and like it much better, I am still not perfectly content. I have exaggerated in places, anticipated in others, missed points in others. I am letting you into the secrets of my trade, every writer comes up against similar snags—those of us who are careful & who take our work seriously, peg at it until we get as near perfect as we possibly can; those of us who are careless and who don't care a hang for quality but only for money, just let the work go out tant bien que mal[1]—but not so can we hope to build upon our reputations. I literally wear myself out over a book, too much so I suppose, but there it is. When I tidied aways your cloths one night—prepared your stocking for putting the next morning, folded your crepe de chine combination— or whatever you call that long thing you wear—you said to me: "Ar'nt you methodical, my Johnnie!" Well, darling I'm like that over my work—I want every smallest sentence to be very tidy. And this child— since its ours—must have very special care—I can't see it go out with a button undone, with its left shoe off and its face & hands dirty!

Tonight I am really feeling more cheerful, and why? Because I've been serving you a little. I've been to my solicitor, Harold Rubinstein,[2] who has heard from his opposite number in Paris M. Georges Hollander of 41. Rue Condorcet, about your French naturalization. Hollander says that this should be able to be accomplished without too much difficulty—he has had some particulars about you from Rubenstein already. It appears that the firm of Hollander is very well accustomed to dealing with these matters, is, in fact, the very firm we want. In addition to this my friend Rubenstein assures me that it is an old established firm of excellent standing in Paris—this latter is a helpful and most important point—we want a French firm, not a Russian, my darling, Rubenstein is as certain of that as I was. The French, bless them, pay more attention to themselves which is, after all, only natural. I took the opportunity to ask Rubenstein about possible English naturalization—that is what I

---

1. More good than bad.
2. Harold Rubinstein (1891–1975) was a solicitor with Rubinstein, Nash & Company. He had defended *The Well of Loneliness* in the prosecution of 1928. His papers relating to the case are archived at the Harry Ransom Humanities Research Center at the University of Texas at Austin.

should have liked of course. But hopeless or nearly so, my beloved. Five years residence in England at least, at the very least, and Rubenstein says very probably longer before they would even begin to consider my Chink-face's naturalization. Also great difficulty to get permission for so long a continental residence in England. Well, sweetheart, your John is very fond of France & the French who gave a home to "The Well . . . ." when it was persecuted and homeless, and who made its author feel very welcome.[3] And now perhaps France will give a home to something far more precious than: 'The Well . . .' and will make Soulina welcome— Soulina whose true home is in my heart but needs an outward & visible country. Rubenstein tells me that once you are French you will be able to come to England and pratically stay as long as you like, just think of the relief this will be, Soulina—it will make us feel so much nearer to each other. Pray to St Anthony, begin at once to ask him to see this matter through for us—tell him how very urgent it is—he will listen, I am certain that he will listen for he was always a most pitiful Saint when on earth and he has remained one. Superstition? Oh, no, only common sense—if the dead survive—the good and kindly dead—then they now have more power & a greater will to help us. Go and find a church in which there is a statue of St Anthony—nearly every church has one— then light a candle to him & say a little prayer asking him to help with your naturalization, and do this with faith, with the faith that moves mountains.

Darling, I am sending you four handkerchiefs in a copy of The Times[4]—you will find them hidden neatly in between the pages—not all together but scattered about I expect—look carefully right through the paper. And papers that you receive (except Punch[5]) will perhaps contain something, so if one arrives always go carefully through it. Punch I shall send you, perhaps every week, because I know how it makes you laugh—but first I am going to laugh at it myself—I feel througherly selfish over Punch I can't bear to let you have it until I've seen it! No more of this tonight—I'll finish in the morning.

---

3. Jonathan Cape, the publisher, had sent the plates of *The Well* to Paris before the English authorities destroyed the copies Cape had printed in England, so the book was indeed a French book in that ironic way.

4. This was to become a common practice to avoid customs duties on small gifts John and Una sent Souline.

5. The popular satirical magazine was one of John's favorites.

December 6th (8.45 am)

A letter from you with my morning tea, bless you. Beloved, about Liza: I should much like to write to her, but I see from your letter of yesterday that you'd really much rather I didn't. Why, dearest? Does the idea make you feel shy?—I'd hate to make you feel foolish in any way, and perhaps embarassed when you were with her. I'll tell you what I'll do: I'll write the letter and let you see it before I send it—if you think I may send it when you've read it, O.K. But I promise not to send it until you've read it. It will only be a very simple and reserved little letter.

I note all you say about my photographs—I am going to have the two beret ones reduced. When the one has been taken in the grey-green cape I'll send you one if it turns out well and then that can be reduced also. I am going to our photographer next week to arrange for your own photographs to be sent out to you & to be taken again myself. The handkerchiefs that I am sending off today are not exactly the same design as Lizas around the edge, I couldn't get the same, and two of them are larger than Liza's, but they're very fine linen & I hope you'll like them. Punch, which also goes to you, is very dull this week—only one funny picture: that of the motor that has turned upside down.

Petral Hahn.[6] I'm terribly glad that you've got some. Brush you hair before putting it on—its about time you did look after yourself—or rather that large bit of John that's Soulina.

Your John

[Talbot House]

December 10th 1934

My dearest love. Today two letters from you because none yesterday— it being Sunday. Your letter of 9th came this evening. I say no & no & no to your doing floor duty. Firstly it is much too straining for you physically and secondly it would entirely spoil our time in Paris. Dont please even think of it—I won't have it for you. Beloved child, you will get a job eventually and whenever you're out of work you simply must let me help you. Do you want me to go mad with worrying about you? You don't? Very well then stop being 'rebellious' and that at once; if you

---

6. Souline's hair was very thin. Since their first meetings John had been urging Souline to use this hair restorative product.

don't then I'll take away the smart collar and put on a shabby old rattier one, on which will be engraved: 'This is Chink-face—please beat it!' Darling, darling, you who could not write a letter when we met now write such particularly dear & consoling things sometimes—Yes, press very close to me and be shealded against the hardships of life. Alas, that I can't shield you more—that is my only sorrow and it is a very real one. But some little protection I can give you and all my love. I'm sorry the hospital dance was not amusing, or at least not as amusing as it might have been, because I like you to have some recreation. By the way Darling, how much is an orchestra seat at your Paris theatre? Let me know this and I will send you the price of 2 seats every now & then— you can take Liza or anyone you like. This will give me pleasure—a great deal of pleasure.

These are my questions which please answer:

1) What is price of theatre seat?

2) Have you found the case of your ring?

3) Do you know of a really first class hair specialist who could treat your hair?

As I told you on the telephone, our child has at last cut its 3rd tooth.[1] But I am not going to write this book in chapters at all, I've decided. It will be written in numbered sections. The action is too swift for chapters. And, dearest, if the book ever gets itself finished, you are not going to like the man I warn you.

Emblem Hurlstone[2] is a psychological study of a man who avoids all pain—physical & mental—until in the end he is made to face it. Something of this I told you when we were together. The love story came to me at Sirmione—& on the way there as I also told you. No, you are not going to like Emblem though you will pity him in the end I hope. Why must I always write about people who are not perfectly normal? I do and I know that I do. This book is of course a perfectly normal love story—thanks be. For though hundreds of people would wish me to write again on the subject of inversion, I have—at all events at present— no inclination to do so. I feel that I have said all that there is to be said in 'The Well . . . . .' Surely anything else that I might write on the subject could only be an anti-climax. But the truth is that I am strongly

---

1. The third chapter of the book John was working on. In the event, it turned out to be what Una referred to as a "tractor" novel-a novel John worked at while gearing up for her real work.

2. Both the tentative title of the "tractor" novel and the name of the protagonist.

fascinated by abnormal psychology—even slightly abnormals, as is the case of Emblem Hurlstone. I wonder sometimes if you will like this new book. It is far from easy to write I can tell you. That my meeting with you and all I suffered before we became everything to each other inspired the book there is no doubt whatever. You woke me up and the process was very painful indeed, and out of the pain this book was born.

Darling no more tonight. I will finish tomorrow.

This is tomorrow—Dec. 11th

Your letter of the 10th came this morning also the French translation of my book—not a bad translation on the whole, I think, but words left out I can see by just slaveing through a few pages—& of course they are very important words that have an important meaning. However, not a bad translation on the whole—& thank you beloved for sending it so promptly. Oh, my darling—don't cry I simply cannot bear it—my Darling I am always with you in spirit—& thank God I am now right in your life—you are never alone any more my Soulina. At the very moment my arms are round you. Again I say <u>no</u> to floor duty—no, no— Your health is too precious—I will never consent to any work that is so over tiring. Darling I must stop & go off to Cooks—I want to enquire about tickets to Paris—whether I can get them at Dover pier—I think so—Also I want to get some French money—for sending you tips!

I love & adore you

Your John

[Talbot House]

December 17th 1934

My most dear love. Two letters from you this morning because none yesterday it being Sunday. Beloved, this morning I have sent you a telegram because yesterday I simply could not write. I was working all through Saturday night—woke up after only a few hours sleep feeling very tired. Went to midday Mass and bombarded Heaven on your behalf, came home and after lunch felt like all Hell—nerves standing on end! Then I had to go & see Dodo Benson,[1] the writer, & a years

---

1. Novelist Edward Frederick Benson (1867–1940), best know for his Mapp-and-Lucia novels. He had acquired Henry James's Lamb House in Rye.

old friend—then—oh—then I was very inconsiderate to Una—said something in the end that I should never have said. She has been rather nervey these last two days as she is sometimes once a month since her opporation, and I deserve to be beaten for not having taken this into consideration. I would have done had it not been that my own nerves get pretty rotty when I'm working. There was a scene which left me so shattered that I couldn't attempt a letter to you. It was largely my fault though not quite all. Its all over now and everything's all right—I only tell you because I want you to know why I did not send you a letter. Your two dear letters that came this morning have <u>comforted me</u> and soothed me beloved—I want you to know that they have acted as a balm—its as though you had laid your cool hand on a wound and had thereby stopped it throbbing. I bless you for your two letters, Soulina. So you read & reread my letters to you—those from Sirmione must have been pretty desperate—I was half mad with longing and very near despair—no, never shall I forget last summer—I think that I suffered the tortures of the damned—if the damned suffer more then there is no God, at least there is no God of Love & Pity. But of course there is such a merciful God and so I feel sure that no one's in Hell, as many another has felt sure before me. My daily life—I have no real life—this life is a dream, a dream of Duty. I attend to business, I see the many friends who close in around me when I'm in London—and who I must see for publicity's sake since we live in a vulgar age—yes we do—and no writer can dare to drop out of things these days, for the best of us are so soon forgotten. I have been with Una to one or two plays—first night & otherwise—all dull & unreal, all terribly boring because you were not with me. I have kept my patience with a journalist who interviewed me for nearly two hours for a theatrical paper called: 'The Era.' I have shopped—done a lot of necessary shopping, such as ordering a case to be made for the little Ikon you gave me & which I so greatly value that I want to take it everywhere with me. What else except work? Oh, I dont know, my dear, just the usual daily struggle of life—of life spent away from the beloved. You are life you are hope—you are joy—you are peace—there is nothing but you in the world anymore—nothing but you, my Soulina. About my telephoning to Paris. Don't ever be frightened because you hear that you have been called up every half hour or so—that is one of our English methods. If one remains in the Exchange does that for one—they continue to call until they get the person, so when that happens dont be frightened. I have got Liza's letter that you returned, it came by the last post the night I called you up. I have sent it to Liza who should have got it by now, and I greatly hope that she'll answer. So your restless Princess is on a mountain top again, but this time—praised be—without my beloved. Darling, they must have pots of money! No, I really don't think I like her—I feel that she's utterly inconsiderate & selfish. I have been meaning to say something about your books, darling, those that got spoilt by your central heating. I remember telling you that that might happen, I noticed the grating when I was with you. Now listen. I want to give you new volumns of all that were spoilt—I shall like to do this, I shall love to do this, beloved. I can't bear to think that your hard earned books have been ruined— when I come I will buy you new ones. I am sending you a letter from the Father Guardian who has charge of our little Saint's Shrine at Crawley.[2] I have ordered 6 masses to be said for my intention—my intention being your naturalization—your happiness and your health, Soulina. The cheque he speaks of was not a bribe to Heaven, but a little donation for the expense of the masses and also a donation to the very poor friars who live on the charity of the faithful. I asked that the <u>entire community</u> of brothers should say special pray[er]s for my intention. I could not get your actual name mentioned because you are not of my Church, but I've written & told them all about you and you will be prayed for as my Intention—this is how we get round the foolish old ruling that only Catholics can be prayed for by name. All the same I have many & many a time heard the priests pray in Church for all Christian Russians who suffer through the Bolshevic devils.

So now we have two active lines in our hands—one in Heaven and one on this wretched old earth—St Anthony and Hollander—what a combination! I want, oh, I do want your naturalization. This morning I go again to my dentist—nothing to do but to scrape off tarter—not you—the other kind, my beloved! He finds my teeth in excellent fettle. I am very particular about the mouth that has the great priviledge of kissing Soulina. Dear, dear one, I must stop. I am only alive because I shall see you now very soon. But I wish that we could be together at Christmas. I shall go to our Christmas mid-night Mass and receive my Communion for you that night. Think of me if you are awake round

2. John had been in contact with the religious community at Crawley where there was a shrine devoted to St. Anthony, the saint whose protection John sought for Souline and for their love.

about 12.30—I shall be receiving Communion about then. Poor Lord—I shall tire Him out with prayers for you—I often think how tired He must be—so tired & discouraged of us all & by us all—but no doubt he understands our woes and our failures since at one time he shared them. Anyhow He must be pitiful of you, and proud of you too, because of your courage. I am—so why not God, my Soulina? I love and adore you—it is for your sake that I am doing my duty and will do it—God & Soulina helping. I am all right again this day—all right, do you hear? There is nothing to make you worry. I love you now and to the end and beyond—I love you—love you—love you.

Your John

[Rye stationery]

Dec 21st 1934. (Evening)

Beloved—I am througherly ashamed of myself for having written you such a depressed letter on my arrival. I should have remembered that you want to be cheered & not harrassed with my heart aches. Your letter of 19th posted on 20th came very late this afternoon—it should have reached me this morning—the Christmas posts are always mad, and goodness knows when we shall get each others letters. Thank heaven I called you up last night and heard that you are not ill. My dearest—my very dearest, I have kissed the bed in the spare room because for on[e] night you lay on it. Am I an extremist in love? Yes—say you, as you said last summer. Well maybe it is so—but better blow either hot or cold as St Paul preached. Very deeply do I love you, and have from the moment we met I do believe. If you and I have not met before in a past life then "I'll eat my head!" That and that only can explain what has happened. Do you know that you're never out of my thoughts day or night except for the few hours of sleep? And during my sleep I expect I dream about you though when I wake up I can't remember. Do you know that I only want to talk about you—or Russia—or something else that is near you? I think that you have obsessed me, yes I do—what would happen if you came to me one day & said: 'John I don't love you any more!' Will that happen? It might, for love is a curious thing and no one can ever force it to come or to stay when it wearies, either. Or suppose I should say to you one of these days: 'Soulina—I don't love you any more.' What would happen then? Beloved, dont get anxious—I am playing at torture, thats all beloved. Shall I tell you what I think would happen to me? There would come upon my life a great and terrible darkness so that my soul could not see any more—so that I might not be able to find God. Sometimes I try to envisage such a happening. I say to myself—(try to make myself believe it) 'Soulina has gone right out of my life—I shall never see Soulina anymore—she and I are divided for ever & ever.' But I have to give this horrible morbidity up—this abomination of the immagining, because I can't bear it, Soulina. Then I say: 'Soulina loves me—<u>she loves me</u>, and so long as we love there is no distance, no death and no possible seperation.' And this helps me to bear what must be born[e], so much better is my fate than if you did not love me, or if for some reason we two had had to part while still loving & longing for each other. Oh, my dear, my dear who I love so much—why you were sent to me I do not know, for my love is very often pure pain, yet not for the whole world would I be without it. The greatest pain is the thought of you alone—you feeling cold & desolate it may be, you feeling tired and my arms not there, you feeling sad and my kisses not there, you feeling lonely and my voice not there—this is pain, this is pain that brings tears to my eyes because I can scarcely bear it. Then it is that when I am here in Rye I look over to France and send myself out until you must surely feel me. At such times desire is not with me, beloved—but a great tenderness that is more than desire because the spirit is stronger than the flesh—and this tenderness is of the spirit. Good night my own self—my other self—I kiss you many times very gently.

December 22nd (early morning)

Darling love. I add a few lines to this and then I shall post it—the only safe post leaves here at 10.45. am. I am breakfasting at the Mermaid Inn[1] as they are sweeping the kitchen & parlour chimneys. I shall post this even before breakfast to be on the safe side. I am more hopeful & cheerful after a good nights rest. By the way beloved—before leaving London I went to the photographer and arranged that the two prints of your photographs that are owing to you should be sent to Paris. Let me

---

1. An ancient inn dating from early Tudor times. It was frequented by Elizabeth I when business brought her to the ancient area called Cinque Ports.

know when you get them—I think I have ordered the ones you wanted—the two I myself left and that are on my desk this moment.

Your little precious Ikon looks too lovely, it is in a brown leather case lined with bright blue velvet—I shall show it to you in Paris. Your photographs are in a very swank double leather travelling frame on my desk (as I said) your little Russian cross is round my neck and you—oh you—are sitting in my heart beside an enormous fire of love. There seems to be enough of you, one way & another—don't you think so my darling Chink-Face? Bless you—be as happy as you can until we meet and so will I—I am going to try to think only of our meeting. What is the matter [with] your patient—can't you tell me? Anyhow I do hope she'll get well—I expect she will with your nursing

Your John

[Rye]

December 23rd 1934 (night)

Heart of mine. This is the letter that I shall post tomorrow—Christmas Eve. I shall also send you a telegram because it is your Saints name-day. In order that the telegram may reach you I shall be down at the post office in the Hight St when the doors open at 8. a.m., as the lines are always so congested at Christmas—at the same time I shall express this letter. Darling do stop worrying about work—if it comes it comes; if it don't, it don't. Of course you can try floor duty but don't please take it on for long as I am afraid you can't stand it—really you had better wait for special work. Unless I hear from you to the contrary I am coming to Paris on Jan 15th We shall go to the Hotel Lutetia. My present idea is to stay more than 10 days or two weeks, and in order to do this I have promised Una that I will make a point of seeing some of our friends while I am there—go about with her a bit. This only wise in any case. It is bound to get out that I am in Paris and everyone will begin to wonder why I never go to see them. Anyhow, wise or not I don't care so long as I can stay longer. Anything for peace and being near you and with you.

Another reason for seeing people is your naturalization. One never knows who may prove helpful and I want to leave no stone unturned. Oh, darling—I simply can't believe that I shall hold you in my arms again so soon—that I shall feel your arms around me—You will never know how I miss you. Its the little every day things that I miss—having meals with you, hearing your voice in the early morning, seeing you in the room when I come in—all the little dear simple things that love makes so wonderful. And then, my darling, there is the other thing—the passion that I feel for you and that needs you. Oh, yes, there is that I don't deny it. I want you terribly sometimes Soulina, for although I love you with my spirit and mind, I love you also with my physical body. I love you all ways—yes, all ways, my darling.

Alex Wolkoff[1] has been here all the afternoon and has only just left—she had tea & dinner. She was staying near by and so she blew in. She is getting too fat as she does sometimes, but for all that she is rather lovely. Una mentioned you as another White Russian who was a nurse at the A. H. [American Hospital] in Paris, whereupon a young man who had come with Alex—a man called: Radon Breakwell said at once "A Russian nurse? What was her name?" We told him and he says that you nursed him when he was in the hospital with a very bad throat that they thought might be dip.[2] He says that you took night duty. It wan't dip. but abcesses, he says. I nearly fell on his neck & kissed him because he had once contacted with you—he is very nice, very nice indeed, but the moment he said that he remembered you I thought him a marvelous person. And Alex—we talked Russia—Russia—Russia, and because she was Russian I actually gave her some of the orchids my fan had sent me[3]—Alex loves orchids, she always has. I gave them to her not for herself at all but because of you, Soulina. I nearly said: 'Here Alex, take these orchids because of my Russian.' How surprised she'd have been. I nearly said: "You're very beautiful Alex, but my Russian seems more beautiful to me—your eyes are rather Chink but hers are more so—anyhow I'm so desperately and hopelessly in love with a Russian that I must give something to a Russian, so thats why you're getting the orchids!" At dinner she made me talk to her in English and she answered in Russian—but that made me feel homesick for you—I stopped it for it made me feel so homesick. From her I learned that her difficulties are as big as yours when it comes to a visa. She also only has that Nansen

---

1. A White Russian émigré who had settled in England. John and Una had known her for several years.

2. Presumably diphtheria.

3. In an earlier letter, John had mentioned the arrival of a huge mass of orchids sent by an unknown admirer of her work.

thing[4]—no pass-port, only the damned thing that you have. She is never allowed to leave England for France without all hell—she had to wait 4 weeks for her French visa this very summer, & then she could only get it for 3 weeks. Her work, poor Alex is terribly dreary—She's a kind of filing clerk at the Imperial Institute of Entomology—where she sits all day filing reckords about insects—buggs etc! She lives with her parents who weap for the past, and who try to make a living by running a restaurant. What a life—and her life began by her birth in the Tzar's Summer palace—(I can't write its name)[5] and now she files reckords of the ways of virmin! Darling, I am outraged for your poor people. Beloved—but you are safe in my heart, you have a big fire of love to sit by. I am all yours and you are all mine so that both you and I are more lucky than Alex. When next you are in England I want you to meet her. Darling, but a more earthly fire to dress by—alas, that my heart's fire can't warm your dear body. <u>You simply must</u> get in lots of wood and warm your room up in the early morning. I am going to look for another room for you, but meanwhile you must warm this one.

Una was apalled when I told her that I thought your room must be stone cold in the morning. She ordered me to put in a gass fire at once! She was really terribly nice about it, and she wants to come with us to look for rooms. She adores looking at flats & houses. I think that it will be kind of you if you let her come around with us—it will give her a lot of fun & pleasure. I am kicking myself for not having thought of the heating of your room in the early morning. That was utterly thoughtless of me, beloved; but don't please punish me by getting a cold. You can't take care of yourself at all, can you——

My darling love I must say good night, and God bless you—it will soon be Christmas Eve. Every thought and all my enormous love will be with you, surrounding and comforting you on this our first Christmas eve—beloved.

Your John

---

4. The "Nansen Passport," issued by the Nansen Committee of the League of Nations to the more than half a million Russian émigrés who were stateless and without travel documents. The Nansen established identity and could be used to obtain visas and other travel documents. However, because of widely differing economic and political realities in individual countries, Nansen holders faced a variety of restrictions in their attempts to travel.

5. The Livadia Palace in the Crimea.

December 26th 1934
(Boxing Day)[1]

My beloved. Yesterday being Christmas day, the 'golden Saints' were evidently disposed to be kind to me for I got **two** letters from you with my early tea. You have no idea how this helped me to get through the day. From your letter of 22nd I gather that you are already on floor duty and the letter of 23rd confirms this. On the whole (since we could not be together) I am glad that you were up at the hospital. I simply dreaded the thought of your possibly spending Christmas day alone in your room. I'm so glad that the two photographs of yourself reached you safely; but I can't understand about you not getting a letter from me on 23rd—if Punch arrived then why not the letter that I posted at the same time? But I expect that you have got it by now—no one can cope with the Christmas posts, they are too maddening. Punch I sent you from London together with a letter. My memory is that I posted them both from London on my way down here on Dec. 21st. (I have not missed writing to my beloved for one day.) Then darling I wrote to you when I got to Rye and that letter you tell me you got in your letter of 22nd. Never mind, I am sure the missing link will turn up in the end. So you are among all those new people—so new they look too [small?] and so crumpled on their first arrival into this world. Personally I have a secret liking for all new things—fledgeling birds, puppies, kittens and babies! And this I will tell you, my Soulina—had I been a man I would have given you a child—as it is I am angry that I cannot do so—I much long for an impudent Chink-faced brat. Jolly for you if I had been a man! Never mind—don't be scared, it will never happen—at least not through me, more's the pity!! So you need calling down, being quite out of hand. Very well I'll beat you when I get to Paris—trouble is that I really believe you'd like it. Only wait, my beloved, the day may come when you get a glimpse of my fearful temper. Did you suspect that my temper is fearful? It is when it starts—I loose all sense, its a kind of madness—ask Una. The night I got your first letter from Zurich I raved about the flat like someone demented—very nearly I sent you back your

---

1. December 26 is called Boxing Day in England because of the custom of giving faithful employees gift boxes on this day. In earlier times it was the day of opening the almsboxes to distribute donations to the poor.

cross—I was beside myself, beloved—I'm glad now that you were not handy to beat, for indeed I do think that I should have struck you. But try to be good until I come, otherwise there'll probably be wiggs on the green[2] with Miss Handley, & that I do <u>not</u> want just now because of this matter of your naturalization. Am I working? Yes, but not very much-indeed not enough; I feel so restless, so disturbed in my mind as well as in my body—longing incessantly for you, thinking only of you and our coming meeting. If I must scold <u>you</u> for your lack of self-control, then you must scold <u>me</u> for the same thing, Soulina. I much wish that you'd <u>will</u> me to work for you, beloved.

Una has begun to read: 'The Proud Servant'[3] aloud to me—and I'm going to like it. Darling, I didn't thank you enough for sending it—but I was awfully grateful, indeed I was & am for so lovely a present. As I've told you your miserable present from me is four pairs of our pyjamas which I'm bringing. But your birthday present I can send before I come, for that will be a book that I want you to read if you have not done so already. Have you read "Elizabeth and Essex." by Lytton Strachey?[4] Please let me know at once. It gives a delightful picture of England in the time of Queen Elizabeth—and this cottage that you love is of her time. I shall get it sent out to you direct from the shop, and will write your name in it when I get to Paris—now darling do let me know whether you have read it.

Oh, my beloved—my little beloved—how I want you at this minute! Yesterday there was a cocktail party here. I showed your little Ikon with great pride to several people who understand such things—Darling, everyone raved about it—you know, don't you, that its a real beauty. Now that it's in a smart little case it really looks like a jewell. Alex Wolkoff has just arrived—I can hear her talking to Una—she has come in for a pre-lunch drink. A nice creature, but like you inclined to get depressed—to subside into the White Russians. Oh, Soulina you have entirely ruined my Christmas. As a matter of fact there was lots of fun going and had you been here I could have througherly enjoyed it, but

---

2. "Wigs on the green" refers to a row or a fracas. In the eighteenth century when men wore wigs, a public brawl or fight would result in a number of wigs being thrown on the ground.

3. A historical novel written by Margaret Irwin and published by Chatto & Windus in 1934. It fictionalizes some of the events in the life of James Graham, Marquis of Montrose at the time of Charles I.

4. Giles Lytton Strachey (1880–1932), man of letters and intimate of the Bloomsbury circle of Cambridge and London. His study of Elizabeth and Essex was published in 1928.

because you were not I kept on getting gloomy. Every thing that happened that was really amusing made me long for you to be here to share it—every moment I was thinking of you, longing for you, fretting after you. Truth is that you are now my real life, and that I have pratically no life without you.

Oh St Anthony, please, please, please, let Soulina get her French naturalisation! Darling—damn your lovely fellow Russian—I simply must go in and be polite. I kiss you very many times all over—not a bit of your body that I'm not kissing. You don't know how desperately I'm wanting you—I keep thinking of your beautiful skin, white hands—Oh, Hell! now an entire party has arrived—the noise is awful—I simply must stop—no peace to go on—beloved.

Yours—yours—yours—

John

They have all gone. I have lunched at the Mermaid with Una, the maid being out. Here I am back again writing to you! You asked me in one of your letters how Nellie the Grand Duchess[5] was getting on. She is intolerable—more a Grand Duchess than ever—now we have to order special food for her! My love, my love—I did wish you could have been here for the rowdy party this morning—had you been I should have througherly enjoyed it. This evening we are motoring across the lovely marsh to dine with Edie Craig's niece Olive Chaplin[6]—but with you so far away its all nothing but sadness. January 15th January 15th! I cheer myself up by writing the date—my darling.

John

[Rye]

December 30th 1934

My darling. I have missed Mass this day in order to work, and here I am not working but writing to Soulina. I just had to ring you up last night, firstly because you are getting a stye! Secondly because I longed to hear your voice and also felt worried generally about you. Oh, my dear, my

---

5. One of John and Una's many dogs.

6. Edy Craig (1869–1947) was the daughter of the famed actress Ellen Terry. She lived at Smallhythe (a few miles from Rye) with her lover Christabel Marshall (the novelist Christopher St. John) and their friend Clare (Tony) Atwood, a painter. From 1929 on, she hosted an annual Shakespeare matinee on the anniversary of her mother's death.

dear—you said in your last letter that if I didn't tell you at once that I still loved you, you would go mad—well I think you'll remain sane if your sanity depends on my love—it is I who sometimes think I'll go mad with wanting you so much, Soulina. What happened to start you feeling so doubtful? Little fool, don't you know yet how much I love you? If you don't then I'm afraid that you never will. How much you must always indulge in self-torture! Letters are likely to be delayed again owing to the New Year, as I told you last night, so don't think this time that I've ceased to love you. Moreover if I get seriously ill—too ill to write myself or send you news somehow, Una has promised to let you know, so now please try to be at peace, my darling. The year is fast coming to its end—I am sorry to see it go, for this is the year that brought us together. We found each other in 1934 and therefore let it always be remembered. It has been for us both an amazing year—a year I think of very grave import, a year of great pain and great joy. Its strange, but I feel as though I were you, as though I had lost my innocence to love, as you lost yours, my Soulina. I felt that first day when I came to your room as nervous and shy as a boy of 16—and oh, what a doing you gave me—Good God, I shall always remember 1934 if only for that—what a doing you gave me! I have thought about it so many times since—I was torn in half by desire and pity. Do you remember how I fed you that night? I fed you from my plate as though you were a baby. I can see you now, sitting hunched up at the table, all broken and sorrowful and terribly anxious, and you spoiling everything through sheer nerves and through being so terribly overexcited yet apprehensive—a most fatal combination. Darling, darling, you must have suffered like Hell—I could have weapt over you, my Soulina. Dear, innocent, passionate woman that you were—you don't know how tender I felt, and still feel when I think back on that first time and remember. How can you ever dare to doubt my love? I'm not sure that it isn't a most deadly insult! I have had many women, as you know, in my life, but no one quite like you, and I adore you. Darling, I am all on fire for you this morning—I keep thinking of the joy I have in your body—my own body is througherly unruly this morning. If I had you here, and we two alone, I would show you whether I had ceased to love you—you'd know all about it in less than ten minutes! You will know all about it when I come to Paris. I feel rather cruel with love this morning, tender and cruel—a queer combination. Rye is blissfully quiet again, praise be, the Christmas people have all gone home or else are attending to their usual duties. Darling I simply <u>must</u> get down to work. "For men must work and women must weap" At least this unhappy invert must work, but Soulina <u>must not weap</u> I wont have it. I love you, if anything too much, Soulina

Your <u>John</u>

<u>PS</u> <u>Your Annual visa</u>. Please don't do anything at all about it until we get to Paris. Una has an idea that it might be obtained direct from the British Concel in Paris—& if so this would simplify matters in the future. She is going to call on the Concel herself. In any case its as well that we should get to know him. Have I made this quite clear to you, darling?

1935

Nineteen thirty-five began hopefully for John. She would manage to be with Souline for almost half the year, first in Paris from January 15 to March 25, and then in the South of France, Italy, and Paris again from July through mid-October. John began to provide for Souline financially on a regular basis, and helped her move to a larger, more comfortable flat in Paris. During this time John's sexual passion and intense desire to be with Souline never abated. Nevertheless the letters reveal tensions and frictions, particularly Souline's growing resentment of Una's presence and annoyance at the importance of writing and literary affairs in John's life.

[Rye stationery]

January 3rd 1935

My darling love. You letter of New Years day has come. Sweetheart I knew that you'd all go on a bat on New Years Eve. Its not the things that one does occasionally that hurt one. Your sly reminder of Folkestone made me laugh—yes, I was <u>very</u> drunk, and a nice thing too on your first night in England—my only excuse is that 3 glasses of champagne drunk during dinner aught not to have done it. Truth is that seeing you again had made me half drunk already—maybe you have that effect on me, I think so. I do love to hear about all that you are doing at the hospital and so on—it makes me feel nearer.

This morning comes a letter from Cooks saying that my tickets for Paris are waiting for me in London—<u>Darling—my tickets for</u> <u>Paris!</u>

Meanwhile I am working breathlessly—not a moment to write you a proper letter. Must get a certain amount of our book off hand before I get to be near you—when I'm with you I'm fearful of not working at all

105

because I'm so desperately in love. This morning my typist is thundering away—making publishers copies of as far as I've gone—thats how I do it so as not to loose time, because generally I'm such a slow worker. Oh, darling how am I going to wait until the 15th? I shall start from London—shall probably go to London on 10th but this I will let you know later on—write here to Rye until I tell you not to. About the hairdresser. I am very pleased with you for having found a man who gives treatment—yes, I am very pleased with you indeed. Treatment you must have so find out what he charges. I'm tired of your letting your hair go to pieces. Its my hair now & I want it looked after. No more—I must post this then get to work at once—Lord, how I long to be happy & idle!

Your John

[Talbot House, London]

January 12th 1935

My darling love. Yesterday not a moment to write you, so I sent you a wire telling you this fact, but also confirming the last and <u>final</u> arrangement which is that you come to the station to meet us. Now if, for any reason, you should be unable to get to the station after all, then come on to the Lutetia and drink hot soup—but I shall expect to see your beloved Chink face at the station, oh, blessed be God. Chink-face, can you believe it? Three days and then I see you—not even three days and nights, only two days & nights and then one day & a bit of the evening!

You ask if you shall stop writing until I come—but dearest there is only one more letter that I can get—the one on Monday morning, and that I am hoping to get, because if I don't, then in my present mood I shall think that something awful has happened. What a strange ridiculous, wise, cruel, kind, painful, joyful, and altogether incomprehensible thing is LOVE. Have you ever stopped to consider how very queer it is that two human beings should be so indispensable to each other that they can't get a moments peace or happiness apart? And what is it that attracts people to each other—that makes two people come together irrestably [sic] together out of the all the world? Oh, what does it matter—I love you and you love me and thats that—and I'm too excited & happy to think, to write or spell English. I know that my spelling is quite mad and that my writing looks drunk and I don't care a hoot—no I don't. I so much adore you that I haven't any brain left except to adore with. Sometimes I laugh to myself when I think: "If my fan-public knew the condition to which I have been reduced by a Chink-faced Tartar what would they say?" If they knew that instead of sitting grandly on a mountain peak waiting to be found, I had come down with a flop and was kissing the feet of one called Soulina—oh, well. . . . . Apropos of feet: Artificial silk stocking in white are unobtainable, at all events at the "best" shops, so I have got you 6 pairs of the real silk ones—nice & thick—they look serviceable to me. Darling, I got size 9 1/2 which I hope is O.K. And I also have your pyjamas with me—Pray for me at the customs! Here also it is fearfully cold. I hate the cold and am hoping that it will subside while I am in Paris; but it will take more than the weather to make John cold when once I have you in my arms! So Mrs Baker sends a fat cheque—how fat? I shall ask this when we meet. Dearest, you have got over her, haven't you—friends by all means, why not? But I require every scrap of your sentiment if you please! Do you know when I heard that she had sent you a cheque my heart turned over. Rediculous of course. Rediculous, wasn't it, Soulina? You shall tell me just how rediculous when we are together. Good Lord—to what have you reduced me—I am as jealous as a school boy!

Oh, my love, my love, joking apart, I am so much yours that I am no longer myself I sometimes begin to think—No more now as I want to catch the post. My heart & soul goes out before me to prepare you for my coming—I am just one big longing & loving—just one big joy & thankfulness—

Bless you for having been put in the world to love me, my Soulina.

<u>Your John</u>

[Hotel Lutetia stationery]

[undated]

Waited until the last moment, darling, but now I simply must go as I am taking Una to dentist. We shall not be gone more than about one hour all told, as he is only going to look at her tooth today. Darling, will you <u>please</u> wait here until I get back and then dine here? I am unhappy, somehow and feel that all is not quite well between us, though why I do not know. Please, <u>please</u> wait for me to get back. Don't go away again.

John

John and Una stayed almost two and a half months in Paris. During
their stay, John bought a bulldog puppy, Boulinka, which she left with
Souline until their return in May. At this time Souline was suffering from
a severe sinus ailment. As always, Souline's health problems caused John
almost excessive anxiety. The letters resume from London on March 26.
John and Una were then packing up and selling the Talbot House flat.

[Talbot House stationery]

March 26th 1935

My little little child. Here I am back in London and because you are not
here I think it the dreariest city in the whole wide world. But in any case
it always seems dark and misty and dirty after lovely Paris, and how
much more so when it means seperation from the beloved. Your dear
telegram that I found on my arrival went a little way to cheer me though,
and like you I am holding firmly to the thought that I am coming back
to you very soon, just as soon as I can get my affairs in order and this
entirely hateful flat off hands; indeed, as we all know, I am only here
now in order to get back the sooner to Soulina.

Some unknown fan who was too tactful and considerate to give her
or his name had sent me masses of white lilac and blue iris in time for
my arrival so that the sitting room looked almost festive, there was a
card with the flowers on which had been written part of a poem about
Spring—Spring, God save the mark, it is most damnably cold in London, in this England in fact—I noticed the chill the moment we landed
at Dover after a wonderfully good crossing. But the flowers were nothing
and your telegram was all—even as you are all my beloved. I saw the
blessed orange coloured envelope lying atop of a mountain of letters and
I leapt at it. All the evening poor Una has been struggling with my post
among which there were at least three completely mad epistles from
members of the public—but raving! My little child, where are you and
what are you doing? That I should not know seems so terribly wrong. I
can't feel that there ever was a time when we two did not belong utterly
to each other. When I am away from you I feel wounded as though you
had been torn out of my very flesh & bones.

I am too tired to write more tonight & so must stop. I will finish this
tomorrow. I kiss you all over, and tired as I am I long for you. Are you
longing for me? I think you are.

March 27th

Sweetheart. I add to this letter sitting in my beastly study surrounded by my partial unpacking. The sun is out but as always a faint and sorry mist hangs over London. Life—this life—has begun again: letters from the public in the post this morning and the telephone bell ringing every few minutes. Una's cold is fairly heavey and she sounds as though she might be voiceless for two pins. She is quite furious as there is so much to do. I have made her inhale with all we have, namely: Friars Balsam.[1] She has no temp so doubtless all will be well—if only the telephone would stop ringing! I am thinking of you all the time—at the back of my mind, no matter what I am doing, there is always "you—you—you." It may be that I shall get the longed for letter from you this evening. You won't get this until tomorrow. I have so much to get straight here, so many posessions to put away and so little room that I must stop writing and get a move on. I love you and I will come back to you always—always. I am only living to be near you again.

Bless you my honey-sweet. Take the greatest possible care of my body. Don't smoke, don't drink, don't go out in too light a coat & catch a fresh cold—in fact "Use your common sense!" You know how I worry about you so you do owe it to me to be extra careful. After your treatment always take taxis—but I have told you all this a million times.

I send you myself.
Your John

[Talbot House]

March 27th 1935
11. p.m.

My own most darling love. Your first dear but disconsolate letter came by a late post this morning and as soon as I could get out I sent you a telegram as I knew that you would not get any letter from me before tomorrow, though I posted one to you early today. My beloved, well did I know how miserable you would feel and I warned you that it would surely happen. And ever since I left you great waves of misery at our seperation have been sweeping over me from time to time, and great fears that you won't look after yourself as you should do for my sake,

---

1. A common cold remedy used as a nasal decongestant.

for indeed if you love me then you must show your love by taking care of the creature whom I do so utterly need and adore. For this you know, my dearest, I am forced to be here in England attending to financial and other business before we all go South. I simply must try to let the flat and I implore you to <u>promise me</u> to take every care of yourself—write & tell me you will do this, my Soulina? I beg of you to go on inhaling every morning if the doctor wishes it—also to put the drops in you nose & use your spray, also to keep clear of cinimas & not to smoke yourself, in fact to do what you can to keep fit and well so that while I must be away nothing will go seriously wrong with you. And for God's sake don't drink spirits because you feel desperate at our seperation—drink red wine & not too much of that. If you want to get thinner don't starve yourself, thats dangerous, very, for you. Just cut out potatoes, butter and white bread, also all sweets and cakes, and go for good long walks with Boulinka. And by the way—I wish you would go & take some snap-shots of him in the vet's garden. That would be awfully nice if you will do it and send me the results (if any!) <u>Then I want you to go to your dentist and be good this time please darling.</u> And last but <u>not least</u> I want you to find out whether Rouad[1] is a good surgeon. This latter is very much on my mind—I am worrying about it terribly, so please write & let me know the result of your enquiries as soon as you can. Now there are three things that I want you to do. 1) photograph Boulinka. 2) Go to a good dentist, and 3) Enquire about Rouad as an operater.

Darling—I have been rushing about all the afternoon, from 2 'till 6 have I been at it. And now listen—I went to my Bank and instructed them to pay over to your Bank Frs 750[2] on the first of every month beginning April 1st. They will make the payments from here always on 1st and will write you each time that they have done so. The money should be in Paris on 2nd or 3rd of each month and you must tell your Bank to let you know that it has arrived. Your rent is due April 1st also I believe, and that you will have paid into your bank as usual, and will be told by my bank that it has been sent. Always my Bank will let you know that the rent money, and also the Frs 750 on first of each month have been paid into your Bank, and if for any reason you are not let

1. The doctor who was treating Souline for obstructions and abnormalities in her nasal passages. He eventually performed the minor surgery alluded to in this passage.
2. Approximately $250 in current purchasing power.

know that the money has been sent there you must write me immediately.

Be a good child and don't adopt a family of White Russians please. If you have a few centimes in hand because you did not have to spend much last month as I was in Paris, put the money aside or spend it on a few theatres. Darling, I forbid you to allow anyone to wangle the money out of you—yes I do, so now you know! Oh, my honey-sweet you are never out of my mind for a moment, and I think of your strong white body and the great joy that it takes of me & of my body, and I long to feel your arms around me and to feel my arms around you and my mouth on yours. Sometimes it seems to me that one almost touches the spirit of the beloved in moments of intense physical passion—strange that I feel this & yet I do. It is as though the flesh must melt, be burned away by the intensity of its own desire and by the rapture of its ultimate fulfillment. For surely the act of physical love is only a kind of mad desire to get closer to the creature one loves. When you say to me, as you do so often, "I don't know what to do, what to do to get nearer" you really mean that the physical act is not enough to satisfy your craving for complete oneness with me—that's what you mean my beloved. And indeed it never is quite enough in spite of its ecstacy, because there is no perfection of union while we are still in the flesh. But it's our most intense expression of a longing that is really of the spirit, at least this is my belief. Oh, my darling, if only I were beside you tonight— I will finish this letter in the morning. I kiss you many times my Soulina. Before I go to bed though I must tell you that I found some relief in shopping for you today. I have bought you a white berret and and a black one, both small like mine. I have bought you a gilt Razor like mine. I have bought you a case of scissors—a family of scissors, father, mother and child all born in Sheffield where the really aristocratic English scissors come from[3]—this case is red leather and they themselves lie on red velvet. I have bought you an ivory hand mirror in which to see the back of the Royal Chink-Piggie's[4] head and the angle of its crown worn slightly over one ear. These things I will bring with me to Paris when I come and offer them to the Royal C—P—on a purple plush cushion with gold tassels—on my knees of course. Presently I

---

3. The Yorkshire city famed for fine cutlery since the fourteenth century.
4. This was to become John's favorite term of endearment, in later years often shortened to R.C.P.

shall buy the R.C.P. some pants like mine, and if it can think of anything else that it needs or would like will it please let me know at once. I also looked a[t] gold bracelets but concluded that there are better in Paris—we'll see.

<u>March 28th</u>

Only a few lines this morning as I must dress & go out. Your letter written after your treatment has come by first post, beloved. Thank you, thank you for your love. Darling do please be careful <u>not</u> to catch a fresh cold—it might undo all the good of treatments and the very idea makes me anxious. Also my honey-sweet don't get too depressed and don't snub Liza—I like you to see her.

Soon, God willing, I shall be with you again. If you long for me I long for you—but more than I can express, my beloved. My arms feel empty, my heart feels empty, my soul feels empty. God bless & keep you.

Your John

Always dress warmly <u>after a treatment</u>. Always put on your muffler and take a taxi by order of John.

[Talbot House stationery]

April 1st 1935

My dearest love. I got home here to find your two letters (one written Saturday & the other Sunday) awaiting me. About the dress that I have bought you: if it don't fit because my R. C-P is too fat then never mind—R C-P shant have it. But I will not buy any more clothes for you—I think that, as you say, its rather a risk perhaps. Only please wait to get your cloths until I arrive in Paris—we will choose the cloths you need together. I can't possibly send you your new dress my dearest because of the customs, you will have to wait for it until I come over.

[Sidescript on left margin, probably written on April 2nd] I must stop now & pack papers from my desk. Your always adoring

John who misses you every moment of the day & night.

Dearest & most loved goose—my pictures, but <u>no</u> I am not going to sell them & this I told you in a recent letter. Some of them are of considerable value—i.e. the Sargent drawing of Mrs George Batten singing[1]— the portrait of Chatterton (only one in exsistence)[2] the big portrait of Count Molina[3] and so on; while as for the little picture of which you speak in your letter and which you had the instinctively fine taist in art to admire when you were here with me, that is not an agnarelle but an oil painting by no less a person than Sorolla the (to my mind) very great Spanish painter.[4] Darling I believe that picture has a big value now that Sorolla is dead—no my most R. C. Piggie I will not give you my Sorolla, no I won't, it is going to be stored with the other pictures.

Gloves—I will buy them for you but I doubt if I shall dare send them in a newspaper—I think they will be too bulkie & that you may have to wait for these also until I come over & bring them with me. Meanwhile go and buy yourself a pair or two of Spring gloves and let me know how much they have cost & I will pay you for them. I command you to do this!!

I am so glad to hear that Bulinka is well, fat and seems happy—thank you darling for having taken him for a walk.

And dearest, I am glad that you dined with Meg and that you like her & her young English girl—of course you shall introduce me to the girl when I come back, but I do not feel that she will be my R. C. Ps rival! Meg is so nice, so jolly and so trustworthy that I am honestly glad to let you become friends with her. You see, beloved, it is not every one that I know in Paris to whom I would trust you—far from it.

I suppose you played ping-pong with Na-dine[5] today. She's all right my dearest but please, oh, please be jolly cautious what you say to her or before her. She is the person above all others who simply must not suspect our relationship. Via her and Natalie[6] it would be all over Paris

---

1. John Singer Sargent (1856–1925), U.S. portrait painter noted for his elegant portrayals of the Edwardian age. The painting is of Ladye, with whom John lived for eight years.

2. Thomas Chatterton (1752–70). English Gothic poet most famous for his "fake" fifteenth-century poems attributed to Thomas Rowley. The painter and portrait remain unidentified.

3. Carlos Maria Isidro de Borbon, Count of Molina (1788–1855), claimant to the Spanish throne.

4. Joaquin Sorolla y Bastida (1863–1923), painter and illustrator.

5. Nadine Wong, a Chinese émigré who was a former lover of Natalie Clifford Barney and a member of the Barney lesbian circle.

6. Natalie Clifford Barney (1876–1972), the expatriate American writer and salon hostess.

in 24 hours. Please be very careful of what you say about me—Na-dine will question you, pump you, I feel certain—but no one can be more wise and silent than you, oh, my Soulina.

I have sent out and procured a tube of codoforme (Botol) which I am going to take—I have the hell of a cough—tickle, tickle, tickle until I am nearly mad—a devils feather in my throat. If I were in Paris I should fly to our Dr Ruaud—you may tell him this. My own doctor is coming to see me tonight to be certain that my chest is quite clear—I am sure it is, so don't worry. I hope the headache you speak of in your Sunday letter is better and that is had nothing to do with your sinus (I can't spell this either) Set my mind at rest anent[7] this when next you write, please my darling. Don't feel sad about my breaking up this flat—dearest I am not taking another flat in London because of you. Don't you know that I am keeping myself free in order to be near you—? Surely you know this, you must. I thought that you would be over-joyed at my giving up a London flat because it would leave me so much freer. And do remember that you could never live in London because of the climate—but never would I risk you in this vile air. No more tonight dearest—I kiss you many times.

[Talbot House]

April 5th 1935

My own darling. Have just got your letter of 4. Yes, my heart is inside your own—please go on pressing it with those most perfect hands that I do so utterly love, the touch of your hands sooths the aching that comes always with seperation.

I am greatly relieved that your new cold seems better; glad also that you sent to see Lifar—I think that I gave you the money for the seats, didn't I my dearest? If I did not let me know what you spent and I will send it. Thank you for letting me know that my Bank have sent the sums due—they sent, I suppose, the Frs 1300 for rent, and also the monthly Frs 750—making Frs 2050 in all. Let me know if this is the sum they mention when next you write, and I tell you again to see that your own Bank lets you know that they have recieved the money—this [you] must always do.

Oh, darling what a rush I am living in in my efforts to get all in order

---

7. Regarding; concerning.

before I return to my R. C. P. Yesterday was a fearful day—every thing I wanted to buy was out of stock—thus berrets had to be got from the warehouse, knickers also, yes and other things, and time going on apace & the shops flustered and doubtful as to getting the things by a given date—almost as maddening as shopping in Paris! I have ordered a new over-coat, same as the shabby faun one but dark blue this time, it should be very smart. I have ordered two flannel suits, a grey and a blue. And a pair of faun coloured trowsers for St. Maxime. My tailors are horrified at my present proportions—I can't get into last years trousers, can you believe it? So this is what comes of happiness! You may tease as much as you like about my massage—you may always tease as much as you like. An enormous and most powerful Sweedish woman comes every evening and kneeds me and pummels me and picks up handfulls of me while assuring me that I am not fat! She causes me agony but I grin and bear it—my body (your body) is as soar as a boil, but massage always does me good and from time to time I have it for the sake of keeping in condition.

This morning I go to my dentist for a clean up & general over-haul, which reminds me that I hear not one word about you going to the dentist—kindly go at once—I love your teeth and I prize them. After the dentist I to Harrods[1] to order some open-neck shirts for the Summer, then I go to the City to see a stock-broker, then I come home & pack up more things. Tomorrow Saturday morning I go to Rye until Monday, returning by an early afternoon train, but please go on writing to the flat as before—in fact always write here unless I stop you. (My heart, my dearest heart I love you.) I am much relieved that you have your papers from the Hospital—I thought that the director would not desert you somehow.

Here the weather has returned to mid-winter. Snow yesterday and bitter again this morning. For God His sake dress warmly and obey my orders otherwise you'll be ill again, as I do not doubt but that you are having the same weather. Oh, for the South and you—sunshine, heat and you. Eat well beloved, at least two _real_ meals a day. Darling I must stop—can't help it I must or I shall miss my dentist appointment.

I send you all of me

Your devoted and most loving and longing.

John

---

1. One of London's largest and most prestigious department stores.

John as an adolescent with her American cousin Jane Randolph and sons. Marie Visetti is standing (left).

Formal portrait of John in late adolescence. She wrote to Souline of her misery during those years.

Studio portrait of John at the beginning of her literary career.

John as she appeared at the end of her life. The dog Fido is on her lap. See letter of June 27, 1942.

John in her fifties. She had sent Souline a number of photographs similar to this.
Courtesy of the Estate of Radclyffe Hall.

John at the Forecastle. She was an avid newspaper reader, especially during the years of World War II.

The Forecastle, John and Una's cottage in Rye. For John's many descriptions of the cottage and its setting, see the letters of 1934 and 1935. Courtesy of the Estate of Radclyffe Hall.

John's study at the Forecastle. The photograph on the right of her desk may be the only surviving photograph of Souline. Courtesy of the Estate of Radclyffe Hall.

John's bedroom at the Forecastle. She and Una had separate rooms. Courtesy of the Estate of Radclyffe Hall.

The guest room where Souline would have slept. Courtesy of the Estate of Radclyffe Hall.

kicking against the pricks and frowning at me & feeling defiant, a motor you are not going to have my beloved. In any case I could not afford it, so let that be a comfort to you. As for us, I don't think that Una & I will be very popular when we arrive except, of course, with our personal friends—this because I do not think that England will enter into an alliance with Russia, a fact that the French will probably resent; but I have met such resentment before when in France and there has been some political difference of opinion—the French are quick to feel resentment, but it passes as quickly and as you know I like them, and if your naturalization comes off, then, in a way, they will become my people. I suppose you have not heard anything else about the naturalization, have you? When I come over I shall come prepared for all eventualities as far as may be. I shall bring as much money as I can muster in a letter of credit that can be drawn on in any European country, and this because I am the sole owner of a very Regal-C.P. these days. No, but nothing melodramatic is going to happen really, but I want to be on the safe side, darling. Personally I think that the world has gone mad, and above all I think that France is mad to pin her faith to present day Russia. An enormous army with no gentlemen to lead it, with no dicipline to speak of and no traditions, an army with no roads or railroads to back it, with probably no adequate depots either, an army that will have to operate across so vast and unhappy a country in which food is scarce and clothing is scarce, in which harvests fail and peasants starve—Ah, no, it will surely prouve a delusion. Its very size will be a disadvantage. France is wrong to want a Russian Alliance unless I am much mistaken. But these are not things for you to say even if you agree with me, which as likely as not you don't. Anyhow, my heart's dearest, I am behind you with all I have now and always—this thought comforts me so let it comfort you, and in any case I'm not seriously worried. Only once again I warn you to be cautious of your words and actions at this critical moment. I suppose Mrs Baker will be back tomorrow and that you will be seeing something of her; I don't resent this as much as I did because now—or so it seems to me—no one could come between us. I feel as though we were now so much one that nothing and no one could come between us even for a moment. I feel that you have given yourself to me absolutely—Am I over-confident, my beloved? Be careful of the ring with Mrs Baker—remember that Una gave it to you. I rather hate having to lie about it, but lie we must—she can be very dangerous and I feel that she could be extremely jealous, and that would make her even more dangerous, and we have the hospital to consider and above all your naturalization. Shall I tell what may happen? She will probably sense that something has changed your feelings towards her, that although you are still very fond of her, of course, the excitement, the schwermrie[1] has gone from that fondness, and this she will miss because she liked it. She will probably try to get you back, to make you crazy about her again, to make you a willing slave again. She may try to appeal to your gratitude and pity—may say that she is ill and so needs you—I know it all, my most dear, and I warn you. Now listen, she has no claim whatever on you—she worked you to death and that is no claim, she played on your emotions and enjoyed the results—you flattered her vanity, my little Cosak—you who went pale and red by turns, who thought of yourself as her second lap-dog! Well, now you are not a lap dog any more, but a R.C.P. with a crown over one ear and a wide gold collar around your neck on which are engraved these protective words: "I am I, and I belong to Johnnie." And on the other side of the collar, on the side that no one is allowed to see, on the side that you wear against your body are the words: "I love Johnnie & Johnnie loves me—and Johnnie is the one who <u>needs me</u>" So now you know all about it beloved. Be nice to Mrs Baker, by all means go & see her—send her some flowers if you really want to—but remember that you are no longer free, no longer at her beck and call, no longer unable to say: "No" to her. Well, thats enough about Mrs Baker, but write and let me know all that happens. I must to bed, its past 2 am and I have to be up by 7.30. How I do love and love you, Soulina.

Your <u>John</u>

<u>April 13th</u> Good morning my darling. It is 8 am and I am going to bath and dress having had my breakfast already. Then I am going out—first to my bank and then to Cooks to take the tickets for Paris as this is the last free moment before the move and its less fag to get them while in London. **The tickets for Paris!**

Your own John.

Una sends love and says she would have written—Oh, she has just called out that she is going to write to you now.

---

1. Probably *Schwärmerei*, a German expression for romantic passion or enthusiasm.

[Rye stationery]

April 20th 1935

My own dear love. No letter yesterday, but my reward this morning when I got that of 17th and 18th. Darling, didn't I tell you I was working? I think I did in the letter you mention written at 2. am., but not in the telegram I sent you. Una said to me 'I'll write to Soulina & let her know that all is well'; for she knew that I'd not had a moment to write as she saw I was sending a telegram to you & asked why—so I explained to her. Did it annoy that she should write? Surely not. Dearest child of mine, why can't I live in the same town with you? Because I belong to my own country to some extent I suppose—all my business & so on being in England. But why do you think that I have not taken another flat in London? Because I <u>must</u> be free to be for long spells in Paris near you—because I can't endure our seperations. A certain time in England I shall always have to spend, but as short a time as possible in future. I am glad that your Doctor patient is better. And bless you beloved for the lovely words at the end of your letter of 18th. 'I am not alone now in the world, there is someone who cares for me.' Yes, Soulina, there is someone who cares for you so deeply that the love is pain as well as deep joy—so that never again need you feel lonely—and maybe this is why you came into my life, so that never again need you feel lonely.

Na-dine. A tiresom Chink but well meaning. Too pushing though, which is not at all Chinkie. But of course she is not an R.C.P., they only posess the <u>perfect</u> breeding. She is not entitled to wear a crow[n] slightly over one ear or any where else—she is one of the common pigs of Paris. So Natalie is returning alone. Strange that, but when we get to Paris she is certain to tell us all about it. Why did we warn you against strenuous dietings? Because you said you were doing it, darling. If you're fat I shall love you just the same. Anyhow, I'd hate you to get too thin—I adore the feel of you as you are, my darling.

Weather here very bad but warmer this day—but so much wind & rain—its disgusting. All the same Rye is wonderfully lovely in Spring, and down here at the very edge of the cliff hanging over the marsh, the birds never stop singing—Oh, why arn't you here to share it all with me! All beauty makes me so sad these days unless I have you at my side to share it.

Many sailing vessels come & go on the river—a sight I adore for I dearly love ships. In one of my past lives I must have been a sailor!

One thing you say in your letter of 17. You tell me not to 'abuse' Unas kindness—Darling—I don't understand exactly. But the next time she wants to write to you like that I'll try to stop her, though the only result will be that she'll feel left out and offended. Never mind—I love—love—love—love, Soulina, and I think I really do know what you mean—its your natural good breeding and delicacy of feeling. But believe me I did not suggest her writing—so don't misjudge your unhappy Johnnie! She wished to do it and I simply did not stop her—thats all oh, heart of my innermost being. She genuinely likes you, Soulina.

I kiss you from head to foot.

Your John

I don't suppose this will reach you until Monday.

[Rye]

Easter Sunday—1935

"Christ is risen——"
"He is risen indeed."

My dear love. When we got back from early Mass this morning, Una wanted to send you a telegram wishing you a happy Easter. I had had the same idea but had thought that being Sunday, it would be impossible in our benighted Sussex. However, after many struggles I got myself connected with Brighton—miles away—and then Una wrestled with spelling out the difficult name of Souline (S. for shin, O. for one—U. for universe—and so on) and the still more difficult name: Francisque Sarcey. The half-wit at the other end of the telephone line promised to get the telegram off at once, but whether it will ever reach you I cannot say. Wind and rain continue, with fine spells in between—such a bore as one gets wet to the skin in two minutes. Darling, I am working as though posessed—and so I am posessed by inspiration—thanks be. But darling, I have a great surprise for you—it is not the book about Sirmione, no, it is quite another book and quite another story. This is a story that I have had in my mind for a long, long time; it is about the very poor, the very poor of this Sussex. You see, having lived among them I know them inside out, and the book is my best work—yes it is that.[1] For some years this book has been nagging at me, and now it has taken me completely. Why could I not get on with the book that came to me after that terrible

---

1. This new book was *The Sixth Beatitude*, published by Heinemann in 1936.

first parting with you in Paris? You are so naturally asking me this. Well, I'll tell you, oh, heart of my heart. <u>I am too near it all</u>. The emotions are so much in me still, so much in me that I can't hear the records of the folk songs I heard sung at Sirmio[ne] without feeling the anguish that I felt last summer—for indeed it was very terrible anguish—the anguish of not knowing what was going to happen to you and me—I shall never forget it. Darling, another thing, love is too near—I can't seem to get it into the right perspective when I try to reduce it to words and phrases. You have filled me with love to over-flowing, but it must overflow back onto you, it can't and won't overflow onto paper. At one time I did honestly think that it would—I wrote & told you so, I remember. But now for ages I have know[n] that I have failed. I didn't say anything about this in Paris because I thought you might worry about it. But you must have noticed that when you spoke of the book, I was often very silent, my darling. Was I worried? But yes, I was terribly worried—for a time I thought that my talant had left me. This was pretty awful, for a writer's talant is to him, at all events, very precious. Do you know, before I met you I was dry—as dry as bones—then I fell in love and that stirred the fluid again, that awoke me, energised me, made me come alive—and I began writing, but <u>not the right book</u>. Maybe I had to set the wheels working—maybe that book was a kind of oil, anyhow the wheels are now working smoothly. You are disappointed. You are saying to yourself: "Oh, I see—I have not been John's inspiration. Probably I don't count at all in John's work!" Little fool—but you are my inspiration. It is owing to you that I can work now—owing to you and your love, Soulina. You give me vitality, can't you see this? Haven't I told you an hundred time that before I met you I was writing nothing? What does it matter which book I write just so long as it is a fine book and worthy? And so, beloved child of my body, beloved child and woman in one, if my letters are sometimes rather brief you will know why—won't you, my beloved, for this book is coming through very fast. Adam's Breed[2] came that way, and that is how I like it. When ones work is sticky it really half kills one—it is like a long and difficult confinement. But I'll probably knock off all work while in Paris on my way down South— yes, I'll knock off all work for those two weeks. I'll have to, my darling, because I want you terribly, Soulina. You are like a fire in my blood these days. I must and will have you in my arms. If, when I come, you

2. The novel for which John won the James Tait Black prize in 1926.

were to deny me I think that I'd kill you, its like that, my beloved. Sometimes when I am writing my book and thinking about my poor Sussex people the desire for you gets me by the throat, and then I write well—I use some of that force—I force it into the channel of my writing. But that wouldn't do if it went on too long—it would ruin my health and finally my work—so be kind to me when I come, Soulina.

I wonder how you would endure being with me when I am working at this terrific pressure? I am irritable—I can't eat my food, and sometimes I just fly out over nothing. I know this you see, but I simply can't help it. Una has had to endure it for years—and they say that one can get used to hanging!

The story goes that H. G. Wells[3] threw his ink pot at the woman he loved, one morning, because she dared to go into his study and ask him some perfectly innocent question.

"Hell take you!" he is said to have screamed. "Don't you know that you are living with a genious?"

I know the feeling—but if it were you I think I'd want to get up and kiss you. That would be the danger—I'd want to make love instead [of] concentrating on work. You'd have to keep me in order, darling. Are you sorry that you've fallen in love with an Author? Believe me, as writers go I am an angel! (I have just spelt Angel—Angle) My spelling is getting more grotesque every minute. The 30th it is coming so near. Won't you please come to the station and meet me as you did last time?—Do, please do if you can—I'll see you sooner, & every hour, every minute counts to me. I am coming by the same trains as last time. Gare du Nord at 8.35—I think, but I'll let you know the exact hour later. Meanwhile, please write at once & tell me whether you think you can come to the station and then on to supper as you did before. Oh, Soulina, please, please. Darling—how I love you! I know how much I love you by just these little things like wanting to see your Chink face at the station. Don't you dare to give me up—don't you dare. But of course you won't dare—if you did you'd crush me. I'm going to get cramp in my hand in a minute. I must stop. God keep you and bless you, Soulina.

Your John

---

3. British author (1866–1946), a prolific novelist who offered to defend *The Well* during the obscenity trial.

April 27th 1935

My own darling love. Four days and we shall be together again—I shall see your most darling face & have you in my arms—I can hardly believe it! Beloved I want you to come and sleep at my hotel if, for any damn reason, this new case of the old gent with pneumonia is still dragging on when I arrive. I could be with you every evening up in your bedroom and stay until between 1 & 1.30. Sleep with you I dare not for fear of comprimising you, & that badly. But it does seem to me that life at the hotel would be less of a strain on you if the case is still on. When this one is over I hope there won't be another until I leave for the South. Oh dear, my darling how difficult it all is for both of us, and we so much in love. If you were asked why you were at the hotel you have only to say that you are staying with friends there—that would do, wouldn't it—darling? I think it would. If work has come to an end & you are free—then I expect that your room would be our best refuge as it always has been. This longing I have to spend the night with you—it is a posotive craving. Yes a tormenting craving. And so unreasonable of me—Good Lord, why not one pair of lovers in an hundred can do that—no they cannot. Nor have I wanted to share a whole night of sleep with a woman since I was 20—maybe I am in my second childhood! Dearest it is the gentle, happy famaliarity of a bed shared—to know you to be asleep & contented beside me—to sleep close up against your warm, firm body—that to me is the peace of Heaven. But we must get what we can. I am not engaging a room for you the night of my arrival—I am waiting until I can talk it over with you and hear your views on the subject. Oh, darling I do long for you so consumedly. This letter will not go out now until 9.15 pm. I am afraid because I am late in writing, as up to now I have been sorting cloths & beginning to pack my trunk, paper case etc. But you must forgive me darling as you will when you stop to think that all this is really in order to be nearer you—you—you. Oh, those two months down South together! Heart of mine are you very tired?—This sounds like a fairly heavey case. Never mind, if you are too tired when I come we will love in Spirit! But a little love in body, too, please darling. I will be all consideration though—I always am, arn't I? Yes Johnnie. Today I sent you a telegram of Easter greeting for the Russian Easter tomorrow. It had to go off today as everything is closed here on Sunday. I am only living until I see your face at the station. I kiss you all over

Your John

John and Una stayed about two weeks in Paris before they headed for the Riviera where Souline was to join them. Souline's discontent about the arrangement à trois, however, had surfaced in a major way. John's letters of May and June are full of torment at the thought that Souline might indeed not come South, as she seems to have threatened.

[Beauvallon]

May 19th 1935

Darling. After I had posted my letter to you this morning, in which I begged you to do all in your power to persuade those in authority to give you your card in time to come here on 14th; and, moreover, to bestir yourself at once about it—I got two letters from you by the same post: the one written on the 17th, the other on the 18th.

What is the matter? Your letters are so cold, so withdrawn—they might quite well have been written by nothing closer than an affectionate friend. Also they are filled with depression and discontent. Is this one of those moods of yours—the moods in which, for some reason, you like to hit at me? Or have you been drinking too much—I ask this, my darling, because the tone of your letters reminds me of those I received when you were in Zurich. The last two letters, and indeed the one I got yesterday, are disjointed and unsatisfactory. You know my dear, I can't do more than I am doing to make life easier for you. I spare you all I can while sparing myself nothing, yet it is so obvious that you are not contented with what I can do—the discontent leaps at me from those letters. If this is a mood for God's sake get over it—nothing has changed since I left Paris—I am still the same Johnnie who loves you. But you must stop hitting at the Johnnie who loves you because the whole world won't go just your way—though what is the matter at the moment I don't know. There are surely times, oh, my beloved Soulina, when (as the old London Palmist said) if an Angel came from Heaven he could not please you! You have never once expressed the least regret at the probable delay in your joining me out here, nor do I consider that you've done your best to find some way of hastening matters. You've just collapsed & done nothing at all. I've very near feeling angry, dearest. But perhaps you'd rather not join me here? Really I shall begin to think so if you don't take trouble about it yourself. In your place I'd have asked a thousand questions, but you asked nothing at all, it seems. What does this mean? Don't you want to come? Or are you anxious to worry me—if thats what you want you've succeeded.

Two things stand out in your letter of 17th. You appear to be trying to get a case, yet I told you that in your present state of health <u>I did not want you to work before you join me</u>. Useless, it appears, for me to advise, for me to express a wish to you. I gave plenty of money until the 14th, and after that (if you are not here) we'll see. But I <u>do not</u> want you to take work now, not before the 14th at the earliest, & by then I still hope that you may have joined me. The next thing is this: you say that your friend has guessed our relationship. This you sandwich in between other things in your letter, as though it had little importance. You don't trouble to give me any details even. No please (1) Exactly what did she say? And (2) exactly what did you answer? And (3) why will all your friends know very soon? I want you to try to answer these questions & when you do so try to answer them <u>fully</u>. I hate having a statement thrown at my head without explanations—I do, darling.

<u>Your letter of 18th</u> What's this rot about a pension, and your only coming to me out here for a month, and you paying for yourself—its the damnedest rot—thats what it is, my Soulina. This Beauvallon consists of this hotel—there are no pensions only this hotel. Moreover, you may only want "a bed" as you say, but I'd like a comfortable one! Moreover again, it would never do for me to be seen coming out of your pension at all hours of the night, (if there were a pension.) As for paying for yourself—I won't hear of such a thing, you are coming to stay with me as my guest—we've been all over this matter before, so why have you raked it up again? And why have you now decided to come only for a month? I won't hear of that either. Whenever you come I expect you to stay until I go back—we will travel back to Paris together. Is it Aix en Provence that is frightening you perhaps? Are you afraid that I'll want you to nurse me? I may not go to Aix en Provence at all, and if I do go I shall take you with me, but not as my nurse—I wouldn't let you nurse me. Yes, on second thought I believe I am angry. Listen—<u>You must bestir yourself and find out more, much more about your card, and this immediately</u>—you really must, Soulina.

I dare not give up your room in this hotel otherwise I may not get one at all, but if you are so anxious that I shouldn't have to pay for the room before you come, then why don't you help me by making every effort to find out something?

I'll be honest with you darling, I am not very pleased with Piggie at the moment—no I am not—I think its being very inconsiderate and lazy. When, oh when, will you understand what it means when an author is writing a book? When, oh, when, will you understand what it means to love anyone as I love you? When, oh, when will you spare me, my Soulina. Sometimes I think that the answer is: Never. Well, my dear I intend to write this book, so please, if you love, stop tormenting. I simply will not have you upsetting my plans whenever you feel the least bit moody—You are not to blame about your Card, but you are to blame for not troubling yourself to make the proper enquiries about it. You could quite well have asked a few reasonable questions when they told you to go back on the 22nd. You could quite well have asked one important question, namely: When you do go on 22nd will you then be given your card, or failing the card a recipisse.[1] But no, you asked nothing—or if you did ask you have not troubled to tell me.

I am writing a Book. I love you and I need you—I can't be happy here until you come. Pull yourself together, Soulina.

I'm the first artistic brain-worker that you have known intimately I think—and so probably you don't understand the tension in which we creative people live during the time of creation. But you've got to try to understand it, my darling.

No more cold, moody, discontented letters please—please. They upset me and I will not be upset just now. Do you want to ruin a piece of fine work? Your health I order you to tell me about and always at once. But such things as your Card you should make every possible effort to get smoothed out so that they need not upset our plans—yours and mine—I think, dearest, that that is your duty—always supposing that you love me. Look here, do you want to come to Bauvallon? Honestly, I am beginning to wonder. I can't think that youve ceased to love me since we parted—youve hardly had time, have you darling? Then why these cold letters—so stiff, so forced, so unpleasantly reminiscent of Zurich. Has the Princess arrived in Paris?

Dearest love—I kiss you, but I beg you to be good. I think that Una

---

1. Receipt.

wrote to you today, making still further helpful suggestions anent your card—do please take her advise—she is wise, she thinks quickly, and she wants to get you here. She howled when I told her about the pension, not with laughter but with horror, darling. No, my dear I don't treat my beloved like that—a smart hotel for me, a pension for you—but in any case there is no pension.

I await your answers to my three questions, and also I await the result of your visit to the Commissariat. Which please go to <u>at once</u> They can't eat you!

Your tired and discouraged

<u>John</u>

This will be posted tomorrow, Monday morning.

Beauvallon

<u>May 25 1935</u>

My dearest love. It was a great relief to get your letter of 22nd. I had had no letter since the one I got on Tuesday. The principal thing in life at the moment is that I shall have you with me again either on the night of the 14th or the morning of the 15th—unless you should take the night train on 13th in which case it would be morning of 14th! Darling, I knew at once from the tone of your letters that something was happening, and I knew that I had not done a single thing except be on earth!

Darling, try to remember how very very much I love you and then you will realize how much you can hurt me—oh, but terribly, Souline. When we are together you shall try to tell me the unpleasant thoughts that came like black demonds [demons] into your mind as soon as I left you—such thoughts are better out than in—I will listen and you shall tell me, my darling. Oh, I know its hard sometimes, darling: first I'm with you and then I'm not, and so on—but what can we do? Before I came I think that your life was terribly empty—I know my life was before I met you, in spite of my devoted affection for Una. If we are to meet we both have to make efforts. I think I could tell you hear & now a good few of those thoughts that you found so depressing—but I'm going to wait until I have you in my arms. Only do try & remember this—nothing and no situation can be perfect—everything in this world has its drawbacks. I feel certain that I have many drawbacks—and those, I suppose, were what you thought of after I left you in Paris. But

I do think oh, most beloved child of my heart—I do think that one has to weigh things up—one has to weigh one thing against the other—I mean this. On the one side of the scales is Johnnie with all Johnnie's drawbacks of disposition and circumstances and so on. On the other side of the scales is life without Johnnie—never to see me any more, never even to hear my voice scold a little—life as it was before we found each other—no, not quite, because now you know another life—the life we are having as lovers. Beloved—when you feel angry and blue because Earth cannot turn into Heaven—when you wish that I were a man who could marry you & thus give you more protection—when all the black thoughts leap into your mind and wound you until you must turn and wound me—when this happens, weigh me up—weigh our love on the scales against what life would mean without it. Peace—peace—my sweetheart—my honey sweet, it is peace and not war between us. The description of your struggles to get your Card—the waiting, the crowds—the whole thing, too awful! It makes me unhappy to think of it even. Today I am wiring a piece of advise, it is this: As you need a doctor's certificate for your holiday—I would like you to ask Ruaud for it at once. I'll say as you do: "One never knows" he might get ill or be called away—I do feel that this is fearfully important—If you can't see him because you are working then write, but as you say you have seen him no doubt you've arranged all this with him already. But just in case you have not I am motoring tonight into St. Maxime to wire you this very morning. We will talk all we want to quite soon now, darling, and you shall tell me more of your little friend who has guessed that we are lovers. We are not her business are we, my Genia? But I cannot think that she'll go around among your friends and talk of a thing about which she cannot be really certain unless you or I tell her, darling.

Oh, I understand all you feel—yes I do—and I want to put my arms around you and comfort you as I write this. Comfort you for being a little White Russian who must bear with so many ridiculous restrictions. Comfort you for having a profession that you hate—and for which you have no vocation. Comfort you for having had to go through ill health and anxiety all alone—without anyone who cared very terribly what happened. Comfort you for every sorrow and pain that has come into your life since the day of your birth—yes, and if our situation often makes you sad, then comfort you for having met Johnnie.

Dearest, but try to be of good cheer—try now that we are going to be together so soon in this divine place to feel calm and happy. I was

really getting along all right until you wrote me those damnable letters—
and now once more there is peace between us.

I kneel down and kiss both of your hands, my Souline.

Your John

[Beauvallon]

June 7th 1935

My dear Love. June 7th and in a week you come. Yesterday there was
no letter from you—doubtless because the train did not wait for the
mail bags—they think that this is what happened here in the hotel, but
are not certain. Today I got two letters from you and was made happier.
Yesterday we took a lovely drive, over the mountains to a place called
Vidauban where we lunched. Had you not been coming the beauty
would have driven me into a deep melancholy, but as you are coming I
consoled myself by thinking that we will take the same drive again when
you are here. "I can show all this to her;" was what I kept thinking.
Love is a strange thing, my Soulina—it intensifies all beauty, turns joy
into pain, and pain into joy—if the pain is endured for the sake of the
beloved.

Last evening there came on me a great tenderness for you—a great
tenderness almost free from passion. I thought back on our first meeting
in Bagnoles, then forward to our next meeting in Paris—to that lunch
together when you could not eat, and afterwards in that sitting room—
I thought back to those hours (our first hours alone,) when you were so
terribly uncertain and frightened: "I don't know how to kiss any other
way . . . ." you said, do you remember, sweetheart? Then I thought of
my coming to your appartment after my terrible summer at Sermio[ne],
of your terror even though you greatly loved—and I thought of that
evening when you sat at supper all crumpled up and in despair, and
when I fed you as though you were a child, and consoled and reassured
as though you were a child—and I thought of the moment when I had
to leave you alone for the night, when of all other times I should not
have had to leave you alone, but should have been able to stay beside
you, making you go to sleep in my arms, making you feel my love &
protection—but instead I had to leave you alone . . . . .

And I thought of how virginal & innocent you were, how ignorant of
physical passion—you the most passionate of all women. Oh, Soulina it
is a wonderful thing that has come to me through you, for I was your

first lover. Through me you are now no longer a child. Wonderful, yes, but terrible also—terrible because so achingly sweet—I [a] sweet pain in the very soul of me, filling me with such a tenderness for you that I feel as though I could scarcely endure it. Step by step—very quietly I led you towards fulfillment. And this had made you doubly mine. It has made you an integral part of my life, so that never can I let you be uncared for again. I found you a virgin and made you a lover; a most blessed responsibility I have taken—a most sweet and dear burden that I shall bear to the end & beyond, Soulina. I have made a new discovery through you—I find that to take an innocent woman is quite unlike anything else in life, is perhaps the most perfect experience in life if real, deep love and tenderness goes with it, if with it goes the will to protect, the will to hold & the will to keep. Your dear innocence was a revelation to me—I had never met anything quite like it before. And this is why there are many moments when I want to hold you in my arms and weap for the tenderness that I can't express, that I find no adequate words to express—and so it was with me all last evening. Yes, beloved, and so it still is with me this morning. My Soul—my heart—my desire and my love—trust me; you are no longer alone, such as I am you have me while you want me. You must have been waiting for me I think, and I bless you because you did wait, Soulina.

I send you my faithfulness, my devotion. I send you my care and my protection. I send you the great urge of my desire, and the even greater urge of my tenderness for you. I ask you to remember when life seems hard & when we are apart, that I love you so much that I could not visualize life without you. That your innocence when first you gave yourself to me is a golden chain twisted around my heart—a chain that I hug to my heart, beloved. And now you are coming to John who is waiting, and you and I are one flesh, one Spirit—and all this is amazingly strange but true. And I love you so much that I can't express it, because its beyond all words.

Your John

[Beauvallon]

June 10th 1935

The 10th of June, my dearest love, and in four days from now you'll be coming to me. Soulina, it seems to good to be true. Your telegram saying that you'd got the receipt made me go almost crazy with joy. Yesterday no letters because it was Sunday—and today being fete very possibly none either—but your telegram is always beside me on my desk, and soon, soon I'll be kissing the beloved hand that writes the letters, my darling. All the same I am longing for a letter. Yesterday morning you got only a few lines as I had to be at Mass by nine. I felt that having bombarded heaven with implorings that your papers should be in order, I could hardly miss Mass—but I wanted to go because I was feeling so grateful. And now, somehow, I am rather more hopeful about your work-card—though I don't want you to count on getting it too greatly, for I hear on all sides how difficult it is. Your land—too splendid if you can really sell it, or even a small part of it, but do be careful that your Russians have got the money to pay you. Thats the snap these days in selling to White Russians—they mean to pay, of course, but they can't always do so; arn't I right, my beloved? I'm glad that your little Sauvage is being nice—I don't think that she'll try to question you about me. Can she really help on your naturalization? If she can you may imagine how I shall bless her. Ruaud wrote to Una the other day, saying that he was pleased with your condition, but expected to see you when you were free—it was in answer to Una's letter. This hotel is filling up now very fast—all rooms are book[ed] for July and August—but they still let me keep my work room. I only just secured your bedroom in time, and you know that its been engaged for ages. You ask me why our love is so intense? That I cannot say, my honey-sweet—some force in us both that having come to life is doubled in strength because we are lovers? It may be so. But falling in love and loving is one of this world's greatest mysteries. We meet hundreds of people & then comes the **one** person and the thing has happened and nothing can stop it and nothing can ever undo it. But the pain of such love—that makes you ask why? I think because all great emotions are one. This is hard to explain but I know what I mean. The circle meets in all great emotions—its a part of that curious Oneness that I feel—that I tried to write of in The Master of the House, and probably wrote of extremely badly because its a thing that lies just beyond the conscious mind—its always just out of reach, yet its there—in us, of us, and all around us. The placid, contented and painless love is not love at all as you & I know love—its something that has a certain beauty, of course, but it isn't love, its affection. I sent you a wire on Saturday in answer to yours—a wire of rejoicing which I hope you received. I knew that this Whitsen[1] was going to delay our letters. The weather continues to be quite perfect, but the evenings & nights are rather cold as always. Everyone bringing coats down to dinner because now we dine out on the terrace. I now spend a great deal of time window-gazing when I go into St Maxime or St Raphiel—window-gazing for the cloths that the R.C.P. will need and which I am going to buy it. Everything can be got much better here than in Paris as I have told you. What fun we're going to have, Soulina! Una is keeping her eyes skinned too—she's being most awfully darling & helpful. And shes getting quite plump—can you believe it? This air—this grand air full of sea & pines and sweet smelling maquis—I want it for you—and your going to have it for weeks & weeks. Shall we all come & live here forever? No, I'm joking. But really one can't help wondering why one lives in cities and gets iller & iller, when the good God has provided the sea & the sunshine, the mountains, the pines and the maquis! Yesterday I got my arms badly sunburnt—no rose without a thorn, is there darling? Jolly painful, you'll have to be awfully careful. You'll have to go very carefully at first & use plenty of oil, though oil didn't save me, but this morning the worst of my trouble is over. My nose is as red as a beetroot, I warn you. If when the train comes in to the station you see something that looks like the rear light on a car, you'll know that its my nose and that I am behind it! It will brown in the end, but its not brown at present. A shady hat you'll have to get at once—I can lend you one on your first arrival—I can also lend you shirts to wear with your pyjamas until we can go & buy some. People wear quite simple open-necked shirts—men's shirts sometimes & they look very smart and I think that they aught to suit you. I've already sent you a list of the clothes that I think you should bring—but do, do buy a trunk. Good Lord, I'm going to miss the post—I must stop—I love you a million times over. I can't express how much I love you.

Your John

Souline joined John and Una at Beauvallon on June 14th. They remained on the Riviera until mid-August, when they travelled together to Sirmione. Souline's anti-Semitism created a major falling out with Mickie Jacob, and the month's stay in Italy was not altogether peaceful in other

1. Whitsuntide, Pentecost.

ways as well, as there were considerable frictions over political views. On September 15th all three returned to Paris, where John and Una stayed a month before returning to Rye on October 16th.

<u>October 18th 1935</u>

My own dear Love. The second morning post has come and gone bringing me no letter from you. I know that you had to be at the hospital early yesterday morning which may account for your not having written until late in the day—I pray that I get a letter from you by this evening's post. I am so anxious to hear Dr Fuller's report.[1] Here there is much confusion. 1) our telephone is out of order and so far the fault has not been found. Oh, yes it has, the man has just arrived to say that all is now O.K. so I am now available by telephone to you. Please let me know the moment <u>your</u> telephone is working— 2) The frigid-air is out of order, a man is working on it at this moment with no result so far. 3) I have many repairs to do to the cottage owing to the recent great storm. 4) I have just heard that my mother has pernitious anemia. & she over eighty! I cannot pretend that this seriously affects my heart as she and I have been so wide apart for many years. Still I am pitiful and shall naturally have to go to London for the day & see the specialist. I am afraid there is little hope for her from what the doctor writes. I could have wished that she would go quickly & painlessly in her sleep, the poor, angry, cruel old woman. Anyhow she is in a nursing home & all possible is being done for her. I have no idea whether it will drag on or not.[2] I shall probably have to see her—maybe that is my duty—anyhow I forgive her her faults towards me and I hope she forgives me my faults.

Yourself, my precious, my life. I am missing you terribly. There are moments when the ache is so awful that I could cry out. Last evening at about 5 this happened—the longing, the need, the tenderness—the mad desire to see you & touch you. It is all here as it always has been in the past—I do not get accustomed to our separations. And once more about my mother. Dont think that because she is dying this means that you are to keep any facts about your own health from me. I am honest, my

---

1. Souline had developed renewed lung problems, including some bleeding from the lung. She was being treated by Dr. Fuller.

2. In the end Marie Visetti outlived John by two years, dying in 1945.

dear—I am no self deceiver, and I hate falseness. My poor old mother's death will not cause me grief. All I want for her is a peaceful passing. Therefore this happening has not added to my worries at all, and therefore <u>your health</u> is to be fully discussed with me in your letters. If I really thought that you would keep anything back, I think that I should collapse of strain. I trust you to report to me truthfully and fully. The political situation goes from bad to worse—yet I do not think that Italy can afford a European War. Here in Rye everyone I have spoken to so far, wants peace to get on with their jobs—they do not approve of Sanctions. France has failed to keep the peace though. I suppose she will have to submit to the bad bull tacticts of England—Mad John Bull!

My love I have missed the morning post. This letter goes out at 2.45. It takes my heart with it across the Channel. I love you, I cherish you, I am all, all yours. Be of good cheer my beloved.

Your John

[Rye]

October 26th 1935

My own dearest love. I now reply to two letters—that of 24th & 25th. First, darling, I want to say that I cannot always catch the 10.30 am post—if I have been working the night before I don't wake up in time, therefore you mustn't worry if my letter does not arrive by the first post in Paris. I can always catch the 2.45—short of some unexpected rush, in any case I will write every single day, & if for any reason I cannot, I will telegraph.

<u>Curtains</u>. I strongly advise your getting the extra one at once and having it added. In a previous letter I told you why it is very unsafe not to see to this immediately.

<u>Your course.</u> I am glad you have started the typing unless the course tires you. I approve througherly of your bringing your typing up to standard. I advise also your hiring a typewriter for homework—this will keep your hand in. Later on if you find you are going to be a good R.C.P typist, I will buy you a smart little portable machine. The shorthand <u>no</u> not for the present. Why? I will tell you. Shorthand is a most trying study, also unless you perpetually keep it up it goes from you. Later on perhaps you might do it, but for the present I would rather you concentrated on the typing which will be useful in all circumstances. One thing

at a time and not too much strain, please beloved. I don't mind paying more for you to learn shorthand later on if you need it.

Cooking. For some strange reason this delights me—I think its such a good thing for a woman to be able to cook, even if she has no need to do so. Don't laugh. I am laughing a little myself—as I write this I feel that I am thinking like an early Victorian man: "A woman's place is the nursery & the kitchen." No—but there's something homey about the thought of you frying ham & eggs! Though I pity Liza & the roast chicken!

Concierge. I am glad you are making a friend of her—Go on making her give you motherly advise—I like to know that there is someone there who would keep an eye on you in my absence if you were not well or something.

But I hope that your course, your cooking & so on, won't make you get careless about your ear treatment. I <u>insist</u> that you keep that up, darling. Health first and everything else after, please.

Yesterday I saw my mother's doctor. The situation is not satisfactory, it is this: My mother, though over 80, appears to be responding to treatment. Result precisely what I should have expected, she is once more being a devil. The doctor tells me that in the nursing home they are being driven very nearly demented although they are most long suffering. This has always happened in nursing homes—on two occasions they refused to keep her until I got down on my knees to the matron! The doctor says that never in his life has he had to tackle anyone like her. Being better she now threatens to get out of bed, and her violence is almost impossable to manage. I asked him what was to happen in the event of her getting really better after some weeks, and he said that as far as he could see she would have to be allowed to return to her hotel. I want her put into a perminent home where she can be properly taken care of, but as he points out this cannot be done without her consent which she would not give. Nor will she consent to live out of London in a climate—say somewhere on the South coast of England, where she could get pure air & sunshine. He pointed out that I have no authority over my mother any more than he has. I asked him what he thought was likely to happen if she pulls through this time. He says that <u>if</u> she continues to respond to his treatment she will return to her hotel and take up a more or less normal life with a blood count of round about 70. She will probably drag on for an indefinate time then get a recurrance of the acute trouble and die—but the dieing will be a slow process. Were she younger they might try blood-infusion, but not on a woman who is over 80. Neither he nor I know about her affairs. Me she so hates & has all along, that I dare not question her, even. I don't know who her solicitor is, or indeed if she has one. The present fear is that the nurses won't stand her. A flat with a servant and a perminent nurse is out of the question—no servant would stay & no nurse. This is why she now lives in an hotel, she simply cannot keep her servants. While she was very weak in [and?] ill she was tamer, but now she has broken out again, it seems. She's so cruel—so terribly cruel, Eugenia—no mercy on anyone in this world, and violent over nothing and filled with hatred. The truth is that she is a borderland case & has been for years, according to the doctor. But not technically insane & so we can do nothing except let her go her own crazy way. Its all too terribly grim and depressing. Una was with me when I saw the doctor and I must say was wonderfully helpful. Sooner or later my poor mother will die as her desease is incurable as you know, but meanwhile the whole thing's a night-mare. However, I have you, my beloved. My beloved, my heart, my love & my comfort—I bless you and greatly do I love you. My love reaches out to you day and night. Yes, you are right, people don't matter, it was only for your sake that I wanted them at Christmas—I thought that Baby[1] would amuse you. He is coming, or so he writes, & I think I'll get hold of one other man if I can. But what matters is that we shall be together. This letter wont go till the 2.45 post. which means that it will reach you late, but I wanted to make it long, my darling, after the scrappy three lines yesterday—I have always so much to tell you.

Una says please go & get the electric fire—go at once she says, and so do I.

God bless you my dearest—I kiss & kiss you.

Your John

P.S I enclose two good critiques of The Unlit Lamp.[2] I greatly value French opinion. I thought you would like to see these critiques.

---

1. Unidentified.
2. Though this was the first novel John wrote, it was not published until after *The Forge*. It is a veiled study of inversion with a protagonist who sacrifices herself to the needs and demands of her conventional family.

[Rye]

October 29th 1935

My darling love. I follow up my few lines of this morning. Tomorrow, Wednesday, I am going to London until Friday—my address will be The Royal Court Hotel. Sloane Square. London S.W. I have wired you today telling you to continue writing to Rye—this as your letters might miss me in London. But, as I shall not get your letters until I return here, I have asked you to telegraph me in London if anything urgent should arrise, and please do not fail to do so. I have to go up to attend a big literary party given by my publishers, and also I have business anent income tax & so on to see to. All rather a bore but it can't be helped. Meanwhile the pulling down of some of the old cottages is making a fearful mess all round us—and I am perpetually scolding the men— what a life! But, oh, my heart I am very very homesick for you, and now that my book is finished[1] I am longing to do nothing but make love to you, which is natural. However I must stay here till you come because of attending to the endless details in connection with publication & so on. The public who read us all neatly bound up—price 7/6, have no idea what the making of books entails, have they, beloved? My darling The Forge.[2] It was not my life with Una, though I used up some few amusing incidents that actually happened to us. I never write my own life—I could not, though my own life often gives me ideas which are used up in a different set of circumstances. This must surely be so with all authors. My chain[3]—are you that? Perhaps, but if so I adore my captivity, and in return I place a chain of love on your heart and attach it to the chain that you have bound round mine, which means that if either heart should try to free itself both will die, for the heart is the source of life and as delicate as life itself. Therefore we two are the loving captives.

---

1. *The Sixth Beatitude*, a novel set on the Romney Marsh, John's beloved Rye landscape. It details a year in the life of Hannah Bullen, a working woman who faces her difficulties with a vision of oneness with nature, a theme dear to John's heart.

2. John's first published novel (1924) is a roman à clef modeled in part on the artist Romaine Brooks and featuring a restless English couple, Hilary and Susan Brent, whom critics often see as a fictional portrait of John and Una, though as the passage in this letter makes clear, that was not John's intent.

3. The central motif of *The Forge*, the chain (love) that binds Susan and Hilary despite their several (and sometimes shared) unhappinesses.

The wind is blowing up to a gale—in Hastings[4] this morning the great waves of our grey English sea were dashing over the street. This grey sea is the one I greatly love—the blue sea of the South is too tame and too unreal, nor has it got the true salt smell. What are you doing at this moment I wonder? That's the hardest part of these long seperations, not to know what my other heart is doing—it always seems so wrong to me somehow. I am love sick, I am only half myself, in a word I am utterly unhappy without you. Oh, dearest do take care of your health— You mean so much, so much, so much. Do you realize how much, Evguenia? And now the book has left my keeping—I shall not see it for more than a week, and you have helped me to write it. If you hadn't come walking into my life I know that this book would never have been written, and believe me it is fine, it is that, Evguenia. Its got the strength in it that you have given—Hannah Bullen is alive—I know it. You shall read it in type before publication—I am having an extra copy done so that you'll be able to read it without hurry. I'd have let you read it as it was written except that that would have spoiled it for you, you would not have understood my writing, all full of crossings out and corrections, especially as this book is such difficult English—No, I want you to be able to do it full justice—I am very proud of it, as you may have gathered! Darling, I do want you so terribly. Your voice on the telephone; I love to hear it yet it makes the wanting, the longing worse than ever—its so crazy to be hearing you speak and yet not to be able to take you in my arms and kiss your mouth and your funny Chink eyes, and you[r] hands that to me are so lovely. God bless you sweetheart & keep you always faithful, and loving to your

Johnnie who loves you.

[Rye]

<u>November 3rd 1935</u>

My darling, darling Love.

It was on Friday that the great sadness came upon me, growing more profound as the day went on, until I could have weapt coming home in the train as I have already told you. Now I know that I was catching your mood in addition to my own, for your letter of the 1st reached me yesterday afternoon. From 5.30, until 12 oc last night I stayed by the

---

4. A city on the English Channel about ten miles west of Rye.

telephone trying to get you. Every half hour I had you rung, but as you know I did not succeed in getting you until this morning. I have reported that you returned home at 9, and a call has been put through to Paris, but Paris can throw no light on the mystery. I wish you would take the matter up with them direct, for indeed I had a most miserable night, full of presentiments, doubts and fears, all of which I would have been spared had we spoken. What am I to say to you my Evguenia? There are words in your letter that you should not have written. You will tell me that you didn't mean them seriously, and this I must believe—yet the thought was there—the flashing thought that should not have been there, oh, you who say that you love me: "Just now it seems if someone came and soothed me and took me away far, so far that not one human foot has ever been there—I'd say yes and follow." Would you—would you—would you? I wonder. You see how the little pin prick of doubt creeps into the mind, Evguenia. You are a passionate woman whose passions I've awakened, whose physical longings I have awakened, and when they are upon you and I am not there you grow cruel towards me for not being with you. And this I endure with a certain understanding. But would you give way to the impulse of the moment and give what is mine—would you do such a thing and be faithless, could you, Evguenia? I can't always be with you as you know very well—my work, my career, my powers of earning all necessitate certain times spent in England. You, on the other hand, can't come here for long owing to the difficulties of your passport. Like a man, a sailor I have to leave you. For five months of every twelve, the men in our navey have to leave the women they love behind them. No wife ever goes on a cruise, beloved. I have never left you for so long since I've known you. Think it over, my torment, my misery, my desire—think it over. I bless you for the love that makes you long for me, but don't use it as a weapon to wound with—thats very cruel Evguenia. Am I taking you too seriously yet again? Perhaps—but this time it is really your fault. And now listen. Suppose that I feel as you do—half mad at moments through this deprivation that the circumstances of our lives impose on me. Do you think you're the only one who suffers? Because if you do I assure you you're wrong. I suffer hell, you make no mistake. But I couldn't go near anyone but you—it would be a complete impossibility. No one but you has the power to ease me. I'm half crazy for you at this moment. And last night when I didn't know where you were, when I longed to hear your voice and could not hear it, I thought I'd go mad. Thats my share of our burden—

every ounce of the burden I share with you. Evguenia write to me explaining those words that came into your mind—they haunt me. Have you been faithful heart of my heart? Do you think that during some enforced absence of mine, you could ever be unfaithful?

Your mood may be "only a passing show" but what might you do while the show was passing? Everything hurts me when you're not near me—music especially seems to hurt me. Oh, but all beauty is pain without you. When will you understand how much I love you—how much my body craves for you, Evguenia? When will you understand that such love is terribly easily wounded? Of course you need tenderness and care, and from me you have both to overflowing, and well do you know this when you let yourself think. No one <u>could</u> give you more than I do—not because I must, but because I adore you. Long for me, long for me when I'm away—long till you could cry out with longing, even as I am longing for you. Suffer as I am suffering now—thats Love, thats Love, my beloved Evguenia. May your dear white passionate body desire me until it spills over with the wine of its desire—but only for me, only, only for me. It is mine and all its desires are mine, and I alone have the right to sooth it—no one else in the world—do you hear, Evguenia? Surely I am mad to fear—to suspect, if I am then write and heal my madness.

Yes my book is finished—yet not really finished for now comes the all important moment when, seeing it for the first time in type, I must sit and calmly pass judgement upon it. If I fail in this my work may be ruined. What can I do to make you understand? It is joy, shere joy when you write that you love me and long for me as I am longing for you. It is hell, shere hell when that passing thought—that damnable thought catches hold of your mind—that thought of some possible other creature. Who might take my place and usurp my rights. You belong to me, and don't you forget it. You are mine, and no one elses in the world. If I left you for 20 years you'd have to starve. No one but me has the right to touch you. I took your virginity, do you hear? I taught you all you know about love. You belong to me body & soul, and I claim you. And this is no passing mood on my part—its the stark, grim truth that I'm writing.

Evguenia—beloved—my life, my all, write quickly, and give me some peace until you come. I want you—I am all on fire with longing, I'm crazy to feel you in my arms—to feel your body against my mouth, to hear you cry out with the pain of passion. Oh, my God—its not safe to play with me just now. Suffer—suffer—why not? Don't I have to suffer? I wanted to spare you and not write of these things, but now I have no more the desire to spare you. There are times when I could cut my body to pieces because of the longing thats in it for you. Times when my nerves are tortured with longing. Times when I cannot sleep for longing. As I write this I don't know what to do with myself for the craving I feel to have your hand on me, your body pressed hard, hard against my own, your mouth on my mouth. I could kiss you till you bled—I could tear you to pieces Evguenia. But for Gods sake let us try to be sane—in a little over a month we'll be together. Help me to be sane—I do implore you, by writing and saying that you'll always be faithful. Don't you love me enough to be faithful, my beloved?

Your tormented
John

[Rye]

November 10th 1935

My darling love. I have now heard my book read aloud from A. to Z. and think I can say that I am satisfied. Certain small details I have to attend to after a little more consideration, but for the rest I find the work good. Audrey Heath[1] told Una (behind my back) that she considers this book of yours and mine to be equal to my "finest writing." But today I am filled with the deep depression that will sometimes come after months of work—a kind of empty and hopeless feeling. If I only had you here the feeling would pass—you would kiss it away, my beloved. I would like at this moment to be lying in your arms with my head on your breast, perhaps going to sleep after a deep and fulfilling hour of loving—only in this way could I find peace. You would fill me—would fill the aching void that nothing but you can ever fill since I met you more than a year ago in Bagnoles. The weather remains unspeakable— wind and rain and a sudden spell of cold; even this cottage is hard to heat, the wind gets in through the very walls by the cracks in the ancient timbers. I think always of you and only of you, and now Una does not seem to resent my talking of you, and this helps me a little. Today I

---

1. John's literary agent.

prayed for your naturalization if its God's will and for your wellfair. Once French so many things should be eased—your coming to England being the most important. As it is I feel so terribly cut off when I have to spend some time in my own country. But of course we're not really cut off from each other—its only the feeling, Evguenia. I think of your little bright homie flat that is waiting for me in Paris, and of the hours that I'll spend there with you—just you and I—the world forgot—and this thought always consoles me. Darling, we'll go to that pot-house in Passy[2] and eat the big, none too good ham sandwiches, and drink the very excellent French beer, and forget that there ever can be seperations. Or better still, we'll find a new pot-house to go to in your own district. That will be fun—we'll find a new pot-house. There is something I want to say about Una. I know that you feel that she has exagerated reactions and that you dislike such reactions. Now listen, if you will only try to remember that Una is not English but Irish[3] it may help you to understand her better and thus not to feel irritated. The Irish are the most emotional people that God ever created in his wildest moments! They are Celts of the Celts—nothing in the world like them—not even White Russians, beloved! Look on her as Irish and she won't get on your nerves half so much as if she were English. As a matter of fact I'll now tell you a secret: your John is part Celt and thats why I'm a writer—to be an artist one must have Celtic blood for it gives one immagination. My very large dash of Celtic blood, however, is Welsh not Irish.[4] But the Welsh are also an immotional lot, which perhaps is why you find me a good lover. My dear—I'm so glad to know that you feel well—keep fat please, I prefer you fat to thin—but fat or thin I adore you.

Must stop now and discuss business with my agent who is leaving later this afternoon. I kiss you many times as always, my Evguenia.

Your John

---

2. On the Right Bank, just off the Trocadero Gardens. Passy, once famous for its monastery and red wine, is now best known for its cemetery, burial site of many Parisians famous in the arts.

3. Una's mother, Minna Gordon Taylor, was the granddaughter of the second Baron Castlemaine of Westmeath.

4. The Welsh connection is not made clear in the biographies of John, but presumably it would have come through the female line, since the Halls were originally from Lancashire.

[Rye]

<u>November 14th 1935</u>

My own darling love. Your letter of 13<u>th</u> has come. I have missed the first post as I slept late this morning. Our letters seem all Bulinka these days. Yes I know that you are chaining him now, and don't be snappy about my warnings—of <u>course</u> I know that you look after your things, but I also know your very tender heart for Johns and Bulinkas and such like creatures, and the harm is done so quickly, beloved. As I wrote yesterday, the dog's life does not please him and he has a side being just pure dog—there are dogs & dogs—take Jockey, for instance, his love for his mistress made life tolerable to him even in conditions none to favourable. Bulinka would be happier in a kennel of other dogs with plenty of games and a constant relay of ladies. Away with depression about your hair—it improved out of all recognition last summer and it will go on improving. Your teeth will now be properly looked after and they also will be saved, so away with depression! Of course I well know that your age is 100, that your teeth are only black stumps in your gums, that you're bald on top of your head & thus are compelled to wear a little lace cap, that you walk with a stick and have swoolen joints—all this I well know and yet I love you! Are you joking as I have just been joking, when you talk about making a "fictitious marriage"? Darling I must send you: 'Foreign Bodies'[1] a book based on fact I believe—in it such a marriage is arranged and you will derive what became of it. Anyhow the idea seems to me revolting. Beloved, darling, heart of my heart—well do I know that if I were a man & free I could give you a country—but don't rub too much salt into the wound—the wound's painful enough as it is, believe me. And who knows but that your naturalization will come, its too soon, much too soon to despair of it, darling. I was talking to a man the other day who lives in Paris & knows all the ropes about your naturalization. He said that you bring 1) a nurse, and 2) a resident of 13 years, and 3) of the breeding age (God help us!) He did not see why they should refuse it. But he said precisely what old Hollander said, namely that its not wise to try to pull strings until its refused or too long delayed, so apparently Hollander was right. This man migh[t] eventually be able to help us—he's John Reese, the man who published The Well—rather a soldier of fortune perhaps, but

1. A tragicomedy by Nikolai M. Gubskii, published in 1932.

a man who knows more about most things than anyone I have ever come across. When we meet I will tell you all about him.[2] Meanwhile I am yours for what I am worth, I might be worth more in all ways save one, and that is love. My love will not fail you and let that comfort you my dearest heart. All the care I can give you my beloved shall be given. Today I am going to look at rooms for the blessed day of your coming.

Your John

[Rye]

November 18th 1935

Darling Love. I feel that I was rather angry in my way of writing about Olga this morning. Of course I did not hear exactly what words she used, but I gathered from you quite enough. I was angry because it seemed so damn mean to come to your flat and try to make you feel unhappy and uneasy—I still think that jealousy played a large part, I expect your flat looked comfortable and pretty—Yes, darling, the morning I wrote in anger. How dare she torment my R.C.P? And really what business is it of hers? You see I am getting angry again, but never mind—only I think her a cat. The next time she says anything you just laugh in her face and then give her a drink or something. Really they none of them matter a hoot. All I want is that you should keep your position at the Hospital pending your naturalization, that I do think is rather important. And by the way—are they all so pure? If they are its because the've not had a chance to be anything else, says Johnnie.

Beloved, this is the Day of Sanctions. Black Monday. The Day of Shame for England.[1] I am deeply depressed when I think of my country, and here, indeed all over this England, there are many who feel as I do. Personally I don't think the Sanctions will work and then what will happen none can tell—I hope the whole thing will just fizzle out, but the shame will remain and not easily be forgotten.

My dearest heart. I think of you so much—I want to be near you always, I want to stand between you and the world—I am standing between you and the world from now on, indeed I stood between you

---

2. John Holroyd-Reece, head of Pegasus Press at the time of the publication of *The Well*. He and his wife Jeanne were to remain close friends of John and Una and of Una after John's death.

1. Sanctions on arms sales and on financial and economic interactions imposed by the League of Nations against Italy for aggression against Ethiopia.

and the world from the very first moment I met you. My darling, my poor, poor little White Russian—I kiss you, I rock you in my arms like a child & tell you to sleep and be at peace—Deeply, deeply I love you and as deeply respect you. You have all my love & my respect, Evguenia. I will finish this letter tomorrow.

<u>November 19th</u>

Sweetheart. Your naughty R.C.P. letter of 17th arrived this morning, but so did your good letter of 18th. Your naughty, grumbly, discontented letter was "the morning after the night before" I expect. I am so glad that you had a jolly time at the ball all the same. And how interesting it must have been to spend the day with your friend who had actually known the Tzar & his family. I told Una and she says she would so love to meet the girl in question. You know how much Una feels about the old imperial Russia and the tragedy of Catherinburg.[2]

Beloved child, I <u>am</u> so sorry about your having to part with Bulinka, but believe me it is best for the dog & for you. Well do I know the energy you have expended on him and how disappointing it must be to have to send him back. I have already told you that in my opinion no one could have done more or done better than you. I do hope that you are not going to be a bad R.C.P. and feel aggrieved over this business— you mustn't my darling because that would be foolish and would worry your devoted John. I have long known that B. is every man's dog— maybe he is all the happier for that, though personally I don't like it. A dog is so much trouble at best that the least he can do is to give devotion—but like us every dog has his special nature—some are devoted & some are not. Anyone who plays with B becomes his god—and this he can't help, poor Bulinka. Dearest, had he been your own a thousand times over it would not have made the situation any better. At the moment you are longing for a house in the country, but the mood will pass because <u>I don't want one</u>. I want nothing that entails too much responsibility—no thank you, my darling, I want to keep mobile with the responsibility of a White Russian on my heart. I want to be able to move about when circumstances demand it and to carry my R.C.P with me in a basket. Cheer up darling—we meet in a month from today, God willing, Oh, how I long for you Evguenia. How I long & long—my most precious love try to get some happiness out of my exsistance—out

2. Ekaterinburg, where the execution of Tsar Nicholas II and his family took place.

of our life together. Its not perfect, our life, but so few things are that. I fret so when I think that I can't make you happy. Indeed I don't know what to say about it. I can only hope that if you look back on what your life was before I came, you will find that now it's a little less dreary and less hopeless, I can only hope this my beloved.

Your John

Souline's visa was finally granted and on December 19, she joined John and Una at The Forecastle in Rye. They spent the next month in a round of holiday parties, visits with friends, and sightseeing, leaving in mid-January 1936 for Paris. John and Una would not return to England for another eighteen months.

In February 1936 Souline was hospitalized with a bleeding lung, and when she was well enough to travel, they all left for Grasse, an old city in Provence about twelve miles northwest of Cannes, returning to Paris in June. Souline had become increasingly unhappy at the ménage à trois, and on June 22, 1936, she and John had a monumental fight, with John raging through Souline's apartment tearing up or breaking everything she had ever given Souline. They soon patched over the rifts, however, and in July the trio moved on to Merano, a town in the Italian Alps only a few miles from the Austrian border. They remained there for more than seven months while John began work on a new novel, never completed. By April of 1937 they were in Florence, where John took leases on two flats, one for herself and Una and another nearby for Souline. The plan was to furnish them in preparation for a long stay during the autumn and winter months. Back in Paris by mid-July, Souline announced that she would not accompany them to Florence as planned. John and Una returned to Rye, and the letters resume.

1937

July 15 1937

I got home too late & too weary to write last evening, oh, you, Same Heart as mine. But on the way through Rye I stopped at the post office, which was just closing, and sent you a second telegram, this time "express" paying double rate, so as it was already past 7 I expect you were dug up at midnight with the wire! The cottage looks more lovely than ever and were you here I could be in heaven, but heaven is not for such as me—at all events not on this earth. Your telegram which was waiting for me gave me much comfort, and now I am looking forward to your first letter. I bucked up after you left me for Una's sake,[1] but oh, oh, the look of your funny, dear back with one shoulder hunched up as you walked away from me down the platform! These things, these great miseries aught not to be, they are all wrong.

The unpacking is still to be done and it is nearly 12, so far all I have been able to do this morning has been to go through draws & cupboards, hurling away things that had lain there for nearly two years. This afternoon I shall tackle the damned trunks. Una stood the journey fairly well. The crossing was like a lake. I thought I was a heaving mass of flesh, but find that naked I weigh just 9 stone which is about my normal.[2]

Can you go somewhere and take out a subscription for the Figaro for me?[3] I want it sent every day for 8 weeks. Of course I will pay you

---

1. This is John's interpretation of fights and tensions and miseries that developed in 1936–37, although Una's journal entries indicate that the three women had wildly differing perceptions of those events. Despite John's term "Same Heart," she and Souline were never again to share anything approximating a same heart.

2. About 126 pounds.

3. *Figaro* was a daily newspaper founded in 1826.

immediately if you let me know how much. Please try to arrange this my darling—do <u>please</u>.

What are you doing I wonder? It feels so lonely not to know, but I expect that you are feeling overjoyed at your "freedom!" But remember "The Same Heart" therefore you must be very, very careful of yourself. No spirits, only good red wine, no getting wet or over tired, no catching cold. I must stop, writing to you saddens me too much this morning because it makes me realize how far apart we are.

Your John

[Rye]

July 16th 1937

Same Heart. No letter yesterday which was natural because you would not have written on the day I left. But now no letter this morning. Will I get one by the second post or the evening post? If I do not I shall wire & pay a reply because tomorrow is Saturday and there is <u>no post here on Sunday</u> and I cannot wait for a word from you until Monday—no I can't. I shall wait for the first post tomorrow morning & then if there is nothing I shall wire. My dearest heart, my own heart, seperation to me is just another word for hell, yes and the sea between us which makes it seem worse somehow. And today a cold wet wind howling as it did all night—no warmth, no sun and but few flowers in the minute garden, so vile has been the weather I am told. Dearest the unpacking is finished all but my paper case, and the trunks are empty and ready to be taken away and stored until I want them again. There is something so final about this unpacking, something so painful, at all events to me. It is almost as though a part of my life had come to an end—the period of our life lived closely together, the period you hated and longed to be released from, yes, and begged to be released from many, many times, often telling me to go back to England. Well, now here I am & you far away and I can neither hear you nor see you nor touch you, and my half of our common heart is aching too terribly this morning, but maybe your half is feeling relief, maybe your half is singing & shouting: "Free! free! free!" Is that so, my beloved?

Darling, this cottage is full of reminders, of reminders of those early days of our loving. There are the little presents you once gave me: the small silver Icon beside my bed—the one I gave back then asked for again![1] This was the very first present you gave me, bringing it over to England with you—I am not counting the precious cross for that was more—& love letters. Then there is the little brass & enamel triptic which also stands beside my bed, and on my table just in front of my eyes as I write, is the little silver cup in which, so you said, they sometimes put honey in the old days in Russia—reminders—reminders.

Those were the presents that came from your bit of our heart at a time when you were deeply in love. Three years ago and how much has happened since—things bitter and sweet. Oh, Evguenia, Evguenia—there are no words, no words to express what I feel. I can only say to your half of our heart: "Love me, cling to me, understand me. Understand my love, my desire to protect, my anxiety, my poor broken life." No one on earth can know all this but you, since you are the reason for my joy and sorrow. Ten oclock and no letter from you. A great pain in this loving—a very real pain to love so consumedly, so entirely. And I think sometimes that had things been different my life might have been so contented, so peaceful. Could there have been friendship between you and Una . . . . . I think of what might have been but what is not. But never again will we live three together, this I have promised so do not fear it. I shall try to work and I have much to see to—the weeks will pass, but today every hour seems like a year. Darling, if you love me then write every day if only a postcard. A postcard—is that too much to ask? If so it is the price you must pay for having a love such as mine.

God bless you and keep you and make you love me.

John

[Rye]

July 17th 1937

My darling R.C.P. Same Heart. I have just had a most dear letter from you by the first post—the one written on 14th. I am so glad that you are getting all your cloths in order, sorting them and so on. I will address my envelopes as you suggest, but I have been most diligently copying the address given on the Pension card and that says: "Neuilly—Paris." Once again, darling, what is happening about your naturalisation? When you

---

1. In the terrible confrontation of June 22, 1936, in which John tore up letters and pictures, the icon Souline gave her in 1934 was angrily returned.

answer this letter please let me know. And tomorrow is the 20th—the day you go about your visa—I do hope you will get it tomorrow, but if nothing has come through from Rome make the Counsel keep his promise to wire, all of which I have said to you in nearly every previous letter, but I shall feel rotten until that visa is on your passport so that's that! I have little news except that the weather has turned fine & I hope with you also.

Andrea[1] spent the whole of yesterday here—as usual she is out of a job and I think her husband is a flop. But she insisted on marrying him against all advice and so there is nothing to be done or said. She is loyal to him which is as it should be. But I fear that she & he have done something that has antagonized his family as no help seems forthcoming from that quarter which is—to say the least of it—strange, the more so as his father is very, very rich and his mother, Lady Warren, has quite a sufficient private income; also Andrea has produced the only grandchild & a boy at that. I cannot understand any of it but I suppose I will never be allowed to know the true facts.

It was somewhat disconcerting to hear Una continually calling Andrea: "Evguenia." She seemed incapable of doing otherwise. Every few minutes it was "Evguenia this, and "Evguenia that . . . " until at last I said: "My dear, your child's name is, or used to be, <u>Andrea</u>!" Quite naturally A. showed some curiosity about you—where & how we met you, what were you like, and so on. I should think that she must have thought Una had a case on you as your name was forever on her lips! It was too funny, and of course it will all go back to Viola & Co.[2] Terrible and pitifuly worldly old Minna[3] is now yelling that she fully intends to go to France as soon as she is allowed to travel. She is bored to death with England, it seems, and proposes to go abroad <u>with a nurse</u> regardless of the expense to others. The whole attitude of mind is very deplorable and she but two years off 80! Also at moments she fears "Hell Fire" but does nothing to be more considerate & less selfish. In every way it is horrible & tragic and is giving even me the horrors. Die she will <u>not</u>. She

---

1. Andrea was Una's daughter. Although there had been something of an estrangement from the time that Una and John became lovers and life partners, Andrea did periodically maintain contact. She had married an actor, Toby Warren, and at the time of this letter she had recently had a child. She died in an automobile accident in 1961.

2. Una's sister. She had married Maurice Woods, a journalist, whom she divorced in 1918. In 1921 she married J. L. Garvin, the editor of the *Observer*.

3. Una's mother.

wishes to live in spite of her maimed and repulsive old body. I hope I am not growing hard, but really the accounts of Minna's mental angle are disgusting. Good, good R.C.P. to take warms cloths to the mountains—this it is doing for Johnnie's sake and the Saints who look after R.C.Ps. will undoubtedly reward it. I am so glad the new coat is smart and warm, I shall think of you wearing it and that will make me happy. Oh, yes, I love you, but deeply, deeply. You are rooted in my innermost being and I cannot tear you out if I would—were I to do so I should bleed to death—One heart—same heart—and no help for it, it seems. And I can now only think of our next meeting and live only for that and next winter.[4] "Its June in January because I'm in love." Or rather it will be next winter. There is still much to do to get ready for Florence—the furniture to sell as best I can in order to buy what I need for my flat—but I have decided not to sell the car—can't get a good enough offer for it.

Thanks about Figaro. Later today I will send you Fr 100 by registered letter, just now I have no registered envelope for money. Must stop at once or I miss the post.

Bless you a million times sweetheart.

John

[Rye]

July 21st 1937

My most darling love. Your letter of 19th came last evening. Now about your naturalization. As you know I am fully prepared to pay the Frs. 3,000[1] on the chance that you get the naturalisation in the end, and I shall not weap or [g]nash my teeth if the money goes for nothing as I fully realise it may do. This seems to me to be our only chance, and therefore you may give him the Frs 3,000 even in advance if he wants it. I am much afraid that if he demands payment in advance there is nothing to do but submit or drop him, and I have a hunch <u>not</u> to drop him, and so, my beloved, if and when you do pay the money you must let me know at once so that I can instruct my bank to pay the sum over to your bank. I am supposing that you will pay it out of what you have at present in your own bank, and you may count on me to repay you that

---

4. John and Una planned to winter in Florence, where Souline was to take a flat near them.

1. Approximately $1020.00 in current dollars.

amount immediately through my bank, as I have said. The words that the affair: "peut marcher"[2] do not convey much but this cannot be helped. Will you write me whether you gathered that you had any chance of naturalisation when this man has pushed forward your dossier? Did he express any opinion regarding your ultimate chances? He is—you will remember—supposed to have consulted someone about your chances. And now listen carefully: You may tell him that the day your naturalisation papers <u>are actually in your hands,</u> there will be another Frs 3,000 for him. That extra Frs 3,000 will only be paid, however, <u>when you have received your papers.</u> You may tell him that it will be a present from a grateful client. But do not put anything in writing even if he should ask you to do so, before you have consulted me. I hope, indeed, that nothing need be put in writing. And do not <u>sign</u> any doctuments [sic] either until you have consulted me. You understand darling that you are at perfect liberty to spent [sic] the Frs 3,000 immediately if he asks you to do so, but the extra Frs 3,000—<u>NO</u>. These will only be paid when your Naturalization papers are in your own hands. If it will not hurt your pride, I would tell the man that your English friends are willing to contribute that extra Frs. 3,000 when you get naturalisation but not before. Darling, forgive me for pointing out that he will then feel more certain of getting the money and will thus really make every possible effort on your behalf. After all Frs 6.000 is a big sum and he may feel doubtful about getting the last 3,000 out of you. I do not want you to speak of your English friend, but of your English friends, this because <u>friends</u> sounds better and we naturally want everything to sound most prim and proper—that I consider to be very essential. Now my sweet, go carefully and carry out my instructions to the letter. Frs 3,000 at once, if he insists; but the extra tip of another Frs 3,000 will only be his when your naturalisation papers are in your hands. And listen again: you must be <u>extremely careful</u> not to convey to him the idea that the extra money is in the nature of a <u>bribe,</u> you are to say that it will be given <u>out of gratitude</u> by friend<u>s</u> who have your wellfare much at heart. I shall expect to get a letter from you about this, and when you write please make everything clear—write as though you were making a report to Dr Fuller! You must try to remember that I am not on the spot and am thus entirely dependant on your letters for information. You will have heard from the man again by now and I will

---

2. Is coming along.

number the questions I want answered, and you will please number your answers as this will help your tired Johnnie.

1) Did he give you any idea as to whether you have a fair chance of getting your naturalisation?

2) When is the Frs 3,000 to be paid? I am speaking of the fee he has asked for.

3) Do you agree to tell him that he will get a further Frs 3,000 as a present the day you have your Naturalisation papers in your own hands?

4) Do you agree to tell him that this latter sum will come from your English friends as a token of their consern for your wellfare and as a token of their gratitude to him for the work he has done on your behalf.

6) [sic] What is the man's full name and address?

This is all about the naturalisation for the moment, except that once again I emphatically warn you not to let that extra payment appear to be a bribe. I[t] must be in the nature of a present made by grateful friends. I ignore the strange ways of France, I refuse to admit them. For me it will be a present that I give him and not a bribe. You may say that I am too nice-minded in such matters, but I wish to remain as I am. A present not a bribe, those are my terms. English I am & English I shall always remain I suppose, but I can't help that. Also, knowing you, I am pretty certain that you also would wish that extra money to have a seemly name.

Your Italian visa. I was much disappointed that it had not arrived yesterday, but after having spoken to you on the telephone I felt happier because I gathered that the Consul was very friendly, that he telegraphed to Rome actually while you were with him, and that he felt no doubt that the visa would be granted in your case. I note that you are calling at Consulate again on Saturday morning and shall be anxiously awaiting your telegram.

All these telegrams. You cannot afford to pay them yourself. Let me know just how much you have spent on them up to date & I will send money.

And now my same heart to answer something very important in your last letter. I am glad you have been to the Hitiavos, glad also the Luba is happy. But I want you to be happy also. Now—if you think that people know that you have someone on whom you can depend, someone who is taking care of you, I personally am glad, and why? Firstly because it gives great pleasure to my love, and secondly because I am pretty certain that your nice Russian friends must be happy to know that at least one of their number has been rescued from anxiety and possible want—I do them the justice to think that they would feel that way.

But yourself, oh, Same Heart. Far from no understanding your desire to earn money, (which I take it is what you mean) I not only understand it but I honour it, whether I am "alone" or not. It is admirable in you and comes from a right and natural pride—I honour you for it. But, oh, but——let us consider the facts as they are and not as they might have been had there been no Russian Revolution, and do let us see if, when we have faced all the facts, you have not reason to be proud of yourself rather than the reverse, if you have not good reason to feel that you can accept my protection without loosing your self respect. Let me try to put your life before you as I see it with the clear vision of a devoted but pratical onlooker who loves you yet in no way minimises your many naughtinesses, your willfulness and your Cosak temper!!!

At 17 you were torn up by the roots in fearful & nerve shattering circumstances. You endured famine, the miseries of the flight from Russia after having been condemned to death.

You found work and stuck to it with the American Unit in Serbia while it lasted. You did not go under as did so many.

Finally, because nothing better offered and you were entirely penniless, you consented to train as a nurse in Paris at the A.H.[3]

You began a most cruel and arduous training when your health cannot have been good owing to all you had endured, and even then you thought of your old father and your stepmother and desired to get them to Paris.

You loathed nursing feeling that it was not your vocation. But did you throw it up? You did not. Against every instinct you plodded on and on and you gave of your poor farthings to help your old father. Your health failed. You became T.B in the middle of your training. Did this crush you as it would have done many another? It did not. You went to a Sana,[4] got apparently cured, came out and continued your training. Was that fine? I say it was.

You broke down again—lungs, always lungs. You had not a penny in the world—not one. You had seen your father die and your stepmother, both of them in circumstances of extreme poverty. Did you also decide to lie down & die? Not at all. Once again you went into a Sana, came

---

3. The American Hospital.
4. A frequent abbreviation for tuberculosis sanatorium.

out and continued the work that you hated—the most terribly arduous work in the world as everyone says, as everyone knows.

You became a special nurse and an admirable one. At first you earned big money but not for long. When in America you looked for other work, you toiled from place to place but found no work. Finally you were forced to leave America. You returned to Paris and again you nursed. You had endless money worries over your flat. You often felt tired, worn out, disheartened, but you never gave in—on and on you struggled, yes, you who had twice broken down with T.B.—you who were brought up at Smolna. Sometimes you had money, sometimes you had not—sometimes you had to think twice before spending on getting good and nourishing food. You longed for many small & innocent things—a Kodac for instance—you could not have them. Your cloths grew shabby, you could not replace them. You were forced to move into that unsuitable room in Passy, you could not consider your health, you could not even consider your lungs, you were probably frightened to look into the future. You saw other nurses growing tired, growing old with nothing to look forward to—nothing, nothing. You would think: "Am I going to grow old like her? A worn out horse staggering between the shafts?" You would think: "The world is a big and lovely place—I want to see it, I want to know life and what this thing is that many have died for—this curious thing that people call love." You had not the means of seeing the world, and as yet love had not come to you, my Evguenia. Did you despare? You might very well have done so, haunted as you were by fears for your lungs and surely by fears for your future. But no, no, you most splendidly continued with your work, taking what offered which was little enough after the great slump of 1929.[5] Poor and none too strong in body, unhappy in the work that fate had forced on you, always looking for other kinds of work, but not finding any other kind in an overcrowded world. Finding that you had only the training for the work you hated, you were yet full of courage. You never said die, you never gave up—you were still plodding on when I met you. You, without one single soul in the world upon whom you could feel that you had a real claim. You—alone—delicate and quite unprotected. Well, Evguenia, I think I know all your faults, but this I do say, you have reason to feel proud. You have put up a truly magnificent fight—I only

---

5. The worldwide economic crisis precipitated in large part by the stock market crash in the United States in 1929.

hope I would have put up such a fight, but as God is my witness, I doubt it.

Then you met me. And what about it? Just this. At the moment we cannot find a job except nursing. Are you able to continue the nursing. I say no because the doctors say no. Fuller would never in the world consent to your doing strenuous special nursing. Bestier & Mineshoffer[6] did not want you to nurse at all, not even lightly—but as Fuller told me "There is no light nursing."

Your lungs have slightly broken down for the third time—it was not very much but it was a warning. Don't you think that the thing is out of your controle, that you have been <u>forced</u> to give up your work through no fault of your own? Because I do.

And don't you think that you now have a right to rest on your oars for a little while longer. Don't you think you have earned that right by years of, to my mind, surperbe courage & endurance? Can you, with your record of courage feel ashamed and humiliated because you take from me, because at last you are: "out of the trenches"? Fool, fool, you are worthy of the V.C.[7] Be proud of yourself as I am of you. No woman should feel more self respect. You have earned the security that has come to you. This is the way I see it, my beloved. You owe me nothing but love, if you feel that you can still give it, beloved. Love will help you to help me, to help my work. Love will make it seem natural & right to accept, just as it makes me feel priviliged to give. Love is the key to the door of contentment.

But still I do think you should occupy your mind—study, I beg you to study in Florence. Only do not expect this life to be too perfect. Let us take from it what we can get while we can get it! You can pay me back for the little I can do in a thousand ways that love will dictate. I give because I love, please accept because <u>you</u> love. When you fret, I fret which is bad for my work. Whatever happens, whatever turns up, I do want you to feel that you can respect yourself. You have been <u>forced</u> to give up nursing, your condition of health has forced you. Of course you can defy the doctors and die—but if you did, I die, oh, same heart of mine, and Evguenia Soulina will have killed me. Be proud of yourself, you are <u>not</u> a failiour, when you say that you are you are merely morbid.

---

6. Presumably two other doctors who had treated Souline.
7. The Victoria Cross, a military honor bestowed by the British Crown.

You are a very courageous woman, and I am going to help you now to study, to occupy that eternally restless mind. You shall start by througherly learning Italian—to speak it but also to read & write it. Well, my loved one I must stop for my eyes have given out.

Be of good chear and love me.

Your John

[Rye]

July 24th 1937

Darling love. Your letter of 22nd came last evening. Well—I am considering all you say anent payment of extra money Fr 3,000. I will write at greater length later—have been working last night. About yourself—if you must be <u>morbid</u> be morbid, but you will never alter my opinion—I think you are Royal Chink Pig, V.C. and Iron Cross![1] Don't worry, Una shall not have any hand in your studies, nor shall she even advise if I can muzzle her. Also I promise not to discuss the matter with her either now or at any future time. I see that your Una Complex is still rampant! Hope you got the Fr 500 I sent you all right. Hope also that you will get that damned visa this day. Did you get my wire about taking a taxi or car to Fathers grave? Was I in time? Lovely weather today after a big storm that has done some harm in the garden.

I am tired but think I have done good work. Bless Liza for being with you. She is a wise and good woman and she has my affection and gratitude. I am stupid with long hours of work. All I can say is that as always I adore you, though you never take my advise about anything, but one forgets that being a R.C.P. you must naturally be **Pig**-headed. Andrea comes this afternoon for weekend, and tomorrow we all go over to Edie Craig's for the big annual Ellen Terry show[2]—I wish you were coming. Darling—darling cheer up, love me, trust me, and be a good Piggie Same Heart.

Your weary but devoted John who loves you.

---

1. A German military honor.

2. Edy Craig was the daughter of Ellen Terry, the famed actress. She and her lover, the novelist Christopher St. John, along with the painter Clare (Tony) Atwood lived near John and Una in Rye. Every summer Edy and company held a major theatrical production in Ellen Terry's memory.

<u>July 26th 1937</u>

My dearest love. This being Monday there came two letters from you this morning—one posted on the 23rd and one on 24th. Thank you, my dearest. Today all Hell has broken out at the Cottage—I have found dozens of leaks that require repairing, so at this very moment the sound of scraping and hammering is almost deafening. However, as you always say the place is quite adorable and while I let Una cling to it one must keep it in repair so thats that. Yesterday the Ellen Terry festival at Smallhythe was really wonderful—they gave a number of scenes from Shakespear all acted by Stars and then an enormous spread of sandwiches, drinks etc. in the garden of Ellen's lovely old farm.

But—oh, but, in the middle of the show there was a fearsome smell of burning rubber, and as the "Theatre" is in an ancient beamed barn with a thatched (or is it **HATCHED**) roof we all began to think of our sins and a possible meeting with St. Peter at the Gate. However we all sat still—very British—and in the end nothing really happened, though behind the stage a battery had fused and was merrily and dramatically blazing! A nice business—but all is well that ends well. I have always thought that Edie's barn would go up in smoke one of these fine days—let us hope that when this happens it will be empty. I had also heard from Olive Chaplin[1] that a <u>snake</u> had been seen during rehearsals—a snake that lived comfortably <u>under the seats</u> and always came out to listen to the music! "What manner of snake?" I asked nervously. "Harmless!" said Olive's new inverted friend,[2] "Don't be anxious John—" she is terribly manly. "Rot!" said Olive, "its <u>not</u> harmless. Its an **ADDER!**" So one way and another the thoughts often strayed—however it really was a very fine performance. Edie, who as you know has been very ill, having recently suffered from 3 different illnesses any one of which should have killed her, has now developed a blocked vein in the thigh, so she was pushed about in a wheelchair. She looks very well, indeed 10 years younger. From Minna, who is staying down in the country, comes a nice long letter, clear and firmly written. She is, apparently, completely recovered. When I shall get up to London I don't know—there is no need to hurry myself for Minna. But of course you will have my address, beloved—if I have not time to write it I will wire you. And you—don't

---

1. Edy Craig's niece.
2. Olive's lover Lucy, called Lou by the Rye intimates.

you dare to leave Paris without telling me. Wire. I cannot be seperated from you by not knowing where you I [are]—no I can't. If you play me any of your common Piggie tricks I shall certainly have a complete nervous breakdown. About this matter of your naturalisation. I do wish you would ask the man outright whether he would like some money in advance. I feel that this would put heart into him. And perhaps he is really waiting for you to actually pay him something to go on with—I have a feeling that this may well be so. Do please ring him up or go and see him before you yourself go off the map and find out if he would like some money. He will probably say no, but I think it would impress him and make him put his back into your business. In any case I am quite willing to risk the money so please take my advise. Do not push it on him, but just see what he says, and give him to understand that your friends can be counted upon for that Frs 3,000 that he has quoted as being his fee. Coste[3] is really no guarantee at all, nor did he wish to accept him as being so. Coste may be charming and honest and all that—but "money talks" and "business is business." Dearest, yesterday I felt so depressed, quite suddenly, that I wanted to die—I felt that I just could not bear our seperation—and then I remembered that you had wished it. Nor do your dear letters sound as though you missed me— not as though you missed me as I am missing you. Darling, do you think that you are still in love with me? Do you think that you really still desire me as a lover? Or am I now just Johnnie to whom you belong and who takes care of you? Darling do you want me physically as I want you? Or has that side of our life grown less important to you. Tell me, tell me, my dearest. Today I am less depressed, but still haunted by the fear that you no longer really want me, that these days you would be quite happy and contented if I were not your lover. Dearest, forgive me if I am foolish, but the fault is not mine it is the fault of my love. I want you—I feel crazy for you sometimes—I want you. Whats going to be done about it? I can wait if I know that you want me too, but something tells me that never once since I left you have you felt desire for me, Evguenia. Has it worn out with you? Tell me. Tell me. God knows there has been enough to wear passion through, only with me it has not worn through—no it has not, my beloved. I am in love. Are you still in love? Sweetheart—Own heart—Same heart, I love you. I love you as a friend upon whom you can count—yes, but I also love you as a lover. Oh, if I

---

3. Unidentified.

could only jump on the boat & come over to you for a couple of days. Why do I submit to this complex of Una's backed up by what was said at that fatal Leonard sitting?[4] I submit because I am afraid—yes, afraid. But in any case you don't want me at this moment.

Your adoring John

[Rye]

July 30th 1937

My dearest Love. This morning at 8.30 I was down at the post office sending you a letter by air mail to Paris and also a telegram asking you to wire me at once your Chateau d'Arcine[1] telephone number. I don't like not having a telephone number and thanks to the ridiculous fact that we spent our last precious days together quarrelling, you forgot to give it to me and I to ask for it. This struck me in the middle of the night and I got up and wrote out a telegram & also wrote you a letter. I hope the letter will reach you tomorrow—I am told that it should. But if it comes too late you will have left your address for forwarding, won't you? In any case you can write and ask them to send it on. My S.H, it was rather a melancholy letter, as lying there in the darkness quite unable to sleep, I felt that the distance between us was about to be very great, and that somehow this was wrong. But my dearest, I do want you to go to the pure air of the mountains—it was my own idea that you should go to Chateau d'Arcine, and I want you to have a lovely holiday, to feel happy and contented, knowing that there is me in the world— Your own John who loves you. But oh, the wicked and the dangerous cold! If you get anything like our damnable weather where you are going then God help you—I think that you will sleep in your new, warm coat! Careful you must be, my darling, as I don't want your holiday to end in disaster. You have promised me to take warm cloths and I suppose you have kept that promise.

Yet again I tell you that on August 4th I go up to Royal Court Hotel. Sloane Square. SW. Write to me there until I stop you. I am certainly

---

4. John and Una had gone to Tankerton, to the home of Mrs. Osborne Leonard, the psychic medium they had consulted since 1917. In these "sittings" Ladye usually communicated with them. In the sitting John refers to, Ladye is supposed to have warned that Souline was "only half human" and that she hated John's work and would soon be out of her life.

1. A resort in the Swiss Alps.

going to be there for a week and possibly longer. I have a thousand things to do in London. I shall think of the last time I was the R.C Hotel—it was with you after Una had left us—do you remember? Indeed, Evguenia, I seldom seem able to think of anything but you. Perhaps some people would call it: an obsession. Everything in me turns towards you. I cannot even work in the garden without thinking: "This would amuse Evguenia." I cannot go anywhere or do or be anything without its seeming to have so[me] bearing on you. I don't know what any of it means, I only know that it has gone on now for more than 3 years and is as strong as ever. My heart is no longer my own—it is yours. Let us resolve never again to quarrell, never again to speak hard & cruel words to each other. If you feel as I do, that we cannot get away from each other, then let us resolve to make the best of it! Dearest, there are some ties that it is almost impossible to explain—they appear to have nothing to do with nationality, with circumstances or age. I think that ours is such an one. Maybe we met in some past life and have met again to work out what the Theosophists[2] call. "Carma" If this is the case then we must take care, you and I, to work it out finally—yes indeed we must. If we failed (as I suspect) in that other life, we must not fail in this one. We must show great forbearance and patience to each other. I sometimes have a queer feeling. I think: "Something very like this has happened before." The nasty things must not be repeated though, otherwise this new meeting will be wasted and we may have to begin all over again next time, and begin with some misery. No, no. You & I are going to get good and not bad out of our meeting & our love. I shall be longing for your first letter from Chateau d'Arcine, the letter that will tell me all about the place, the people, and above all your bedroom. I do hope they will give you the best room. It feels a bit lonely not knowing what the place where you are even looks like, but that cannot be helped. I feel that, always provided you don't play the fool and catch cold, this holiday will do you good. Moreover you should be safe up there whatever happens, and if things in France got dangerous you now have 2 frontiers open to you, thank God. You have also that blessed old English money. Yes, yes, I think I have thought of every-thing—I pray so. In my letter last night I asked you not see the man you

2. John, whose own interest in psychic phenomena is well-documented, is here using the term theosophist rather loosely. Karma, a term properly used to designate an Eastern philosophical tradition's notion of Fate, is not usually a theosophical term.

were once engaged to if he should be once more in a nearby Sanna. Dear love I still ask this. Keep clear of T.B—please—please. Darling I love you so much that even the thought of the tiniest risk drives me distracted for you.

Your more than darling letter of 29th has just come. Your dream—my dream. No good telling me not to want you. Dearest I am passionately in love with you—get that into your head. But I can wait and be faithful—and I will. When we meet again we <u>are</u> going off together somewhere, either in France or when we get to Florence. It will just have to be & it shall be. You tell me not to let Una suspect my state—dearest how right & wise you are, but I am afraid she cannot help knowing. I do my poor best. Oh, if only I could take you in my arms, lie in your arms—fulfilled, satisfied and at peace. I can't help this gnawing desire for you—it comes over me in waves. But you are right—it is bad to dwell on it when nothing can happen. Alas—these bodies that ache for union. Beloved—Oh, beloved. Love me, be faithful to me. I would die for you, Evguenia & you know it. I must stop writing or shall say too much.

God keep you—I adore you Piggie.

Your John

[Rye]

August 24th 1937

My darling—Oh, my most darling. I am so longing for you—yes I am. And this is the time of a great full moon over the marsh when the marsh looks much as I described it in "The Sixth Beatitude" and far away is the sea that divides us, and the sea is silver—and so is the winding river that leads down to the sea. And all is beauty and a vast peace, but I cannot share it with you, so that the beauty hurts me and I am not at peace. Moreover there is no letter from you this morning—I seldom get one by the first post on Tuesday—I don't know why unless because there is Sunday to reckon with on your side—perhaps it is that. No reply from Paris about your visa—why, oh, why are you a White Russian—why aren't you an ordinary person? But perhaps if you had been I should not have fallen in love with you, my bundle of trouble! To move you about is like moving ten ton of bricks, my back aches. Everything I see I refer to you in my mind—wanting to share it with you—

this darling cottage, this darling ancient Rye, the marsh—all—all. It seems preposterous that I should have a big chunk of life quite apart from S.H. and yet so it is and as far as I can see it must be endured—all the same it makes me unhappy. I see in the paper this morning that my little Commandante[1] is said to be lying very, very ill in his "Palace on Lake Garda" and that it is rumoured that he is dying. I have wire[d] to Louisa for news. Well, I have always felt that I should never see him again on this earth, that our long and intimate and affectionate talk would have to be continued in a more peaceful and happy and reasonable state of being. He is such a little and destressed man, may his enormous & anxious spirit make a good & courageous journey when the time comes. I could wish him to die as your father died.

And now to more cheerful matters. Yesterday came a certain actress by name Elizabeth Pollock, and she brough[t] with her an unknown fan of mine. I know E.P. but only slightly, having met her at the beside of Lord Loctain when he was ill some years ago. E.P. has become a mass of make up and breathtaking scent. But in a queer rather frightening way I suppose she is beautiful—marvelous eyes, but looks like a vampire, very long & thin & hungry and passionate!

"I have just come from Sermione." says she.

"Oh, do you know Mikkie Jacob?" say I. And then came the following story.

It is evident that E.P. is dementedly in love with Mikkie. It seems that she travelled back to Sermione with her some short time ago. But listen: the Misses[2] has left Mikkie if you please—refused to return to Sermione only five days before the day of starting. Whether it was because of E.P. I could not make out, but E.P. was full of invictives about the misses—hating her, apparently. She had the hideous bad taiste to inform us that she had slept in Miriam's bed while staying with Mikkie. No doubt at all that they are lovers. Una showed her some Sermione snapshots and she commandeered one of Mikkie—all but pressed it to her heart! Then she thrust it into her bag. Can you beat it? It would really seem that Mikkie must have a most deadly **Sex** Appel—sex appeal Mikkie. What price false teeth, an enormous back and front view, a cockney accent and all the rest! Thank God she hated you at sight or I might have had a most fearsome rival!

---

1. Gabriele d'Annunzio, whom John had visited in 1934.
2. Not Sadie Robinson, Mickie's English love of the summer of 1934, but another named Miriam.

I think, in view of Mike's successes, that I shall try my hand—I am looking about for a victim at this moment! If Mikkie why not John? Surely there must be hope even for me! No, but joking apart, can you understand it? Darling, it does seem that it is enough in itself to be an invert these days to get all the women as crazy as bitches in season— forgive my frank coarseness, but I do think so. Annie[3] has asked me to address a p.c. for her to send you and this I am doing now in a minute.

I enclose Francs 800 for your excursions. Let me hear that you have received them please, darling.

No more now, except that I am all yours and that if I do find a victim I will let you know in good time—don't worry!

Your devoted—

John

Keep this letter handy for <u>future reference.</u>

[Rye]

August 25th 1937

Darling—darling—darling. This morning came a letter from Humbert Wolfe saying that the Home Office has granted you an Annual Visa, allowing you to come & go and to stay in England for 6 weeks at a time. This is the greatest possible tryumph as the annual visa is getting more & more difficult to come by. You may immagine if I am pleased with myself, for the idea of asking Humbert to help was entirely my own. I made up my mind to put my back into it with a vengance this time, and I asked him to lunch at the Berkley. Una was there too and she backed the application up for all she was worth, as I think I have already told you. But when I knew that Humbert had left for his vacation and we had heard nothing, I began to feel despondent, thinking that he had failed me, but no, he had not, and for that I bless him, and never again will I speak against the Jews[1] for Humbert is a Jew though a Catholic

---

3. John and Una's servant.
1. While it is very clear from these letters of the 1930s that John shared much of the upper-class British prejudice against Jews, it is also evident that she indulged those views far more frequently with Souline than with anyone else. This presumably is due in part to Souline's extreme anti-Semitism, probably learned in her formative years as an aristocratic Russian.

jew and pious. I have been on telephone with White Hall[2] who say that the notification of ann. visa will have gone through to Paris. And now I am waiting to get Paris. After I have spoken to the man in Paris I will let you know the exact position by adding to this letter. But what it means, according to Whitehall, is that a few days before you come over to me on Sept 28th you go to the British Consulate. <u>Passport Office. 16.</u> Avenue Hocke, and merely ask them to put the 6 weeks visa on your passport. There and then—no need to apply to London. You will, of course, tell them that you have been granted the annual visa and will present your passport and the usual letter of invitation from us.

<u>Tryumph!!!</u>

(5 minutes later) Just spoken to Captain Jeffs who is back. He has <u>received</u> authority to give you your Annual Visa. He says you have now only to call on him, or on his representative if he is away, ask for your annual visa and get it there & then with the first grant of 6 weeks in England. He will expect you towards the end of September he says, as you are still away. He also says that it is the greatest possible good luck to get the annual visa, as they are getting more & more difficult at Whitehall—I gather that it is no longer easy to get stamped in Paris as you have done in the past—hence the letter from the other man. But now with an annual visa you can <u>always</u> get stamped direct in Paris. He also said that he had written to notify you that an annual visa had been granted. Where he wrote, to what address, I do not know—I suppose he has written to your flat 8 Rue Emile Allez. Therefore please write to the concierge at once and get hold of that letter. It is better that you should have it, though if lost I don't suppose it will really matter—still, get it if you can. Also I want you to write to Captain Jeffs at once, you must always keep on the most friendly terms with him. I enclose a letter to him for you to copy. Now darling, I hope I have made all clear. <u>About a week</u> before coming to me—say on Thursday Sept 23rd <u>go & get your visa</u>—this will be five days before leaving. Your letter of invitation will be sent you later, nearer the time.

I will meet the boat as usual—I think we may spend a night at Dover and go on to Brighton the next day, but all this I will let you know later of course. I must enquire about trains & so on. But on Sept 28th you come to your John—to your John's own country England! The train

---

2. The Pall Mall London site of the Home Office, the equivalent of the U.S. Department of State.

leaves Paris round about noon & the boat gets in round about 4$^{oc.}$ Exact time you will verify at Cooks in Paris please & let me know. Yes, yes, I think we spend first night in Dover at Lord Warden and then motor to Brighton the next morning. I am almost beside myself with joy! Today, having received your letter of 22nd I have rung up my bank and they are sending you about £5 of Swiss money to help you to have something in your pocket—they will post it registered letter today. Re. Geneva expenses you will let me know later. I also received your letter of 23rd Re the expenses of your excursions, I sent you the money myself yesterday, registered letter, so you should be all right. I understand that you think of going to Geneva on Aug 31st and returning to Paris about Sept 5th. This seems a good plan to me, darling, but I am counting on you to give me all details and for money's sake don't fail me. Oh, my own dear love. England & you—you and England—Blessed be God. And now take great care of yourself—don't risk catching cold or overtiring yourself or anything that might interfere with our longed for H.M. And this Prayer at once.

"Thank you good & kind saints Anthony and Expedite for answering John's prayers about my annual visa. Also write to Jeffs as per enclosed letter. Then I do think a few lines from you to Humbert Wolfe—he is pratically a minister, most important to you and friendly to me. I enclose a letter for you to copy & send to him also. No more. I kiss you many times.

Your John

PS Keep this letter handy for referance. I wired you the good news this morning. Let me hear that you have sent letters to Jeffes & Wolfe.

The following letter is in Una's handwriting, the first such letter in the Souline collection, although in subsequent years there would be many more. The reason for this transcription was that John had broken her ankle and was unable to sit up comfortably.

[Rye stationery]

Aug. 26th 1937

My own most precious Love. Una has written you at some length telling you how the little accident happened. I don't care about the pain or anything because you telegraphed offering to come and because you now have that blessed annual visa, until you got that we were so much apart. But I don't want you to change your plans, especially as no doubt you <u>will want</u> a little time in Paris over your naturalization business, and I want you out of Paris by November. Also I do know how you hate being cheek a block with Una. In any case as I wired you last night and am wiring this morning my ankle is better—no pain at all now at times & more movement, from which I judge there is nothing broken, only torn tendons or whatever they are. My one aim is to be quite well when my SH comes to me on September 28th, but well or not you simply <u>must</u> come then as I shall die if I have to wait longer to see you. But of course I shall be perfectly right by then—I know it, touch wood! Oh, my dear, my love and my need I adore you.

Your letter of 25th has come. By now you must have had the excursion money. My bank only sent your 100 Swiss francs yesterday, as the fools went & tried to send coin through post & had it returned, but by tomorrow you should receive the Swiss money—I enclose their letter. Darling enjoy yourself. Tomorrow's—Saturdays letter—goes to you at Pension Coupier. Rue des Alpes 3. to await arrival.

Darling no more now. I am really, <u>really</u>, <u>honestly</u> better & expect to be up in a few days. But meanwhile I can't get to the telephone to telephone you in Geneva. Bless you for remembering to give me the telephone number & telegraph address—My Piggie is getting quite Love-trained.

Enjoy your holiday—no need to worry about me.

Your grateful & loving
John [signed by John]

In the event, John's fractured ankle was much worse than either she or Una had anticipated. John had to be taken by ambulance to the London Clinic where her ankle was broken and reset. It remained very weak for months and she was forced to use crutches. She was later to date Souline's waning passion from this time.

London Clinic

September 8th 1937

Just got your letter of 7th Oh, S.H. So the Baker has turned up again! Well I'll thank the old bitch to mind her own business. How <u>dare</u> she interfere and want you to put yourself on Call—what has it got to do with her? How glad—how delighted I am that you went there smartly dressed—how proud it makes me feel my Piggie—my Piggie, <u>my</u> Royal Chink Piggie! Maybe she is too blind to see your crown & has not grasped that you are royal—she had better go to her occulist & get her glasses changed at once. Darling of course you feel independent. I am glad also that you feel independent even with me. You see it is only through love that I care to keep you—only through love. And once again I promise that there shall <u>be no more living a' trois</u>. When you come here on 28th I would really like you to keep your room in Paris if she will let you have it on same terms, though this I had better leave to you. The trouble now is that I have no idea when I shall get to Paris, and I am hoping that you will stay with me until I can hop & hobble onto the channel steamer—which will be before the climate here becomes dangerous for you, of course. Then once in Paris—if I only remain a day or two I thought perhaps you would tolerate coming to our hotel for those few nights? Johnnie loves you and greatly needs you . . . . . I am not ashamed of this physical need because it is the nature & result of being in love—what will you? But here in England what? For the first week no question—you will have to be quite on your own while I remain in Clinic. Una has a room here so you will not have too close a contact with her. After I leave Clinic plans are vague & depend on my doctors. Only one plan is clear—You & I have our H.M. [honeymoon] You & I all alone—all alone—all alone. But <u>don't leave me—don't leave me.</u> It may be that we will all be able to go to Rye—I'll have to go there to pack at the end of course. In Rye you can go to a hotel if you like. There is the Hope Anchor which is more comfortable than the Mermaid I think. I do swear to you that you shall be free to do as you like about this. We will, or rather <u>you</u> will decide when you come. At this moment I am utterly helpless, tied by the leg. I know only that very often my eyes fill with tears of longing for the sound of your voice and the touch of your hand. It has been pretty dreary and awful. Please come on 28th and take care of yourself! Yourself needs taking care of and has had much pain—even now it has spells of pain & much discomfort. Listen to it, making an enormous bid for sympathy, will you! This question of whether or not to keep your room in Paris—I don't know what to advise. What do you think? Paris being so full you may have difficulty in getting another room. If only I knew my dates, but I don't. Oh, I leave it all to you. In Florence you will not want to come to our hotel while you look for a furnished flat, so will have to find quarters somewhere else. That will be easy. Oh, damn my lameness. Because I must break it to you that although I am not going to be a cripple for life, they expect me to be rather lame for a little while. You see it was so outrageously neglected, for a whole week. Una keeps saying: "I suppose if Evguenia had been here when it happened she would have known that we aught to have had an X Ray at once—she would have known what to do." Never mind—only come on 28th and all will be well. No need for us all to be under same roof. It will be in your hands, get that into you[r] thick Piggie Skull! But please go & get visa on 23rd as arranged, even if dear, darling, beautiful, alluring, seductive, youthful Baker—Cleopatra—Messsalina—Venus, asks you to fly with her to the Fugee [Fuji] Islands!! And allow me to tell you that all this is just pique on your part. You dont care a hoot for Baker—Cleopatra, not one hoot! Where the bloody hell do you want her to invite you? Personally I am praying that you will stay in Paris so as to be in close touch with our ankle. My plaster is cut off on Saturday next & the surgeon examines his handy work. Naturally it is a comfort to feel that S.H. is get at able. Be damned to Baker-Cleopatra. Do you really mean that you seriously want her to take you away with her somewhere at this moment? There will be no chance of my meeting you at Dover, Sweetheart. You will have to come straight through to London. There is the fast train that meets the boat—we call it "The boat train." Hand luggage is examined at Dover. Trunks are examined in London. Be careful to bring nothing dutiable. Una will meet you in London of course if I cannot. Please go to Cooks & let me know cost of journey also time of departure & arrival—I suppose you will come by train we took—twelve something, I think, arriving Dover five something—but I dont clearly remember, nor do I know at what hour boat train gets to London. Go to Cooks soon—the sooner you engage places on train & Cabin on boat the better as everything is so full. Ask for Monsieur Robert at Cooks, telling him you are a friend of mine & Una's. If you can get a second class pullman from Paris to Calais as well as from Dover to London, do so of course. It is one day less than 3 weeks now! I simply can't believe it. There is a hunger in me for you. Do you love like that?

Your John

P.S Perhaps better not bother to keep room in Paris—but you know best. I think it depends on whether you are going to travell out to Florence with me or not—that will be for you to decide. I am giving away my canary! I don't need to tell you how I'd like you to come out with me—how I'd lean on you this time—Oh, you bet I would. On the otherhand I will not urge you—do as you please and I shan't feel offended! If Baker—Cleopatra no longer needs you, Lame-Dog—John does—but possibly this is not much consolation!!!

PP.S Of course buy the Romanian belt you long for.

London Clinic

September 14th 1937

Your letters of 12th & 13th came together this morning, my darling heart. Only 7 days until you come—only 7 days. Do you know what this means to me? I wonder. I am praying that you have made up your mind to give up the damned workcard and take an ordinary one—long, long have I wanted you to do so as you well know. Now let me see what else I want to say—oh, yes, your trunk. I would rather you did not buy it here. You have an idea that everything is so perfect in England—it is not. We can produce no trunk to equal the Innovation in any way. Were you to buy an Innovation here in England the price would be beyond everything because Innovation being a French product there is an <u>enormous duty.</u> Therefore, oh most Royal of Crowned Piggies, I get you to buy a trunk the twin of mine at Innovation in Paris. You will never regret it—there is so much room, and, moreover the trunk is wonderfully light while being tough—never have I had such a heavenly trunk, no never. Cheap trunks are the worst economy in my experience. Thanks for the tip about getting the reduction on our tickets—Una's & mine. About that letter of invitation—as you now know from copy of Jeffes letter that I sent you, it is not legally necessary anymore—you are free to come & go within reason, but Jeffes <u>did</u> say that it might be as well for you to have it just in case a person on this side called the Immigration

Officer asked questions, so I myself worded the second letter that Una sent you, and please keep it in case of need. If that annual visa is not a direct answer to prayer then I don't know what is, because every visa is getting more & more difficult to obtain, and can you wonder with these infernal anarchists [1] wrecking civilization, or trying to on all sides—but they won't succeed because, unfortunately for them, there is someone whom for want of a better name we call: God. But once the annual visa is on your passport, it can, I think, be yours for ever so long as you do not abuse it in any way, which you will not. Darling love, I am afraid you will have a very dull time when you come and this makes me furious for I was planning so much fun and other more divine things. But come—come—I cannot endure our seperation any longer. I am sorry if the change of date has put your plans out, beloved, but it was really principally in order that you should be able to return sooner to Paris & see to your business as well as my own intense longing to see you that prompted me to beg you to come sooner. Also we have so much to discuss about plans, and it is so hard to get things straight by letters. I would have accepted with rapture your many darling offers to come as soon as the accident happened had it not been that I hoped that by waiting I would be less of a crock when you came—that was my hope, my reason as I told you. But now it seems that that hope has vanished— I have had what the hospital calls "a dirty fracture." Well one must thank God that it was nothing worse than an ankle for it was a mighty fall. There is now very little pain—an aching after the daily massage, but not always; every day after massage the plaster case is bandaged on again—it was cut down the front when removed—and by bed time it feels a ton weight & I am sleeping badly. Its all an awful trial and such a bore, but it just can't be helped and I am playing for safety, or rather I suppose the surgeon is—to be lame or not to be lame "that is the question," darling. Your last letter to Una began "Dear Una" instead of "Una darling" she said "Evguenia has gone back to Dear Una" I think she felt hurt for a moment—anyhow it struck her at once. She is threatening, with much laughter, that if you & I both have big trunks (and she genuinely implores you to get a trunk like mine) then she will take **two** trunks, hers being so small by comparison, which is quite true.

---

1. Because there was so much political turmoil at the time, it is unclear just which anarchists John refers to here. It is unlikely that she refers to events in Spain, since there is no other mention of the anti-Franco forces in her letters. Nevertheless, John's support for the old world order as she envisioned it is clear.

I think myself that we should all make ourselves as comfortable as possible—why not? I am all for doing so. Oh, it is cold here—so cold, and my poor thin legs get cold in bed because of the credel [cradle] which is a cold thing—but when I can hold your beloved hand and feel your beloved mouth on mine, all these troubles will pass—you will exercise Pig-majic. I am actually mean enough to be disappointed that Liza is going to Florence before us—I wanted you to be the first to show her the little Dream City, you who could have swanked about as though you were a real Florentine, because you do know the city in a very, very surprizing way considering that you have only spent so short a time there. I used to think that your knowledge of the streets, the short cuts & bye ways (a knowledge so much greater than mine or even Una's) was like a memory—it gave me the queers. Were you ever a Royal Florentine Pig smothered in brocade sewn with emeralds & pearls, do you think? Darling I love you, and I greatly desire you. I want to trip off with you to a desert island & make love for hours on end—until there is nothing left of us. I shall be awaiting you[r] wire anent X-Ray but don't suppose I'll get it for a day or two as they will have to develope. But I feel it is all right.

Your own John

PS Una thanks you for the catalogue on art pavillion—which she says is most interesting. Her letter had just gone when it arrived.

When Souline arrived in London on September 21, John was still hospitalized and would not be released until October 13. According to Baker's account, Souline spent little time with the convalescing John. The ten days they did have together after John's release were spent between London and Rye, with Una moving to either place to leave the lovers alone. On October 24, Souline returned to Paris. John and Una followed a week later, and in November all three arrived in Florence. It was not a happy time for any of them. Souline was restless and longed to return to Paris. John's limp continued to plague her, the book in progress was going very badly, she came down with a bad bout of flu and had something like a nervous breakdown when Souline determined to return to Paris for the summer. The letters resume on the day Souline left, June 4, 1938.

1938

[Lungarno Acciaiuoli hotel stationery, Florence]
June 4th 1938

Well you have left me for a time—a little time, my Same Heart, but all I can tell you is that Florence seems as though it had a gaping wound in its side because you are not here. As for me—but I won't make you either laugh or frown by telling you what I am feeling like at this moment.

Five minutes after I got home your flowers arrived & bless you for them and the card you sent with them. Una also was really emotional over the water lilies. Oh Piggie, Piggie, I do love you so much—too much. You have become to me like a part of my flesh & my spirit. If only [you] can find work out here—I do understand your wish to work but I feel so utterly helpless these days when everything is so selfish & so upside down. But my darling try to remember how much you are loved & cherished and maybe that will make up for all the disappointments, or at least make up a very little. Darling take care of my heart I put you on your honour to do so. I shall wait & long for your telegram. And darling I do hope you will on stay at Vouillement[1] so as to be there when I am as we must be together when I am in Paris, also I feel you are so safe at Voullement. If it is too much for "Pocket" I will send more money, or pay you back when I arrive just as you please—but I much want you to stay on there.

Your over-loving, over-anxious, over-particular

John.

---

1. A suburb of Paris where Souline was staying with Lysa Nicolsky.

[Florence]

June 21st 1938

My darling. Your letter of 19th came this morning. I note that you are
going on Wednesday—that's tomorrow—to St. Malo[1] and returning to
Vouillement on 30th, also that you will let me have the St. Marlo
address—thank you, dearest. But somehow the words "you have <u>con-
sented</u> to my going" sound as though I were a kind of tyrant who
watched your every breath. There was no reason why I should not have
"consented," as you call it, provided you promised to be sensible while
there. But never mind; I only hope that you don't make Liza think that I
am a devil. Dearest you have a false humility sometimes about things
that don't matter, and an enormous arrogance about things that do!! Of
course I should have been amazed & angry if you had not planned to
come back in time to meet me in Paris, which I think you must admit
would have been only natural, but since you did intend to come back,
all was well. These last days here are trying me rather, so much to do &
now very hot—everyone is going away; we shall be about the last to
leave. I do hope from my heart that you will have a really nice, restful
time in St. Marlo and that you will try not to convey a bad impression
of me to Liza. My feeling are being rather hurt anyhow, just now—
again Sandra[2] is asking why you are not saying that you will come
back—she has the misfortune to be fond of you, poor nut! Of course it
is becomming very obvious to everyone that you care less than nothing
for me, because, as I am settled here, they must argue that if you loved
me you would want to be with me. That is the way most people see
love—those who love want to be together and not seperated, no matter
what the circumstances. I grin and speak lightly of your future plans.
Oh, well, it is just one of those things that one forgives, but never
forgets. I again, & for the hundredth time, repeat to you that if I am to
help my mother and look after you I <u>cannot</u> afford to live in France. It
would hardly help any of us if I go bust. I do my best, yes I do, & I can't
do more. I want a little comfort for myself too, as I am not awfully
well—comfort only in which to try to work. Oh, whats the use—you
know all this already. To tell you the truth, Piggie, I am just througherly

---

1. St. Malo is a coastal town in Brittany on the English Channel.
2. Sandra Tealdi, one of Una's relatives. Una had spent much time in her late adolescence with the Tealdis in Florence.

disheartened—just disheartened. I am so sorry you have failed in Exam.[3] We will talk about it when we meet. I can't remember whether in England they tell you the number of marks you have got in any given subject. I know that the Sorbonne has the name for being one of the most devilish exams in the world. I wish you had not wanted to go in for the thing, but as you did, thats that. Oh, I suppose I aught not to have said this—you will tell Liza that (like Mrs Baker) I am trying to stop you educating yourself. I know that everything I think, say & do is misunderstood. Well, it can't be helped. No more now as I am very tired & down hearted.

Your discouraged
John

[Lungarno, Florence]

June 23rd 1938

Darling. It is 4 am. I have been awake since 2 am thanks to the stuffy bedroom and the infernal noise of a machine that makes ice, and as I shall have hardly a minute later today I have come into my study to write to you now. I don't suppose that I shall write more than one or two more letters before we meet, as I am afraid they will take a long time to reach you. I can judge better of that when I get your first letter from St. Marlo. Now listen Evguenia. You and I have been a great deal to each other for four years, and there are times when I think that you still love me. One does not throw away the most precious things of life— you must not. If you make it impossible for us to be together you are going to regret it most bitterly, and this I do know, but then it may be too late. My own life has now settled into a grove [sic], and this must be so my little, little Piggie because of three things: money, work and health. I came here because of you in the first place, and now I must remain here for at least 6 months of every year, at all events for the present. Piggie you infuriate me—yes you do, and yet I remember your saying to me: "Never, never let me leave you." And I also remember how much alone you are—no one but me in all this big and unkind world. No one else to depend on for anything of any kind except yourself. But there

---

3. Souline had sat for the entrance exams at the Sorbonne.

must be give & take, my sweetheart, and nothing is perfect here below. Now I propose that we face up to the fact that neither of us is perfect but that in spite of this we don't feel able to part just yet. Do we? And that being so I think that for both our sakes we aught to stop this play-acting. You have no intention whatever of taking a rotten job in France even if you could get one which is doubtful. No one is going to let you be boss in these days of heartbreaking competition, and that you just must try and get into your Piggie head. Nursing is entirely out of the question as we have agreed—therefore what? A possible complete break with me—no me any more, because my Heart, if I once made up my mind to part from you I should go altogether. In that case, Evguenia, what would your life be? You are at a very serious turning in the road, because sometimes play-acting turns into the real thing before we know where we are, and then it is too late. I still love you, but if you go on tormenting me I may suddenly not love you any more. I once told you, my beloved, that love is as fragile as glass and must not be roughly handled. Also love has a right to expect a fair bargin. I ask for fair bargin from you. I appeal to you once again to be balanced and reasonable and contented. Contented with what I have to offer you. You have not been a good woman to me, my Evguenia, not as good as you might have been. You were not a kind woman to me during my recent breakdown— you could have taken care of me, but you did not. But all this I forgive and so I am not going into the details of those things that hurt me more than I can say. But if, as I think, you have still any love for me, perhaps we can try to begin all over again and make a better job of it this time. I am willing to try if you are. And now I will tell you exactly what is going to happen. I am coming to Paris on 2nd. You will meet me at the station when I arrive on that day—<u>July 2nd</u>. You will stay at Vouille-ment while I am in Paris. You will come over to England for a bit— either coming back with me to England or joining me there—that we will discuss. While you are in England you and I will go off somewhere for a week at least all by ourselves. <u>At the end of October you will come back here to Florence for the winter,</u> either taking the Fossi flat or another with Angelina. While you are here you will do one of 3 things. Enter for a course or courses at the University of Florence, where I hear there are a number of English, American and French students and where there are courses for foreigners—though I don't suppose you would need those as your Italian is now so good. You will probably enter for History of Art, as you have a decided love for and good judgement of pictures. Or, secondly, you will continue your present line of study under the French professor you had last winter, and try for the Sorbonne Exam next summer again. Or, thirdly, you will look about for a job here, using what influence we all have, and the pull of you knowing several languages. But if you want to try for the latter, then it is absolutely essential that you should make up your mind what kind of work you wish to try for; at present I feel that you are too vague about this and it is not a thing that I can decide for you. If you would have perfected yourself in typing you could have worked for me, in that way you would have earned your £300 a year and I would have been spared hearing that you want your own money. I doubt if you can hope to find any job these days that will pay more than £300—indeed most of them pay much less! But you did not feel inclined to do my work so thats that. As far as I go, my Heart, I do not want you to work at all unless you want to. You are mistaken if you think that Una would have opposed your working as my secretary—she might have at first, but not for a long time past. Only of course you would have had to let her help you a bit to get into the work, and this I suppose you would not have liked. But, my God, what a comfort & help it would have been to me, especially with my troublesome eyes these days!

Well, dearest, now you know the programme. <u>And just that is going to happen.</u> And you are going to be contented & reasonable in spite of being a Cossac, (can't spell it) and Florence sends you much love and will welcome you back. And the sun is just awake & is shining. And I love you and need you. I am your duty. And my book needs you and begs you to help it. And try very hard to <u>love</u> me more than you <u>hate</u> Una. If you can manage to do this all will be more than well.

God bless my Piggie.
Your devoted
John.

<u>PS</u> I would like you to talk the whole situation over with Liza; tell her everything, even the conditions I have imposed regarding your allowance. You may tell her what I allow you, if you like. Also you can translate all, or part of this letter to her if you wish. She is, I think, a good friend to you and all women need a confidant. But be fair to me, Evguenia when you discuss me with Liza—this much you owe me. And tell Liza that I much hope she will come & stay with you here next winter.

This impassioned letter ends abruptly, as there is a page missing in the archival collection. It is transcribed nevertheless because it reveals powerfully the soul-searching John was engaged in at the time.

[Lungarno, Florence]

June 28. 1938

My darling love. Your letter of 26th has come. No, no, Una does not hate you. But can we never get away from Una and think only of ourselves? Even if she did hate you, which I absolutely deny, can't my adoration for you make up for any hatred in the world? What does it matter so long as we two love each other? Oh, I know that it would be happier for you if my circumstances were different—if I were free; I know this and I sympathise with all you feel; but am I to be sacraficed to my circumstances? No my honey-sweet, you cannot, you will not do this thing. Why can't we be at peace—Oh, give peace to your poor John who loves you. I can't eat, or sleep, let alone work, for my heart is never certain or at rest. Would it help at all if you tried to look upon me as a man who was already married when we met? Had I been a man I should have married Una and then met you and loved and loved you and found you to love me back—as I have done. The result would have been that I could not have divorced a faithful Una even had I wished to. She on her part would never have divorced me, she is a Catholic & would not divorce Troubridge. So our situation would have been much the same as now, only with more scandle. There are many people living a trois here in this very town, I find, but they generally all manage to keep on terms. That is all you need do, just be on terms with Una. She matters so little to you really, you know—I do feel that you give her undue importance. But now lets leave her & think only of ourselves. Are we ready to part? Think long & think wisely. We have come to a serious & difficult place in our lives, because parting really <u>means</u> parting. Oh, Piggie—my little and lonely one—my Piggie who kicked its way into my heart. Are you meaning to leave the warm home of my heart? The world is so enormous and Piggs are so small. My eyes dare not shed any more tears my darling, & so my heart has begun to weap, and when a heart weaps its a terrible weaping. Piggie I can't believe that we are parting—can you? No one to telephone to, no one to write to, to telegraph to, a great blank, a great empty space in our two lives. John and Piggie both still in the world perhaps, but parted—meaning nothing anymore. Four years—its a big thing to smash, my Evguenia. If you refuse to come back here next winter, to come back to Florence to which I have come solely because Italy will harbour us both in peace, solely because I want you so much and can't be happy unless I am near you. If knowing that I <u>would live in France</u> which you prefer, but cannot do so because of the expense and my diminished income,[1] and that during the winter you yourself aught not to live in Paris or in England, both of which climates would be an awful risk—if knowing these things you won't come back then it must be because you have ceased to love me. Darling listen—that may have really happened, and no blame to you either, for love cannot be commanded. But then it is you who shall say the words: "Johnnie I do not love you any more." And until I hear that I refuse to believe it. Oh, my love that I have held in my arms, whose mouth has so often clung to mine, my love who has cried out my name in love—my little, love once so innocent and frightened—oh, my love, my love . . . . I can't find the right words for this is real stark pain, not a novel. I am half mad with pain—the pain of the body that has grown accustomed to the joy of your body; the pain of the mind that has thought of your welfair day & night now for four long years, and that cannot hope to stop thinking about you; the pain of the spirit that in some strange way is bound to your turbulent, restless spirit. Dear love, I don't want to be melodramatic, but I too have suffered during these four years, I am nearly broken and you alone can mend me. If you leave me I break completely. My beloved, my soul, you came into my life at a time when I had ceased to take love lightly—I have given you all that I have except honour, and never will I dishonour you or myself by parting with my honour. Listen, oh, listen, I implore you, Evguenia. If you have even a remnant of love in your heart for me, then don't let me go, don't turn away from me forever. Because you need me as I need you, and you cannot do without me, or I without you. Are we mad? I think so to talk of parting. Oh God give me words—I can't find words, but surely it must be reaching you, darling? Never mind Una, never mind anything or any body on all this wide earth—only love matters and our clinging together. If you leave me because of Una you can't love me. If you leave

---

1. Some of John's investments had lost her considerable money during the failures of the Depression. She was not poor by any means, of course, but she had never been frivolous and was always conscious of prudent money management.

me I think I shall not go on with life. Why should I? There will be
nothing left to live for and I am tired, but intolerably tired. I would like
to sleep for a very long time, to sleep & then wake up near Ladye who
was always so patient, so kind & so wise. This world without you—Ah,
no, my Evguenia. And why are you thinking of doing this thing? Because
of Una, incredible! She has never harmed you seriously, she was terribly
jealous and hard just at first but not now, and even if she were, will you
kill me because of Una? Because you want to work—but in France there
is no work, of that I am sure & so really are you. Will you kill me
because of work that you have not got and will probably not find?
Because you want to study—that I understand, that I approve of with
all my heart, but will you kill me because here in Florence there is only
the University & not the Sorbonne? Will you refuse to try & study here?
Think what you are doing to this creature that is John and who has
proved its love for you. Come back, come back & creap into my heart,
into the warm faithful home of my heart, but only if you still love me.
Look my darling, my child, my little, little Piggie—I have opened the
door—it is standing wide open. I have made it possible for you to
go—my allowance has made you free—given you your freedom on
conditions that are merciful and all, all for your sake. I could have said:
"No me, no money." but I do not & did not want to buy you—I wanted
you to stay with me out of love—that is why, if it kills me, I have
opened the door. "Never let me leave you John," you once said. Oh, my
beloved—stay, stay, stay; have I been a fool to open the door—will you
live to regret it? Come back to me my dearest, my love. What are
quarrells between two people who love—nothing [a page is missing
here]

[Florence]

June 29th 1938

Your letter of 27th came this morning. Oh, my aching Same Heart. I
have been so anxious & unhappy that I may have addressed my letters
to you wrongly perhaps. For one thing I have spelt St Malo—St Marlo—
God knows why. For another I have added: Brittany, and possibly that
was wrong. This is no fault of yours, you put St. Malo. I/V. France. Why
I did these imbecile things—again, God only knows. However I have
sent you two letters to Vouillement and now this goes there—the last I

shall write before we meet. This morning I wired you to St Marlo express telegram, acknowledging your letter of 27th telling you that I had written every day and—what was even more important—imploring you to tell Liza everything and ask her advice. I hope the telegram will reach you as they seemed never to have heard of St. Malo and had to look it up and so on. In their book it did not appear as being in Brittany but as Isles de something or other—the I/V—I suppose. Well I can only pray for the best. My dear who lays the whip on my back in true Cossack fashion! I am not doing more in regard to the University of Florence than to make suggestions based on what I have heard about it—naturally you will decide what studies you go in for—I suggested art because of your love for pictures, that was all. What is the matter with you—oh, woman of my despair? But I can't write today—I am not able to make you understand, it seems, what life would be here without you. You can face quite calmly life without me, but I simply cannot face life without you—thats the difference; my Evguenia, that is the impossible gulf that lies between us. Can Liza help us? There is just a faint hope that she can—I don't want to do myself in, its against my every religious belief, a great sin and a terrible sign of cowardice, but I feel that I am nearing the end, and a God who Christ told us was a God of Love must also, I think, be a God of Understanding. I am turning from side to side in my prison, in my prison of circumstances that you know of and knew of before I took you; in my terrible narrow prison of love, in my prison of complete and disastrous failure. There is my mother who must be helped and you who need help, and oh, believe me I cannot afford to live in France just now—is that a crime? Think it over, Evguenia. There is England with a bad winter climate for you and the stupid stipulation that every 6 weeks you have to go over some frontier. Only Italy seemed to me to remain, only Italy was willing to accept us both, which was why I decided to settle in Florence—but all this you know already. My work—time is passing and I am earning nothing. Old books pay nothing after a while, or so little that it does not help us to live; if you do not believe me ask any author. This flat has prouved impossible to work in, even last winter my nurses noticed the continual noise, yes, even with shut windows. No artist can work except in surroundings that allow of quiet—ask any artist. This alone was my reason for taking my new flat, in order that I might work and earn money. I can see, between the lines, that you resent my new flat. I cannot understand this but I feel it very strongly—I suppose we are telepathic. But here, if you will come, there

will be money enough for us all, because as you know life is cheap—
cheaper much than in France or even in England. But I am only just
getting onto my feet again after my accident and subsiquent break down;
I work with difficulty and strain, and now I can't work at all, my dear,
because my mind is being tortured. I am asked to face a winter, perhaps
all life without you—I am asked to face loneliness, anxiety, failiour and
something dangerously like despair. I have faced many things before in
my life, and I think faced them bravely, but this is too much. If you have
made up your mind to leave me—because if you will not follow me to
Florence that is what it means, it means that you have left me—then I
don't think I am called upon to go with life. I am perfectly calm and
perfectly sane, I am merely looking things straight in the face. I see one
thing so straight that I cannot doubt it, and that is that you simply
cannot love me. To abandon me now after my long illness, yes, and at
the very moment when I'm trying to work, speaks for itself—I feel no
bitterness & I do not reproach you. Why should I, Evguenia? It is fate,
not your fault that you cannot love me. I know that you very naturally
feel that you want to work too, but reason is reason. I have work to my
hand can I only do it, whereas your work has not materialized and God
alone knows if it ever will in these days of competition. All of which, my
dear, is no fault of mine as you must admit in justice. As for study, that
you can do out here, if other foreign students can, why not you? As for
Una, well Una undoubtedly exsists but really I do assure you that she
does not hate you. If she made you suffer through her jealousy at first,
you made her suffer I do not doubt—your coming must have been a
great shock, and I think you should try to understand this & forgive her.
She is greatly changed as you often admit. I now never expect you two
to like each other beyond a superficial liking—just enough, my dear, to
get along with. But between you two I am being completely broken, and
this is not fair, my beloved Evguenia. You are tightening the ropes of my
wrack too much, you are giving me a most cruel ultimatum that I cannot
accept in honour. If I leave Una you will make your life to mine, that is
what it means in so many words, if I "were alone." After over 20 years
of loyal friendship I cannot leave Una and this you know—you knew it
before I became your lover—I was honest, I did not deceive you. You
accepted the circumstances of my life as they were, while saying that
they were not perfect you accepted them, didn't you, Evguenia? Now
Una has accepted you, yes she has, but it seems that now you will not

accept her. Its all too mad and while I remain sane I feel that I cannot any longer endure it. My life without you is impossible to contemplate, the more so because I am almost convinced that you no longer love me, but fear to tell me so. Oh, my poor little Piggie. I shall see you in Paris & perhaps by then you will have talked things over with Liza. I wanted you to spend the summer in England & for you and I to go away together for two weeks and try to get back into the past—to those days in Passy when we were so happy. But if it is parting that you have in your mind, then England would only be more agony, at least for me, so what's the good of it? Without me to come to you won't want enquiries to be made at the Home Office or anything, though while I am in Paris I will certainly go to Jeffs about one more annual visa—that is, of course, if you wish this. Well, my beloved, I have come to the end, the end of my road is I think in sight. I have lost your love and am going to loose you, I cannot work, Una is terribly unhappy because I told her what you said about her hate—she thinks I am going to desirt her. She is afraid of you, honestly afraid—I have had many tears, and its been pretty awful. But the thing that matters is your love which I've lost. All the rest only adds to my overwhelming burden. But taking it one way and another, my Evguenia, life's a bit too much, thats all, my dear, and I think God understands what it feels like. I am absolutely without hope, you see. Wherever I look I see only darkness—You are going to fail me when I need you most, and because of this my work has gone from me, so what is there left to live for, Evguenia? If I have ever failed you, my most dear, forgive me for I have not meant to fail you—maybe I've been too anxious; too careful of you & your health, but try to remember the awful shock I had about you, loving you as I do, Evguenia. I think you can forgive an anxiety that sprang red hot from an immence devotion. Well thats all, I have written many pages after all—words—words— words that will find no echo in your heart. But always remember that I've done my best. I have failed, but God knows I have done my best, and as always I say God bless you.

Your John

John and Una left Florence to return to England in late July 1938. They stopped in Paris on their way and at that time Souline agreed to join them in Rye later in August.

July 31st 1938

My dear Love. You are naughty and very revengeful—because I was too rushed in London to do more than send you a line, your letter of 29th which I got yesterday was too scrappy for even a common pig to be guilty of, however the main thing is that you should write me every day if only a post card, so you are forgiven. What news have I—pratically none, life goes on and that is all I can say for it. The weather is fine & warm now but so windy, and as I have always detested wind this constant blowing gets on my nerves, but its good, at least, to see sunshine. So your brother is going to the Riviera, oh, well, I suppose its all right in its way, but frankly I do not like it. If I had to live there of course I could because people mean much more to me than places, and if I could be with someone I loved I would live at the North Pole or on the Equator, but the French Riviera always seems so false, I am sure I prefer the Italian. Never can I stand at the window of this cottage and look across the marsh and the channel to France without thinking of you, without longing for you; and never can I walk through the streets of this Rye without grieving that you are not with me. And this is what you have done to me, Evguenia, you little white Russian refugee who I found at Bagnole by the merest chance, by one of those blows given us by Fate in the back, in the dark when we think we are in safety. You have made all the beauty in the world more lovely if you will consent to share it with me; you have ruined all beauty & turned it to pain—to a terrible heart-ache when you do not share it. When you are with me, or at least near enough for me to hear your voice if I long to, my life is full, but when you are away in another town, in another country, my life is completely empty. When you are kind and human and gracious, showing those little courtesies towards me, those little friendly courtesies that one human being must show for another, when you seem please[d] when I try to give pleasure, and happy because of my love and me, when these things happen my day is all bright as though clouds had rolled away from the sun, and I become well again in my soul and better again in body. But when you are unkind, ungraceous and inhuman, when you seem to hate me and to take no pleasure in the life that I am able to provide, when nothing I can do is enough to content you, when your mind strays off after false gods and wild longings and forgets me entirely, then my day is dark, as dark as the blackest corner of hell, and it seems to me that life cannot be lived much longer, so now you know what you've done to R.H. who was once a respected and celebrated author. And this is the power that you have in your hands, that has suddenly fallen into your hands—your lovely hands that are yet often cruel—the power to make or the power to mar, or perhaps it would be more truthful to say the power to <u>un</u>make or the power to <u>re</u>make; and sometime, little mad white Russian of my heart, I pity your terrible responsibility, you who have hated responsibility in the past and have now had it thrust upon you, not by me but by something very like God, for as God is your witness you tried to escape when you told me that day that you wished to leave Bagnole, and as God is my witness it was then too late, too late for I simply could not let you go, yes, but I never sort [sought] for our meeting—meeting you was a lovely yet terrible thing—a blessing, a joy, a fearful disaster. Can you understand all this, little Heart? Can you hear what my heart is trying to say, to make you realize before I go shipwreck? My heart is so burdened that it must speak to yours, it tells me that it has a right to speak to yours, that your heart really loves it and wishes it well and will help it to find the courage it needs to go forward towards work and endeavour once more. Beloved what does <u>your</u> heart say? Tell me. I am lonely, lonely, for I love you so much—too much—I love you more than you would have me love you, and this is the truth, Evguenia. Well, I suppose that love had to come into your lonely and dreary life, into your dear, dear, courageous life, and if that is so it should be a comfort to feel that you have had a real love—the kind that comes seldom and to very few people. Whatever happens in the future my beloved, you can say "I have had the real thing, yes I have. I have meant the whole world to someone, yes I have." And it may be that this will be your consolation.

Your none too happy
John

[Rye]

August 10th 1938

My Same Heart. Another 5 days only, I can scarcely believe it for I am oh, so much in love! How I hope that the weather will clear up—now it is like a Turkish bath, hot and raining, a few days ago it was cold and probably will be again tomorrow, and so it goes on, but then this is

England. I have no news, Rye is always adorable Rye when one just potters about. Yesterday I attended a tea given on the cricket field by the town during our 'Cricket Week'—everyone seemed very glad to see me and made me feel that I was the most important fish in this tiny pond—it was rather touching. Thanks to me the garden now has a few flowers in time for your arrival—all I now do is with an eye to your coming. I wish you had one of those transparant rain-proof skins that everyone is wearing—they come in all colours and they can't be dangerous to wear I should think—honestly you'll need someting of the kind here, but we can doubtless find it in Hastings. No more now or I miss the post.

Your devoted and starving John

Starving for the sight of R.C.P's funny face, & for the sound of its lovely speaking voice (when its good tempered, of course) I have fallen in love with you all over again. I am as much in love and in need of you as I was when I first had the very thought of you before you belonged to me. Love me—love me please.

John

Souline arrived on August 15, and John took her off to the long post-poned "second honeymoon." They went to Malvern in Worcestershire in the Severn Valley about thirty miles from the Welsh border. Malvern held many happy memories for John. She and Ladye had vacationed there nearly every summer, and it was also where she and Una had first made love in 1915—a place that recalled much happier days in John's life. John was not yet to know that this was the last time that she and Souline would make love. Souline returned to Paris in early September.

[Rye]

Sept. 13th 1938

Darling. I am just off to London for the day. I got your telegram about Italian visa and am as delighted as you. Heard Hitler on wireless last night—he is an hysteric, I think an epileptic, a patriot in the extreme sense of the word and a fanatic. He carried over 30,000 people with him—the roars of the people gave one to think. Take care of yourself—these are not the days to run any undue risks with health. So far no news from Whitehall about the English side of your life, and I dare not ring up at such a moment but mean to do so before coming to Paris. I must stop as the car comes for Hastings in a minute. All my love

Your John

[Rye]

Sept 14th 1938

My darling. I write again today to tell you that no letter has come from you by the last post. If you possibly can, will you <u>please</u> post early every morning, as not hearing from you these days makes me anxious. Of course I don't mean that you are to get up & go out especially to post; but if you would only have a few lines ready to post when you do go out—yes <u>please</u>. Have you got my letters all right, or do you think the posts are being delayed? Let me know this. Do you like being away from me at such a time? Well I don't like being away from you. I should come over sooner but for one thing, it is essential that I stand by as long as possible over your affairs at White Hall. I must keep in close touch over this Resident Alian business. Though God alone knows whether you have a dog's chance now that all this mad horror has broken out. If you do get it, it will be a miricle from heaven. However I do not feel inclined to delay my coming beyond Oct 4th as arranged. The news on wireless this evening is rather grim. Sand, they said, was being given out all over Paris for use against fires caused by incendiary bombs; it was also said that France is against a plebesite for the Germans.[1] Here everyone fears the worst—war. Anxious crowds are gathering every night near White Hall where cabinet meetings go on. England has grown suddenly old— people's faces, old and pale and resigned. I went to a party at Edie's this afternoon. Vita Sackville West[2] was speaking at a meeting of "The English Speaking Union" I also was roped in to speak. I saw my friends faces when they were off their guard—changed, grown years older, all that is, except Miss Edie who is happily preparing for her annual jumble sale next week—such a darling, bless her. Olive fearfully depressed as she has two young sons for the killing. Loo drinking whiskey to give herself that manly courage that I suppose she feels to be in the role, yet

---

1. To determine the fate of Germans living in the Sudetenland.
2. English author (1892–1962). Married to the British diplomat Harold Nicolson, she was at various times the lover of Violet Keppel (Trefusis) and Virginia Woolf.

openly saying that she is a coward & can't face up to another war, for which I rather like her. However at another moment (when the whiskey has worked) she announces that she is going to join the air force as a war pilot, when she is expecting to crash earthward in flames! As for me, John Radclyffe Hall, what do I feel? I scarcely know beyond amazement and spiritual horror. I cannot seem to envisage the horror and yet I am haunted by it. No mere words can express this madness that has suddenly stricken Europe. Darling I don't want to depress you, God knows, but these are terrible & dangerous days indeed. If only you could get that Resident Alian blessing, my country will always be decent, always. Once they took you here you would be safe, or rather as safe as I am. Be careful of yourself, of your chest—these are not days to risk getting ill. Be careful of all you do, of all you say, of where you go—the French are given to violent & unreasonable attacks of hysteria. And above all go at once & get your new validity of Passport & new visa de retour. If war really comes you may have great difficulty in getting anything. There is not a moment to lose, not a moment. I wonder that you did not think of this aspect, but when you wrote on 12th you had not heard Hitler's speech of course. You must surely be convinced by now that war is very near. How I wish that I had a letter from you today, a letter written on 13th. It is pretty awful not hearing from you. I will add a few lines tomorrow morning—No on second thoughts I will post this tonight.

Your John

[Rye]

Sept 15th 1938

My own dear. This confirms my telephone message of this morning. By the first post came the news that you had been granted "An Unconditional Visa" which is what is given to enable you to take up residence here in England—that gives you England's protection. I have no words to express my gratitude to God. At a time like the present I had not dared to hope. I am now going to London to make all the enquiries possible as to the procedure etc. and will write you full particulars. I will ask about you working here though I know this will be all right, but after all it is your life, my dear, and you shall know every detail. I have been in Hell—with a capital H. I have not wanted to alarm you but both Una & I have been greatly worried. We could not ignore the fact that with France so controlled by Russia, Stalin might at any moment, in the event of war, demand that France as his ally should turn out her White Russians, especially as some have been turned out already for conspiring against the Soviet. When France gets the wind up she is most unjust and unmerciful. Yes we have been deeply anxious, for if that happened the good & innocent like yourself who have never dabbled in political things would be victimized with the guilty—it might be very like what is happening to the jews!!

War & rumours of war are very dreadful, they make bruits of decent governments. But there is my England & here things are different & no one looses their head and you are safe. I must go.

Your John

I got your letter of 16th last evening. Today being a Sunday, no letter.

[from Rye]

September 18th 1938

My dearest Love. Yesterdays letter was not posted to you until 8 p.m so I do not suppose you will get it until Monday. I had such a long and trying day about Air Raid precautions & many other things that I could not get down to writing to my Piggie, and yet Piggie was forever in my thoughts. Friday evening I wrote you an enormous letter all about your visa, and I enclosed a sheet of clearly written notes for you to keep, and also a copy of Perks letter to me saying that the Secretary of State had granted you a visa "Without Conditions." I think you are being splendid, darling, doing everything so promptly, and this is a great comfort to me. I shall anxiously await your telegram telling me that the English visa is on your French Nansen. When I hear that I shall be more at peace. It is so awful to be away from you at such a time. There are moments when I long to ask you to come over at once and then we all to return to Paris on Oct 4th if there is no war. Do you know why I do not ask you, or have not asked you so far? Because I am afraid that you would say "No" or at all events not want to come—am I right? Today there is only one piece of news: The Duce has made a statement (or rather it is generally understood,) that unless a plebiscite is granted to the Sudetan Germans he will go to war together with Germany, but that if justice is done & the plebiscite granted, then Italy will remain neutral whatever happens afterwards. Yesterday there was what seems to me to be rather an important piece of news: America is about to reconsider its attitude towards her neutrality. No one seems to have taken much notice of this announcement, and I am wondering why; because if America were to come in on our side it would be very grave indeed for Germany & Italy. Oh, but my God! There simply must not be war. My heart aches for the women of Germany & Italy quite as much as for those of France & England. The emotion of love is the same all the world over, and this frightful anxiety is being felt by all alike—in love and the anxiety for those we love, we are all one big bleeding heart these days. God grant that there will be peace & justice. Darling, <u>are</u> you taking great care of my Piggie? Wire, good Piggie Hall (that is suggestion!) Wire, good and careful Piggie Hall who puts on warm coats, and keeps its hoofs dry, and <u>never</u> goes out without an enormous Pig-Umbrella! Also, who goes to bed nice & early and only drinks milk & soda water—a wonderful Pig who is nearly a saint—and oh, so good tempered, gentle and loving!!! Olive & Loo came over last evening and we laughed a great deal over a demonstration I gave them of how to carry an incendiary bomb away on a long-handled shovel after having thrown 30 pounds of sand on it. There were also other equally grotesque suggestions that I was able to demonstrate after my morning interview with Bunder who, as you know, is in charge of the Rye Air Raid Precautions, but who has to struggle with a stupid & lazy council. I know one aught not to laugh over anything so deadly serious, but honestly .. . . . Well, when we meet we will laugh together. I am now full of knowledge as to all those things that one aught to do but which—in most cases—it will be utterly impossible to do. It is a vile day, rain and wind and the last flowers in our two little gardens being blown off. My heart is with you always. I am glad I gave you that extra £10. Now you have £40 to use & hand on if you have to come over in a hurry, or indeed if you find yourself up against any emergancy—I am glad. But remember that if you are in even the smallest trouble of any kind, I will come to you at once.

Your John

[Rye]

Sept. 19th 1938

My darling. At last a hope of real and lasting peace—the news this morning seems almost too good to be believed. No, it is not fear that has prompted England & France to agree, as they have done, to make consessions to Germany and the other peoples who have been suffering for 20 years under oppression, but rather is it a sense of justice and a proper perception of values, and God bless them I say.

I have your letter of 17th, and what you tell me about France & her White Russians is very interesting, and (were it not for the Soviet Pact) very right in a way, but it would have been pretty awful for the young men to have to fight for the Soviet that has killed their families. However perhaps this generation has forgotten much—that is the way of the world. Anyhow you are getting your English visa on today, & the Italian also. And Piggie is being immensely pratical. But please send me the telegram I ask for when you have the English visa on your passport. Darling the strain has been pretty fearful & I cannot write more now. There has been an Anti-God Congress in London,[1] the result was that one hundred thousand Catholic men marched through London yesterday with uncovered heads & in complete silence as a reparation to God for the insults He has received. They marched from Southwick Cathedral to Westminster Cathedral[2]—the procession took 3 hours. Also all the Churches, protestand & Catholic have been crowded with people praying for peace. I enclose a picture of one. There are still rocks ahead, but the worst is over—Blessed be God.

My own—my dear, dear Evguenia

Your John.

[Rye]

Sept. 23rd 1938

Dearest. The news this evening is very grave. I fear that the conference between Chamberlain and Hitler is breaking down. Hold yourself in readiness to come to me here at any moment. Better not attempt to take work until we see where we are. There may be war in a few days. Suppose the French should try to stop you coming by taking away your visa de retour, you can come just the same as Perks has told us that with your unconditional English visa, a French visa de retour is not required by us—you land in England without any conditions.

Calais—Should you have to come, try Dover, but come by any route

---

1. Newspapers reported a large gathering of atheists as an anti-God rally.
2. A distance of less than two miles.

that is open to travellers. Try to wire me where I am to meet you and your plans for reaching me. Have your trunks & all you need handy so that you would loose not a moment.

Your John

[Rye]

Sept 26th 1938

After our telephone talk on Saturday, I did not write to you my darling. This morning I have your letter of 24th. I have sent you a telegram explaining why you wont get a letter from me. There will be war, judging from the news this morning. I still think that you should come over <u>at once</u>. As I knew when I spoke to you on Saturday, there are going to be endless difficulties in travelling. To prouve this I enclose a cutting from mornings Telegraph.[1] My earnist request is that you come now—England will need you. I can't force you to come now, I can only entreat you to do so and thus spare me a terrible added anxiety. Why expose me to that and yourself to a most damnable journey, only for the sake of having your own way? Darling, for God's sake come now.

If you refuse to do so and still persist in this mad & foolish course you are taking, then you will have to get here as best you can & god help us all. The government trains will be crowded with refugees—too fearful. You have been through that once. Do you want to go through it again? I beseach you to wire to me when this letter reaches you, saying that you are coming now. I ask it for the love I have for you—and if you have even affection for me you will come. In any case I am loving you—but please, please love me enough to come at once.

Your John

The immediate threat of war was postponed by the Munich agreement, and John and Una felt secure enough to resume their plans to winter in Florence, arriving there on October 17. They had seen Souline briefly en route, but she adamantly refused to join them except for occasional visits. She did visit in November, but laid down certain conditions for the continuance of the relationship. There was to be no sex, as she had concluded that she might be more "normal" than she had supposed, and

---

1. The London *Daily Telegraph,* a newspaper John habitually read.

she would never live in the same town with John and Una. She then went back to Paris, promising to visit again at Christmastime.

[Via de Bardi, Florence]

Dec. 17th 1938

M̲y̲ Piggie. Yes, the Corrini villa was wonderful, and I thought that the large estates in the real Russia must have been like it only larger. And I thought of you and longed for you as I have already told you. The new dress that you have bought, but how glad and happy it makes me to know that my Xmas present has been spent on a new dress. Foolish and loved Pig—don't you y̲e̲t̲ know how much pleasure it gives me to feel that I can give y̲o̲u̲ some pleasure? Is there any doubt about your coming for Xmas? You say "perhaps I can manage." Oh, no darling, you can't mean that there is any doubt. "The harmony of my exsistance" will you break it by coming?

No you will not, because there is no harmony to break when we are devided. There is not always harmony when we are together, but when we are apart there is a veritable hell of discord. Now listen to me. We are never going to quarrel again—all that is past, it has just got to be past. No quarrells, no recriminations, no reproaches. We have entered on a new phase of our exsistance and we have got to make a good thing of it. But I am not well and I think you must come. I have a very great longing just to see you. Will you please let me know when I am to expect you? Dearest I feel that you love me a little, or perhaps that you are at least fond of me. I am not suffering from a mortal illness, but I am pig-pining, it can only be that. Dearest I swear I am telling you the truth. I don't understand it, no I do not. Sometimes I think that we are one, and then when we are apart for too long the wound of our seperation starts bleeding. Sometimes I feel as though a part of me had been torn away like a limb in battle. God knows what it means, it is not imagination or hysteria, it is merely the truth. Come to me for a little while my dear. Yes come if you have affection for me. No, do not trouble to bring the typewriter in case you have any trouble at the frontiers; I have thought it over & I think better not. When you go back to Paris you will want it. I once told you I would give it to you, but you showed no interest and did not take it, but now, apparently, you think you would like it. Keep it my dear little Piggie, it is yours. It is old but still works well, or it did

before it went into storage. I shall just <u>have</u> to get a new one out here.
Yesterday my typist's Italian machine broke down 4 times and I nearly
went mad! I was struggling to give her dictation. I think I shall buy a
new Underwood[1]—the price is apalling and what is even worse there is
not one to be had at the moment; however they swear they will have one
in a week. Come to me Piggie, don't cry but come. And your health, am
I grateful? God knows I am. The news you give me is simply splendid. I
am so grateful that I cannot hope to express my gratitude to Our Lady
of Lourdes.[2] Do you think she is particularly fond of Paris?!! This has
been a good winter everywhere but in England. Oh my Piggie, my little,
little Pig-child, my heart yearns over you night and day. When are you
coming to your desolate

Johnnie?

[on unmarked paper]

Dear love. Same Heart.
All happiness to you this
Christmas—your first in Florence.

John

---

1. A popular typewriter brand.
2. John is referring to the shrine at Lourdes, France, where the Virgin Mary was
reputed to have appeared. Prayers and devotions to her under that guise were reported to
have worked miracles of healing.

1939

Souline stayed in Florence through the holidays into late January 1939,
but there were almost constant frictions and quarrels. The problem of
the triangle loomed large, and at parting Souline refused to say goodbye
to Una, literally slamming the door in Una's and John's faces. Left alone,
John and Una motored to Viareggio, a town on the Ligurian Sea, to
enjoy a brief change of scene.

Stationery of Astor Modern Hotel, Viareggio

January 25th 1939

Same Heart. I am writing this in bed before getting up—in fact I am
taking it easy. We had a good & uneventful drive here yesterday, but on
arrival found that the basin in bathroom <u>stank,</u> so had to change our
rooms. Now we are up on 2nd floor & have each got a bedroom which
is really much better. The weather is perfect and the peaks are white
with snow which (except that this town is so frightfully ugly) reminds
me of Merano. As I lie here the sun is blazing into my bedroom which is
now at the side of the hotel & thus gets all the morning sun. The more I
think of it darling, the less can I understand why you asked me, just
before leaving, whether I would like you to stay and then when I said
yes, of course I would, but only if <u>you really wanted to stay,</u> (and what
else could I say, what else could I feel?) lit out at me furiously as you
did. Can you yourself understand this, my Piggie? But no matter, no
matter, only when I breath this air, so pure, so life giving, I can't help
wishing that Piggie were to breath it with me. Do you know something?
I cannot help wondering whether your English is at fault occasionally,
whether you express yourself badly, whether you do not make your
meaning clear, either saying too much or not quite enough, and whether

201

you do not understand my meaning. This may very well be, and if it is so then we must try to avoid misunderstandings, which are not only senseless but exhausting. Darling you know what joy I would have had in your staying, but how could I keep you longer when you were so obviously wanting to do [go], I could not accept a sacrafice on your part unless you really felt that you wanted to stay, & that was why I asked you—why I said: 'Yes, but only if you want to stay with me.' Surely you understand how I felt? Put yourself in my place, beloved. It was terrible to me that you left me in anger, though I myself, as you know, was not angry, but never, oh, never let us part again like that, suppose something awful happened—Your telegram to which you had added the word 'love' made me happier, for I felt that the storm had passed, and now I am awaiting your first letter which I pray will be even more reassuring.

I love you, my bad, bad, mad Pig, & so I implore you to be sensible & careful, & not any more to delude yourself into thinking that never in all your naughty life have you had bad colds in Paris! I cannot controle you, I can only advise, & appeal to any affection you may feel for Johnnie who loves & needs you so much—and believe me it is good & fine to be needed—not to be needed by someone who is lonely. You must have your own life, that I realize, but the sad thing is that it must be far from me, or so it seems, my Piggie. Well, come back soon as you have promised to do, & meanwhile take care of yourself for our sake. And let me hear all about your plans, and what you meant when you spoke of 'the doctor,' & whether, in your own opinion, you think it would be sensible & wise to have an X ray taken. I am sure that it would not reveal any trouble with your lungs, but just as a precaution?

Darling, I must now get up & dress. God bless & keep you. Write to me please, and remember that you have promised to tell me at once if you are not well or in trouble. I hold you to that promise—had you not promised this I think I should go mad, so now you know. I kiss your beautiful & cruel hands, first one & then the other

Your John

Viareggio.

February 5th 1939

Darling S.H. Your letter of 3rd together with the Transfer and Dividend Request Form arrived yesterday afternoon. I am so glad to have them back safely. Really they took no time in coming and I thank you for having been so prompt and businesslike. I shall send the papers to the Bank tomorrow morning, and the Bank will then lodge them in the right quarters and all will be done. It will only remain for the Bank to get your Stock Receipt which will come along in due course & be held by them for you.

So Mrs Baker has evinced after all! Yes, but how much? I insist on being told how much—tell me at once!

There is something I owe you. I promised to pay that Russian Solicitor who did your naturalization business and has now got you back your dossier. I am of course supposing that all is now finished, and you have paid him, as you said you would, as soon as he got your complete dossier for you back from the French government office. Therefore dearest, let me know 1) how much his bill came to, 2) what you had to pay Consulate for witnessing your signature. I will arrange to get the money to you and also, as I said, a bit extra for postage.

I am returning to Florence on Friday next, the 10th. Please write here on Tuesday next, and after that write to Via du Bardi 8. as usual.

Darling, what has happened to the money you got for your land? I do wish you could invest that also in War Loan, though there would be a big loss on exchange. But I expect you would rather keep that money in hand. I am hoping to hear from you that you will want me to instruct the Bank to place all dividends on W.L. on Deposit for you until further notice. As I told you, the sum standing on Deposit could, at any time, be transferred by you to a drawing account, but for the moment why not on deposit? Yes—yes—yes. However it is for Piggie Hall to decide this, and Johnnie Hall awaits its Royal instructions!

On Tuesday we go to Lucca[1] for the day. Una is most anxious to see Lucca and it is nearer here than it is to Florence. I could find no possible way to say "no." It would have come later if not now—I would have had to go there from Florence. But although I don't expect you to understand, darling, because you are now so out of love, it appears, I am dreading Lucca like the very devil. We shall have to lunch at the same hotel there being no other—Oh, yes, I dread it. Something very intimate has gone from my life—how can I explain? It is childish perhaps, but many very little & happy things have gone together with the one great, big thing. There are foolish songs that I cannot bear to

---

1. A medium-sized town a few miles east of Viareggio.

hear, or even to think of: "The very thought of you."[2] Yes, and others
that got themselves all mixed up with that first time I left you to go to
Sirmione. Alas, alas, and I want to live now in the spirit, I want to
forswear the body, but like the music it is all mixed up—body & spirit,
spirit & body. As I write I am not in any physical torment, no I am not,
and yet I feel bereaved. And sometimes I simply cannot believe that all
that is over forever between us—it is as though someone had died and
my eyes fill with tears and so does my heart, for I am no fool and I very
well know that the day I was really pretty bad with that broken bone
you fell out of love—my long illness did it; and then when you ceased
to be in love much tenderness in your feeling went too. You see, my
beloved, I know these things for I myself have been a great lover—I
have loved and then grown weary and bored and put an abrupt and
brutal end to the thing just as you have done. Did I stop to consider the
other person's feelings? No, I did not. Well, now perhaps I am paying
for my past and the price is high you may believe me. And yet—and
yet—would I have it otherwise? God help me, I am constantly torn in
two. I am not going to write anymore about all this. You no longer
desire me, you have made that quite plain & you had a perfect right to
do so. Am I jealous and suspicious? Of course I am. I tell myself that
there must be someone else, knowing your temperament as I do, and
then I suffer, doubting your word, I suffer like Hell, Evguenia. But I
have what is left of it all—your friendship. Not yet, & perhaps never
can I say a real good bye and go on living—I don't understand it, I
aught to hate you, but instead I must love you. Your mind is often to me
a closed book, I do not know the workings of your mind. Frequently I
find you unreasonable and cruel, yes cruel, and yet I love you. the bond
is so strong, so frightfully strong between us that to break it would mean
death I do believe, at all events for me. Better friendship than nothing,
that is what I am reduced to. Never to see you again in this life—never
to hear your voice again, not to know what was happening or where
you were! Could you bear it, Evguenia? I could not. I am a woman who
has passed through many things, known many deep joys and sorrows. I
have lived my life to the full, yes I have, but nothing that has gone before
is like this, nothing is or ever has been quite the same—you, you, you—
who are you? What are you? And long, long ago what were we to each
other? I am nearly 20 years older than you are, as you frequently remind

---

2. A refrain from a song by Ray Noble, popular in 1934.

me in so many words, though I do not need reminding. This means that I actually was living in the world before you were conceived, that I had a life of my own when you were non-exsistant! Isn't that queer—I can scarcely believe it. Then a very long way away in Poland there came a day when you were you, when a little squealing baby was being borne— and I, John Hall, knew nothing about it! I think at that moment I must have been in England—yes, I am sure, in England. I was pretty young then with all my life before me, young and carefree; and as selfish as you are! I could not see into the future, Evguenia. Well—be it so, you have found a friend. But dearest, do not batter friendship as you have done love—stop battering, dearest. Do not make hard fists of your lovely, lovely hands, let them be gentle and soothing. This began as a business letter and has ended as what? A love letter? No not that. It is a little bit of my heart. Only when and if you replace me as a lover, let me know— that much you most certainly owe me. Meanwhile take care of yourself, I beg you, and come back to me at Easter if not before—I am very very terribly lonely. And peace, peace—oh, let there be peace between us so that I may get well again. Peace and forgiveness—complete forgiveness. No bitterness, no misunderstandings, my darling. I shall die before you do, I honestly believe, and your memory of me must be good and kind and have in it something of love and sweetness.

Meanwhile I am better in health. Now remember, I go home on Friday—write here on Tuesday for the last time, after that to Florence.

Your John

Viareggio.

Febuary 9th 1939

Darling Same Heart. I write you today because, as I am returning to Florence tomorrow, I shall not have time. Listen, there are one or two things that I want to clear up, and better is it to write them than to speak them because you so frequently get angry these days when I least expect you to do so. This bewilders me, so that very often I leave things unsaid or only half said, or worse still convey a wrong impression.

When we were talking when you were in Florence and you had grown angry over something—over what I cannot any longer remember, I said: "And when I think of you when I first met you—what you were then." And you instantly replied—"Nonsense, I was a general's daughter."

Darling, what I was thinking about was naturally not your social position, not that you were inferior to me, but that I had found you too
terribly alone and unprotected in every way, which at the time seemed
all the worse just <u>because</u> of your social position. It was that that I had
been going to say, because it was that that I hoped to do away with—
your loneliness, your humiliating work, or rather work that you found
humiliating. I wanted to say that your social position, your birth, made
it imperative—at all events in my eyes—that you should meet & know
my friends and be one with my social life, Evguenia.

Another thing. You very rightly asked me where I kept your letters &
I said in my cell, but forgot to say also that the letters that count are &
were locked up in my dressing case the key of which never leaves me. I
may sometimes let Una unlock the case to get money out, but that is all
and never takes more than a moment or two—No one can ever read
your letters that count, I am much too careful. At the Forecastle your
letters are in a locked tin box, and as they are bulging my dressing case,
I am going to get a locked box in Florence—the key will always be on
my chain as is the key of the box at the Forecastle.

Yet another thing. You asked me whether Una knew about your
English nest egg & I told you that she did. It occurs to me that you
might justifyably resent this, might think that such matters are strictly
private between you and me, as indeed they should be. Therefore I
would like to explain how Una came to know about it. She knew
nothing about that £300 before the war-crisis last September. Her knowing then came about in this way. I was distracted by trying to get you to
come to me, and was discussing with Una what was likely to happen if
war broke out—she had had great experience during the last war when,
at its beginning, she joined her husband. We both knew that money
would be a great difficulty, that French money might be refused in
England, and I then said: "But even if I could not meet her because I do
not know where she will land, she aught to be alright because she has a
passbook showing several hundred pounds that she has as a nest egg,
standing in her name at my bank in London. Una then said: "Well, I am
thankful to hear it!" And there the matter ended. But I am annoyed that
in the strain & confusion of those terrible days—to which strain you
must admit that you added—I mentioned that English Nest Egg. What I
have done for you and still do is absolutely between you & me, and I
must say, in justice, that Una never presumed to question me about it.
But I felt that I owed you an explaination, and I hope you will forgive

that slip of the tongue in view of the shattering circumstances at that moment. And my fearful anxiety about you and about our seperation at such a time when others were all rushing to get together! and everyone was fearing the worst—at all events in England, I do assure you.

One more thing that even if you resent it I must say in justice to myself. Speaking of doctors, you wrote me here that any doctor would advise you not to winter in Paris if you had a chance to do otherwise, but you added: "But of course a doctor would not know the circumstances." If by "Circumstances" you meant having to spend the winter in the same town as me, then I ask you, my darling, to remember this: When I thought it my duty to stop your allowance if you persisted in remaining in Paris,[1] I said very many times that the allowance <u>would not stop provided you went to any suitable climate</u>, I even spoke of Grasse[2] or Merano, and I not only said this to you but wrote it, as you will see if you have kept my letters writen after you left Florence last summer and probably at other times also. There was never any compulsion on my part as long as you went to a suitable climate & remained there during dangerous winter months. You see, I love you, and that being so I thought only of your health and not of my own feelings, bitter though it naturally was to me to feel that you did not want to come to Florence and that my taking a flat there had failed so miserably in its object. Well, I had not meant to take this up, but somehow I cannot let it pass, what you said in your letter haunts me.

Never think, never delude yourself into thinking that I am resigned to the idea of your spending the winters in Paris. I am not so resigned & never shall be. But since you insisted, I thought the matter over from every angle and came to the conclusion that if, in addition to all the other risks, I let you remain in Paris without money, the risks would be doubled, and I could not bear it. The continuing of your allowance if you stayed in Paris after I had said that nothing on earth would enduce me to do so, must, to you, have appeared merely like weakness—may even have made you respect me less. But weakness it was not and is not. Thanks to you I had only two alternatives: one to let you fend for yourself during the winter as best you could, probably being reduced to

---

1. This is the first overt reference to the practical control John's financial support exerted on Souline. It is also the first indication that John sought to use that influence as a source of control.

2. A town a few miles northwest of Cannes. John, Una, and Souline had spent several months there in 1936.

nursing of which all your doctors disapprove, probably finding yourself short of money for suitable quarters and suitable food, the other to continue the allowance and thus contribute to your staying in Paris—in a word contribute to your dangerous folly. It was a desperately hard position to find myself in, but I have chosen—and God grant I have chosen wisely.

Well thats that, and now I have got this off my chest and we won't go over it again because, darling, you will be just to me in future, even if you don't want to, my dear, my most unregenerate & unjust Piggie. You have come to a turning point in your life when you have just got to have a sense of values. Never, never before in your life have you had to take such a vital decision. Your friends may say this or that or the other, but only you are able to decide, and only I, in all this big world, am entirely interested in your future and selflessly interested in your well fair, yes Piggie, and this you know to be the truth. It is natural enough, come to think of it, there is seldom if ever more than one person in a lifetime to whom one means a great deal, and we are in luck if we meet one person.

God bless you—I must pack. Take care of yourself.

Your John

PS Take this long letter in the spirit in which it is written—the spirit of love, if I may dare now to use that word—if I may not now dare then call it: affection. No good your feeling bored or cross, it is too grave for boredom or crossness, my dearest, above all it is too grave for anger. I do not ask for an immediate decission about England, but what I do ask you to do is, for your own sake, to think it over very gravely. And don't answer this letter by threatening to tear me out of your life, just answer it calmly. I am not going to be torn out of your life, so no use in our upsetting ourselves—the Same Heart can never be torn quite asunder otherwise it stops beating.

I am glad to be leaving Viareggio—the town is now all noise & dust getting ready for the Carnival next Sunday. On every lampost there is a loud speaker bawling the new Carnival songs from dawn till dark, alright for some people but I am in no mood for such songs, they only irritate and then depress me. So far Viareggio remains very empty in spite of the effort to make us feel light hearted—yes, I am glad to be going. Old Fossi[3] has been very ill, it seems, he and his wife are still in

---

3. An acquaintance from Viareggio.

Florence—he was taken ill when he went there on a short visit. What's the matter with him I do not know, but it seems that he is now better. The weather has been very wonderful here—I see that in Paris you have had "London fogs" which news has not added to my peace of mind as you can very well imagine!

Here I am in Italy, my Evguenia, and my home is your home and always will be—I am yours to come to, and I hope you will come, at all events for a bit at Easter. I would <u>like</u> you to be out of Paris during March, the most damnable month there for colds as you know. But you will decide this for yourself—my wishes will not weight with you I fear—though perhaps they may after all, my dearest. You said that you would come back at Easter, but I would be thankful if you came in March. Indeed you promised to come at Easter, but alas, Piggie promises mean very little. Well, Evguenia, I am your home remember, I am your family, your refuge and your home, your hope in the present and the future. I am indeed all you have, so far, in the world and without me my Pig would be very much alone and Pigs hate it when they feel deserted and lonely. You must carefully take stock of your future, must think many times before you decide to refuse to take out your English Nansen—it will soon be now or never for England. The decission will be so grave a one that you must not shrink from it, must not wobble. The American Hospital could still be kept in touch with, but Good God, my dear, it is much more than that. What is an occasional, possible job at the Hospital when it is compaired with the protection of the British Empire, with the chance (if you wish it) of naturalization in the country that is your soùl hope financially? What is the American Hospital, the life in Paris among Russian refugees however nice, your affection for France, when compaired to your having the wherewith all to live on, and <u>ample provision after my death</u>, and even someday a substancial income unless you do something entirely outrageous which you will not, will you my darling? Evguenia, it is my duty to say all this, and your duty towards yourself to consider what I am saying, to consider it gravely.

<u>Via du Bardi. 8.</u>

March 3rd 1939

Darling. I have your letters of Feb 27th and 28th, the latter came this morning as you posted it, I see, on 1st.

On March 1st I sent you by Registered Post, all the papers about your War Loan, I hope that you will have received them by now. Please let me know that they have reached you safely.

We all feel that Pious XII[1] will make a fine Pope. The news of his election was shouted through the streets of Florence last evening—I should think it must have been one of the quickets [sic] elections on reckord, a matter of a few hours, whereas it often takes days for the Conclave to make up its mind. Our Florentine Cardinal Archbishop, della Costa, is said to be almost a saint, but I hear not at all keen on his election as I had heard that he had very marked political views not altogether of a kind likely to make for peace with the government. Pious XII has travelled all over the world as Papal Legate, which in these dark days maybe very useful to him, also one has always heard that he is the kindest and best of men—I wish I had been in Rome at 7^{oc} last evening to receive his blessing from the balcony of the Vatican, though the crowd would likely have crushed me flat—thousands of people, of course.

I have a feeling that Diane's[2] luck is out. I cannot understand why she can't get work, no I can't. She is attractive looking in her own way, though she has missed that lovely expression and middle-ages look of her mother. But I'm afraid that the truth is that every profession is terribly overcrowded these times—too many people in a world that seems to be shrinking, awful thought! I think I shall write a morbid short story one day, called: "The World Shrinks." And suppose it did begin to shrink, to contract for some reason unknown to science—what then? Also why not? Anything can happen. Here also the weather is a little cold, or rather fresh, but of an extreme luminosity—every smallest house at Fiesole[3] visible from my study window, also all the mountains to right and left of the bridges are standing out unusually clearly, & some have snow on them still. Yes, my Evguenia, a lovely little city and full of nice well bred but simple people. Only spoiled for you because someone called John is living here—and that is what it has come to! Looking back across the years since I first met you, I feel that I am looking at the ruins of what should have been a very fine and helpful and lasting structure for us both, bringing you security and tenderness and love, and to me the great joy of giving your these precious—these

---

1. Eugene Pacelli (1876–1958), elected Pope in 1939.
2. One of Una's Tealdi cousins.
3. A town about five miles from Florence.

In late April Souline and Lysa returned to Paris. Meanwhile John's health was breaking down rapidly, and she finally gave way to Una's pleading and consulted a Doctor Laparicci, who discovered that in her youth John had unknowingly suffered a severe attack of tuberculosis. A second opinion confirmed the TB scars and John was ordered to quit smoking (she smoked over three packs a day) and to undertake a purification cure at the thermal springs in Monsummano, midway between Florence and Viareggio.

[typescript letter—the first]

Via dei Bardi 8, Florence.

June 3. 1939

Darling,

You asked me to send my report and I now do so. The metabolism report I have not troubled to have copied. It is very simple: all my glands are over-active especially my thyroid. The normal count ought to be ten and mine is nineteen. La P. is giving me glandular treatment.

The X-ray report I have had copied for you and I now enclose it. There is also a drawing of the heart and the aorta which I cannot enclose. La P. says my heart is slightly enlarged and that the aorta is enlarged as he thought, but that if I am careful, entirely give up smoking and keep very quiet for a time, especially during the period of my cure, my heart and the aorta ought to normalise, and certainly I have not had any more attacks of that very violent pain which I think must be a good sign.

Now for a most extraordinary thing—extraordinary because I am alive. You may remember that I told you that when I was a child I had been a victim to bronchitis and had once had what was then called inflammation of the lungs. From the condition of the pleura shown by the X-ray it is obvious that I had quite bad pleurisy. I cannot remember if I had much pain when I was supposed to have inflammation of the lungs, I can remember having a good many painful poultices put on, but I was very young and I cannot even remember what age. But the tuberculosis is what is so very extraordinary. You may remember again that I told you that when I was about nineteen I had a fearful cough, night sweats, and grew very thin, that I was taken to a German doctor in

London who specialised, not in T.B., but in recomme[n]ding certain German water cures—I cannot now even remember why I went to him at all. He said that he was not satisfied with the condition of my lungs but he would not actually say that I had T.B. He did say, however, that he wished me to go to a sanatorium in Germany and have an open-air cure. Everyone was unwilling to believe that anything could be the matter with my lungs and so I was taken to a very big general consultant who had known me all my life. He did not consider that my lungs were affected but only that they were in a very delicate condition, but he thought my bronchials in a very bad state and sent me off to make a cure at Bad Ems. The doctor at Ems did not think I had T.B. and certainly I got better there, but for several years at that period of my life I was not over strong. Now comes this X-ray which shows the results of pleurisy, and above all the results of quite bad T.B. Both my lungs were affected, the left in the middle the right in the apex. La P. says that it was a bad case and that I was very ill without knowing it—I can remember feeling very ill sometimes. La P. says that had I started my career as a writer anywhere round about the time when my T.B. was beginning I must have died. But the extraordinary thing is that in spite of the severity of the attack I showed by the X-ray, I cured myself, my fine constitution fought the germs and so here I am. I expect the life of sport which I led later on may have helped, though the sport was so violent[1] that had my lungs not been completely healed by that time I should think it would have been disastrous. Anyhow La P. considers that I am now immune, being vaccinated as it were. If it would interest you I will show you the X-ray when I come to Paris, my lungs are very distressful looking! I asked La P. to tell me quite frankly what I ought to do in the winter, I thought it just as well to ask him in view of this amazing X-ray, but also in view of the fact that I am not well what with this aorta and one thing and another. La P. immediately said "I would like you to go to the Riviera; I would not like you to be in London or Paris." I asked him if Florence would do and he said it was very much better than London or Paris and that yes, it would do because the air was fairly pure unlike the air in big cities and that taking it all in all the climate was very much better. Is it not amazing, don't you think that at the time when the German doctor thought I was threatened with tuberculosis, when indeed I actually had it quite badly, none of the three

---

1. John seems to be referring here to her intense dedication to riding.

doctors took the sputum test? Of course they were not then able then to X-ray the lungs, but they were able to examine the sputum.[2]

[Via de' Bardi stationery]
June 10th 1939

Your letter of 9th reached me this evening. It was I and not Una who asked La P. where I aught to spend the winters, and I asked him the first time I saw him after the X Ray & when he was examining same & reading the report in my bedroom. Una had not seen him alone, & when I asked him that question she was not in the room even. I told you about the winters when I sent you the X Ray report, yet now you write as though it was something new. Also it was I and not Una who drew up the list questions for La P. to answer. So now let us have an end to this crazy digging at Una—it makes me unhappy, so stop it. Jopolina[1] who has seen the X. Ray (which I have not) tells me that any sane doctor would advise a decent winter climate after seeing the picture and studying the report on same. And you always seem to forget the pleurisy—why? It is not a breakout of T.B. that La P. is scared of, but anything that might lead to pneumonia, & this because I have both of my lungs damaged and am in a low condition. But what is the good of my writing all this, only do face the truth: I have trouble with my aorta and a couple of damaged lungs—quite enough to go on with, don't you think?

I could let myself get angry—but am not going to. Only please, my dear, please do try to realize one thing and it is this: I am a woman who is quite capable of managing my own life & always have been. I do not require Una or any one else to manage it for me and I greatly regret the suggestion that I do. When I want to know anything from a doctor about my condition I ask him myself,

Your John.

[Florence]
June 19th 1939

Darling. No letter from you this morning & I expected one. If you had written on 17th which your day to write, I surely aught to have got it this

---

2. X-ray technology was not available until the 1920s. The earlier diagnostic tool was a bacterial culture prepared from sputum.

1. One of the doctors treating John.

morning—perhaps I will get a letter by the afternoon post. Tomorrow at
10. am. I leave by car for my cure. I have a letter from La. P. for the
doctor, and La P. comes to see me after I have had 6 baths. I hope the
cure in addition to getting rid of my poisons will remove the fat. Some
gland is not working properly—thyroid working overtime but this other
has struck—result, I am very fat in spots & very thin in others—I look
rather like this:

Arms & legs & neck very thin,
but the rest of me . . . . !

Please write to Monsummano until I tell you not to. I will let you
know in good time when I am leaving there. You should have got my
letter giving you my address, this morning—I posted it on Saturday but
missed the 4 p.m. post so I suppose it is just possible you will not get it
until tonight or tomorrow morning. The weekend is always damnable
for letters. Piggie—oh, Piggie . . . . . Piggie be a good Pig, a kind Pig.
Piggie I smiled when you wrote in your letter in answer to mine about
my lungs that of course I had cured myself because at that time I had
been young & happy & had had "the money." Darling—there can have
been few youngsters so utterly & miserably unhappy as I was between
the ages of 15 & 20. I thought I told you how unhappy was my
childhood & adolescence. No—it was not happiness that healed my
wounds—it can only have been God's will.

I have had yet another talk D La P. the result of which I will tell you
when we meet—that is if you are interested. I think that now I know
exactly where I stand, at least I know all he knows—or I think I do. No,
dearest, I cannot say that I feel really "upset—", it does not appear to
be that that makes me not want to work. I just do not feel inclined to
exsert myself at the moment. Write to me. Here is the new address yet
again—

Hotel Victorio Emmanuele
　Grotto Guisti.
　　Monsummano.
　　　Toscana. Italy.
I must get on with my packing.

Your John.

June 21st 1939

Dearest of Pigs. I have been into the town to get proper paper & have opened my bottle of ink and am using my proper pen, so this letter looks more sane than the one I sent off last evening. I am writing this to catch the first post tomorrow morning. Your letter of 19th arrived safely by this morning's post, so apparently letters get here as soon as they do to Florence which surprises me. This is rather a lovely place in a quiet, simple country way. The hotel & grotto Giuisti are 1 1/2 kilometers from the little town of Monsummano and further (I don't know how much) from Montecatini.[1] At the moment there are only a handful of people in the hotel as the real season is from next month until the end of October—I am glad of the quiet. This morning I went to the Grotto & remained in the "Inferno" for 35 minutes—tomorrow it must be 45 and after that 60 minutes, also tomorrow I am to be given a medical bath in addition to the Grotto & the massage I had this morning. This bath I am only to have every other day, but Grotto & massage every day. I have seen the resident M.O. and La P. is coming to see me after 6 Grotto. It is the most curious place—one walks down down into the bowls [bowels] of the earth for a little more than 300 metres. The atmosphere is strong & heavey & of course damp, damp. As one enters the Grotto one feel[s] that one cannot take a deep breath—awful. The attendant told me that some people feeling this are too scared to go further. I felt less beastly when I got to the hottest point & sat down & finally began to sweat. I am assured that this breathlessness only occurs at first— anyhow it is obviously a fine means of getting rid of hoarded up poisons, this cure. I was made to rest on my bed—still sweating—for 3/4 of an hour, then I had about 25 minutes of massage & rested again until lunch. After lunch 1/2 hour stroll & then rest again until 4 p m as I wrote you last evening. This air is in itself very calming to tired nerves, it is gentle, kind, good air and so healing I am sure. Also, my dear, your letter was gentle and made me feel quiet & peaceful and so has helped me. Darling about my T.B., it was of course a very fairly bad case as you can judge from the report I sent you and will be able to see with your trained eye when I show you my X Ray. Also there was pleurisy affecting both lungs. All this La P. and Frangoni have explained to me and I never

---

1. The coastal town where John had planned to stay with Souline in April.

see any sense in not facing facts my Pig. La P. thinks that I am a mirical almost, & that even so a little more & I must have died. Well, dear one, I lived to meet you among other things! Anyhow as you say, God willing, the trouble will never now come back if I am not too great a fool which I must try not to be. I am in no way morbid over this discovery, and as I was to be allowed to cure myself I am thankful I did not know of the trouble at the time. I am haunted by only one fear, that in all innocence I may have infected someone—even perhaps a child, but I cannot help it if it happened, can I? I am very homesick for England, and when this revelation occurred, I was actually telling Una that I thought I would take a country house there & settle down for good & all. But I see now that I was not meant to do so; and, moreover, it would almost seem as though I was meant to know the truth about my lungs at this moment & thus saved taking the English home—all so strange it seems. However, 'what can't be cured must be endured,' and given certain conditions I can imagine that I could be very happy in my exile. Anyhow I must do what the doctors advise if I want to avoid possible trouble, because these days I am not so recilliant as I must have been once upon a time. Life has tired me as you can imagine, knowing how many hard battles I have fought from my earliest youth onwards.

God bless & keep you. Yes, I shall join you I am certain sometime in July—otherwise you will have to join me.

Your John

Via dei Bardi 8

July [Souline's handwriting above John's obviously wrong date]
June 6th 1939

Darling. Your letter of 3rd sent to Monsummano has been sent to me here in Florence and I got it this morning. I am glad you have written to Geneva for my letters—there was nothing of any interest in them but one does not like ones letters to go wandering about. You were quite, quite right of course to give me your Swiss address when you did and I am certain they will return your letters at once, the Swiss are such pleasant & careful people. About what you say about your allowance darling, the question of your allowance does not enter into the situation at present, though I thank you for what, I must believe, you meant as an unselfish offer; but as I have said, your allowance has no bearing on the situation and so need not be discussed at the moment. My letter from Monsummano written before I left will have reached you by now. Quite suddenly after my 12 baths I was all in and my face blazing with a most painful eruption, so I came home. I sent you a telegram on Monday evening letting you know that I was returning to Florence—I hope you got it, M. was such a God forsaken place and the hotel without any proper management. I suppose my cure has been a successful one—I hope so. I still feel very feeble & still have this damned rash, though I think it is better this morning. Yesterday it was so bad that I had to go & see a skin man here. I am sick, sick, sick of doctors, and when the kind & rather humble little skin specialist asked me for the details of my case history (as it was his duty to do) I was suddenly very rude to him: "Oh, my god!" I snapped. "I have had every illness under the sun!" He was too much surprised to write anything down after that except my name. I felt I should go mad if I had yet again to go over the dreary record of my neglected and ailing childhood and all that happened after. However I mean it when I say that I do not intend to give any real trouble—only somehow I simply cannot believe that it is me—John Hall who has to be reminded by the doctors that my lungs are badly damaged and that there are certain things that I must never again do in case the time should come when my luck did not hold, especially when I am run down & so on. The Professor who is in charge of M. & who came to see me, as I think I told you, & who heard the trouble in my chest when he listened, this professor was very frank, he gave me to understand that owing to my damaged lungs I should have less chance of recovery than any one with sound lungs given certain illnesses. It is no worse for me than for thousands of others, I am not saying it is, you are in precisely the same poor boat, my dear, but for so many years I have always been supposed to be the strong one, the sound one, the one who took care of people, & this being so I am finding it a really hard task to get used to things as they are. Dearest you will be waiting for me in Paris and later coming across to England for a bit. In Paris we will have our quiet talk—and it must be quiet this time. I expect you have been turning everything over in your mind, weighing it all up as I asked you to do, and I am prepared for anything that you may have to say to me about your papers. I am praying that I shall be able to work again some day soon—that will help. I still crave my cigarettes unfortunately but surely that must wear off in time?

Your John.

Oh, Piggie, my heart is so terribly heavey sometimes when I think of you and of all that might have been. No—no—I have not written that, please don't take it up angerally when you answer this letter.

[Florence]

July 17th 1939

Darling. Two depressed letters from you, the one of 13th and now and this this morning—I don't know what it means but expect that I shall do so when I see you in Paris. Sometimes I also am depressed—I get such a sense of failiour, but I must not give into this, fatal simply! I am so glad that you went to the review—I knew that you would be longing to see it, and it seems that you did so in the best possible conditions, & that has given me real pleasure, Piggie. Darling I am not arriving at 8^{oc} on 21st but at 9.10 according to the Florence American Express. Why do you say 8^{oc} when I took the trouble to send you a registered letter telling you the exact hour—don't you read my letters? But I know there is a difference in time between France & Italy—I think one hour. Has that muddled you perhaps? My dearest, I shall be on the Rome Express that leaves Florence at 2.20 on July 20th, you had better verify for yourself the hour that the train arrives in Paris the next morning. They told me here: 9.10—but whether they meant French or Italian time I do not know—better find out.

Cousin Bessie[1] was buried this morning—I went to the house & then to funeral—very sad somehow to see her little coffin in her own sittingroom. But saddest of all the old, old dog whom she has left behind—I cried quite a lot and am not ashamed to admit it. Maybe you will write to me again just once—a letter that I will get on 19th. This will be my last to you before we meet in Paris, and meet in Peace & quietness of spirits as we must these days—I shall be on the look out for you as the train draws in at the station. If the union of the French & English flags made you feel sad because of me, I suppose that is because you are unhappy about something. Never mind, you shall tell me all about it when we meet—until then—

Your John, & God bless & keep you—

PS I may write one more letter. perhaps—

1. One of Una's Tealdi cousins, whom she had known since childhood.

John and Una left Florence in July, intending to sell the Forecastle in Rye and move permanently to Florence. The outbreak of war in September of course changed all such plans. On their way to England they stopped in Paris and on August 4 arrived in Rye with Souline. After the declaration of war, they still hoped to return to Italy for health reasons, believing that Italy would remain neutral. In November they sold the Forecastle and went (temporarily, they thought) to Lynton, a city in Devon on the West Coast of England. Souline, as a stateless alien and therefore under severe restrictions of movement, was restless and very unhappy. She wanted to get back to France, but in the interim sought work at various occupations, initially as a nurse with the Red Cross, then (unsuccessfully) with the BBC doing war work monitoring radio transmissions, and finally in some highly secret government war work.

1940–41

The letters of 1940 reflect primarily John's long battle against illness, with the dangers and rigors of wartime privations added to that battle. In the first months of the year, she was bedridden with a severe bout of influenza, for which she was treated in London. The war news continued to worry her.

[no letterhead]

<u>Tuesday</u> March 3rd 1940

My darling heart. Your letter has come & I have sent you a telegram about coming up. Saturday would really not be worthwhile, tiring very for you and fussy for me. Sunday <u>no, no, no</u>—always, even in peace time, fearful delay in trains and my hairdresser has just informed me that he tried Sunday trains last week—was all but crushed to death by the troops who get weekend leave—no heat in train & late of course, quite fearful. I could not bear the thought for you & would only worry myself sick. Again, I have looked up the trains & of course the 7 something in morning (3rd class only) is out of the question. The later trains would hardly arrive in time for lunch in view of delays, and then the getting back—oh, no, darling. Now this is what I want you to do: I want you to come up by your usual morning train (8. something) on <u>Friday, March 13th</u>, that is Friday week. I want you to stay until the Monday please. This is the 3 nights you yourself suggested and it may be my last chance of seeing you before we meet at Lynton for Easter. This arrangement will give you Friday to shop, and will also give me time with you & I shall not feel rushed which tires & worries me just now. I am engaging a room for you at once in case I cannot get one nearer the time—we are full up. On this week as ever is [?] depends a

227

great deal for me—I am hoping to see Gillies[1] and hear his verdict about my eyelid—his will surely be the last word, or rather he is my last hope as I cannot get to the great Swiss or Austrians. As for my lungs, I am much put out by the fact that on last Saturday evening that aching started in the left lung, & since then, occasional aching, stabbings, & so on, also on two occasions a <u>slight pain</u> when I drew a deep breath. I agree with the doctor that it is muscular and sometimes the scar tissue left by the pleurisy, but Dawson[2] will decide; anyhow I feel sure it is not important only a bore. Today for the first time it is really warmer and I think I may be able to go along and have a bath. No, I have not had a real bath yet only blanket baths. Well R.C. P of mine I shall see you on Friday week—a long time to wait that seems but it can't be helped & I shall look forward to plenty of time together & no feeling of rush. I hope you have written for your room to Mrs Weedon[3]—Have you? please let me know—probably I shall have to help you out with your cloths, I forgot to say this in earlier letters. The best shop anywhere happens to be in Brompton Road a stone's throw from here—Giols and Beaumont.

God bless you, & thank you for going to church for me. Until Friday week then———

Your John.

[The Imperial Hotel, Lynton, Devon.]
April 10th 1940

Darling Piggeryroon. I am very "low in my mind" today, not liking the news and all this fearful uncertainty, so my letter won't be very interesting I am afraid. We lunched at Dulverton and saw a much more attractive hotel there [than] the Canarvon Arms—the Canarvon Arms is really too far from the town—two miles—& yet is not attractively situated in lovely country. The hotel we discovered in the town (really a villiage) is The . . . . . even Una cannot remember its name at the moment—it has a nice garden, nice rooms & is run by a nice woman, a lady. She has written making good terms, but we are very comfortable here & the

---

1. Sir Harold Gillies, an eminent eye specialist in London.
2. Lord Dawson, the King's physician.
3. Mrs. Widdon owned the house in Lynton from which John had rented lodgings for Souline.

cooking is satisfactory, also I do like being back in Lynton. It is fearfully cold & a cutting wind—at least five degrees colder here than Exeter,[1] but the air is like champagne (iced champagne!) All last evening & a part of this afternoon I have been unpacking—the bedroom here is big and has plenty of putting away room, thank the Lord; also my little sitting room is not bad & has all the afternoon sun. Dr Staniton, my faithful friend—vet of many years, writes to say that he will go personally & fetch Fido,[2] nothing could possibly be better. I dread the quaranteen for the dog but think now that all hopes of joining him have vanished, the more England is hard put to it to win the war—and win it we shall—the stricter will they become about money leaving the country, and everyone thinks as I do about this, so the dog had better take his chance of keeping fit during the unhappy 6 months quaranteen. I have heard that the quaranteen kennels at Taunton[3] are good—Staniton writes this, so it had better be Taunton. I have asked the hotel here & am told that the Babington[4] will go on for about another month, but why don't you write to one of your Babington pals and make sure?

There are only a very few people about the town, & hardly anyone in this hotel. Tomorrow I am going to Barnstable[5] to the tailor. Remember not to break into that £20 I left with you for anything except the necessity of joining me or some other war-emergency, I am anxious that you keep it by you. About the flats we saw, yes charming, but don't for heaven's sake let yourself in for one of them, the times are growing more uncertain every hour and you are well enough were [where] you are for the moment, anyhow this is my advise.

Your John

[Lynton letterhead]

April 14th 1940

My Piggie. I have your letter of 12th which reached me yesterday. This letter that I now write will not go off today there being no post here on Sunday either in or out. Last night they gave me a very fine bit of news

---

1. The principal town in Devon, about forty miles from Lynton. Souline was living in Exeter at this time.
2. The large white poodle John had bought in Florence.
3. A country town in Somersetshire, about twenty miles from Lynton.
4. Presumably a county festival.
5. The largest town near Lynton, about ten miles away.

at 10–15. It is not in todays papers as it must have come throug[h] too late for the press—Our Navy has done another extraordinarily courageous thing off the coast of Norway and has sunk 7 German destroyers, went and dug them out of hiding & killed off 4 at once, then 3 ran away into a narrow slip of water round the corner, as it were, but we followed & killed them also. And your namesake was there, the Cossack, and well to the fore again—she destroyed one of the heavey costal batteries. It is all terrible & likely to get more so, and when one stops to think of war one is sick at heart, and yet when one reads of such courage and selflessness—risking all for ones country one has to admit that even out of the horrors of war God is able to bring gleams of fineness & beauty, at least that is how I feel about it. Such a pity that the Germans are such dirty fighters—dashing about everywhere with aeroplanes trying to machine gun or bomb poor Harkon & his family,[1] no, really they are too hopeless—don't laugh darling when I say that it seems to me to be very ill bred. My new suit is grey, that is if I can get the material, I am waiting to hear from the tailor—no it is not a dark gray, rather a nice bluish colour. I should rather have liked to see "Women"[2] myself, did you see it as a play or as a film? My work: I have not yet actually started, but I took the bit between my teeth and bought myself a desk in Barnstaple—not a new desk but, of course, not a priceless antique. I have a nice, bright little room to work in here but they simply could not produce an adequate writing table of any kind, though this management is awfully willing and considerate. I really have no news of any personal kind, I think this air is going to do me good though the wind never stops blowing & is as cold as midwinter. Dear Piggie how are you? Truthfully now—how is that cough? Piggie please get to love England very, very much—it is my sincere wish that you should do so, and your doing so would give me such deep pleasure. And did I give you the £1 — 1 — for the three weeks heating up to the end of this month? I think I remember doing so, but let me hear from you about this.

God keep you R.C.P. in these dangerous days.

Your John

---

1. Unidentified—perhaps the King of Norway, Haakon VII.
2. There are so many works by this title that it is impossible to know which is here referred to.

[Lynton stationery]

April 17th 1940

My darling. I wrote yesterday telling you of course to come on Friday—I have taken a room for you already. And for heavens sake bring your mac and wear your heavey brown overcoat—yesterday it snowed nearly all day and today is bitter cold though fine. I am going out riding in a few minutes.[1] Dearest R.C.P. I am very glad that I shall see your face again so soon, and glad to hear that you are well—no cough. I have no news of any kind—I also am well though worried as is everyone else that I meet. I do not like the Italian news much. Nino[2] has written a loving but rather heart broken letter—whatever happens I shall not cease to feel an affection for my friends who are certainly very far from being Pro German!

No more now. When are you arriving please? I want to meet the bus.

Your John

Lynton.

April 23rd 1940
(St. George's Day—"Saint George for Merry England!")

My darling R.C.P. I have your postcard. And now let me say what a very happy weekend I had—I shall, I think, remember it. The French transit visa: as you say it does seem like an irony, but I have a very strong instinct, oh, so strong, that we are being taken care of and guided, and that it would not have been right or safe for us to go abroad—especially do I feel this about you—Every day now every country (if one may believe the B.B.C.) is making it harder & harder for the foreigners within its gates—even though long a resident. In some countries they are refusing to grant extensions of visas when same become due, and of course the question of sending money out of England to anyone who is not English is almost, if not quite, impossible, indeed it really is impossible. Suppose you had gone out of England at the beginning of the war—where should we be now? I ask you. I could not have got money to you, & I would not be permitted to draw enough money (had I joined you) for all of us to live on—a nice state of affairs. Well, my Pig here

---

1. John and Una had resumed riding on the Devon moors, the one form of outdoor exercise John's doctors recommended.
2. Husband of Sandra Tealdi and one of Una's cousins.

you are in my dear country & for that I do thank God, and perhaps one day it may also be your country, who knows? So many almost unheard of things have happened re. your visa & the Nansen—(unheard of because we are at war) that I see no reason why you should not eventually be English.

Winston Churchill who should have spoken at the Great St George's League luncheon excused himself on the plea of work and Duff Cooper spoke in his place—you know, the man we met that night on Lake Garda—Lady Dianna's husband.[1] He spoke magnificently, and I was wondering all the time whether you also were listening in & hoping that you were. I have no news except that I have seen a girl who may do for my typist—I am going to try her on Thursday, she is the one that nice young woman at the post office told me of—what luck if she turns up to be trumps.[2]

I enclose a draft of the kind of letter you must send if you decide to return your badge.[3] Also under seperate cover is a card for sending with Liza's scarf if you decide to send it. There was air raid activity in Paris itself last night, do hope Liza will decide to take her mother and go to the country. Piggie please take care of yourself—these are not days in which to be ill—not even a little ill.

Your John.

P.S. Darling, if as you tell me, you only stayed when war broke out because you had promised me not to go in the event of war—then thank you. By so doing you save me fearful anxiety.

Lynton.

April 28th 1940

My darling. I wrote you such a hurried, scrappy letter yesterday but I had to go out into the country to a farm to look at a pony. Dorothea[1] is little short of a friend of cruelty when in a rage—it is all too long to go into at the moment but I shall never hire from her again and I only wish

---

1. Alfred Duff Cooper, Lord Norwich (1890–1954); British diplomat and cabinet minister, married to Lady Diana Manners, famous beauty and former actress.

2. A winner. The term is used in various card games. In bridge it is the suit the winning declarer designates as the superior suit.

3. Her nursing badge.

1. The owner of the livery stables from which John rented horses. John and Una were so disgusted that they bought their own ponies.

that I could buy all the poor beasts in her stable. Apart from what I myself <u>saw</u> and found out, I hear that it is well know[n] how disgracefully the horses are treated, overworked, neglected and underfed—worked with sore backs etc. When we meet I will tell you all about it. Of course yes, yes my Piggie you are to spend all your summer holiday with me—it was you who said when we lunched together in Exeter that you might like to spend a part of the summer with Iris. I think though now that Cornwall[2] or at least a lot of it is prohibited to alians, though doubtless you could get permission to go there, but it would take time & be a great fuss. I think we had all better spend the summer here in Lynton. Dearest I am enclosing a cutting about these forbidden areas for alians—everything is being tightened up as I knew it would be—I remembered the last war. Meanwhile I am hoping to get a list of the places from our police serjeant as I told you, but so far it has not come to hand. However, I think there will be enough of England left for one R.C.P. & Johnnie to move about in. All the same I am jolly glad that Exeter and Lynton are O.K., what a bore if they had not been. In your place I would rather go constantly to the police (worry them in fact) than make any kind of slip—you will find that everyone will get nervy and irritable as the days go on, including even our sainted police! The feeling against socialists etc. is beginning to run very high, and that pleases me because I mistrust them. The Norwegian news is none too good[3] but I am not really anxious—we always win in the end—its a way we have. I send you a cheque for £26—8—that is £25 for May & £1.8—being 7/—a week for heating. I am so glad that you have decided to send back your badge, much better so I feel. And now you are free to go to the University. Darling I am not going to see Fido for a week or two, not until he has had time to settle down, & then I shall go in the middle of the week; end of the week the worst time to go to kennels, the kennelman might have time off & so on. Again it may be a forbidden area for you—Taunton, I don't know. Now please no Russian Blues over these forbidden areas—as I told you some areas are forbidden to the English. You are immencely well protected thanks to the Home Office, and as you are in every way desirable you have nothing to fear. Una opened the enclosed letter of yours by mistake—she asks me to say

2. The southwesternmost county of England. Its naval importance made it strategically critical and therefore particularly off-limits and dangerous for civilians.
3. After initial successes, the English navy was sustaining heavy losses in the Norwegian campaign.

how sorry she is, but says that her name was more visible on the envelope than yours—the letter seems to have been half round England! Again I say, darling, that I will only go where you can be, so feel reassured about that. No post out today also.

Your John

[Lynton]

May 3rd 1940

My darling. I <u>am</u> so glad that you have sent back the nursing badge, I agree with your having done this, indeed I earnestly wished you to do it, and now you will feel much freer & so shall I. I am glad too that you have written to Iris & shall love to see your Chink face again, yes I shall. The weather today is lovely & I do hope it will be fine while you are here. We will have some long, long walks together. I have no news, everything & everyone is very quiet here, in fact, at the moment, we are the only people in the hotel, but I don't mind this as I have work to do. Anyhow I much love this place as you know. The war news is not good but we shall win in the end without a doubt. Our Italian friends are not answering our postcards or letters, even Isobel has not written, I am inclined to think that all letters to England are being held up in Italy—I sometimes think sadly of those dear people whom I appear to have lost, but it can't be helped so thats that. Una is beginning to have very serious doubts, but still hopes that Italy will not come in against us.[1] The whole thing is such an awful muddle—

Bless you, I must go for a walk while the sun is shining.

Your John

There are no letters between May 1940 and July 31, 1941, because all three lived once again in very close proximity. On June 11, 1940, the prospect of returning to Italy was irrevocably cut off. In that same month France fell to the German army, and Souline was therefore cut off from a return to Paris. She moved into lodgings at Mrs. Widdon's in Lynton, while John and Una took rooms at a cottage called The Wayside, owned by a couple named Hancock. It was not a happy move, as Souline had only part-time work as a French tutor and deeply resented

---

1. Italy declared war against the Allies on June 10, 1940.

her confinement in the semi-retirement of Lynton. She and John quar-
reled frequently and John was often in tears. By August of 1941 John
was in Bath for the painful (and unsuccessful) eye surgery that had been
looming for at least a year. She was never to be really well again.

The Wayside. Lee Road
Lynton

July 31st 1941

My dear Evguenia. As you know, when I obtained for you an unconditional visa, I gave certain important guarantees regarding you to the
Secretary of State, becomming your guarantor, or as they now call it I
am told, your "referee." In view of all this I understand that before you
could obtain police permission to go into another county for a short
holiday without me, I would have to write giving my consent to the
police for you to do so. It appears, however, that this is not necessary as
you have received permission without it. All the same I would like you
to have with you some definate proof that I am your referee, and so I
send you this letter which do not hesitate to show to the authoroties
should occasion arise. I do hope you will have a nice holiday and am so
glad that you are able to have a complete change as you have been here
without moving for so long now. Of course I am rather anxious at your
leaving my protection even for a short time these dangerous days, but I
do feel that you badly need a change.

    Yours affectly

Radclyffe Hall

[Stationery from Francis Hotel, Bath]

August 22nd 1941

Piggie darling. I am writing in bed where I am going to remain for
breakfast as I am resting all I can and enjoying feeling that by doing so I
am not putting an extra burden on anyone. The servants here are nice &
very willing, accustomed to slugs as am I at the moment, this being a
great cure place as you know. The hotel is really very comfortable if a
little old fashioned & the food is good & plentiful enough, I am able to
save some for Jane[1] & now the chef is helping me out—she is well. I

---

    1. One of John's dogs.

am wanting to bring you back 4 pairs of lyle [lisle] thread stockings as a present, the shops here are first class. But before I can buy them you will have to send me 8 coupons.[2] These must, of course, be sent by <u>Registered Post.</u> I do not know if you can afford the 8 coupons but should think you can and stockings you must have. You know, don't you, that as soon as the present coupons are finished you can now take the empty book to Post Office and get forty odd new coupons, but this new lot will have to last for 12 months from the day they are given to you. If you want the stockings send me the coupons by return please, darling.

I saw the occulist, Tizzard, yesterday. He finds my lids: "very, very soar," and yes, they are. He of course examined the upper lids & saw the dry, gritty catarrh, also the lower lids & saw the spasam. He tells me that my only hope of a cure is an operation to lower lids, this he considers would cure the spasam, and probably the dry catarrh, though I do not think he can guarantee the latter, however it would certainly improve it. The operation: it would mean nursing home and bandaged eyes for 5 days. At the end of about 1 week the stitches are removed and I could leave the home, but not Bath; I would have to stay on here for all of another week to be watched by Tizzard for any tendancy of the scars to break down etc. He advises me to be operated on at once, if I consent to the operation, as Hitler is quietish at the moment but, or so Tizzard fears, will presently try to Blitz us to hell! I cannot make up my mind to have bandaged eyes, be in fact, totally helpless for a week and on my back at such a time—it would take a bit of doing. I am so active a person that I don't think I could face it. I should feel like my V.C. patient at St. Thomas' last war who said that he did not care for the feeling of being in bed unable to move when he heard things exploding! It is certainly an unpropitious moment. T. has given me a lotion for daily use & says I may strap my lids down etc, but no hope of a cure except by operation. I cannot make up my mind. If it were a case of saving me from blindness there would be no question of course—Oh, I don't know what to do.

The weather is fine on the whole but with occasional violent downpours. Went to Tizzard in sunshine so minus overcoat or umbrella, had to get them to ring up taxi for me or get drenched to skin going home. No more now as I must get up, go out & do some necessary shopping.

Your John.

2. System for rationing goods in wartime.

PS Never saw anything so terrible and so sad as Bristol—no never—
God help this stricken world.[3]

*In September of 1941 John underwent eye surgery in Bath. Unable to
read or write on her own, Una became her contact with the outside
world, including Souline. The letters from Bath were initially dictated by
John to Una. Editorial superscripts indicate which letters are in Una's
handwriting, which in John's.*

[Francis Hotel stationery, Una's handwriting]

11. 9. 41

Darling your letter of the 10th came this morning. I am terribly sorry
about the dog[1] and think it was caused by her letting him walk about in
the rain as I saw many times, probably did not realise that she shd have
dried him carefully every time the way we do. Poor foolish old woman,
I'm afraid the dog will die. I am glad to be back at the hotel pending my
second operation, or rather, I think I may say my third, but our room
into which we have been moved is much smaller than the other & after
a bit we are to be turned out of this one it seems & shoved up to the 3rd
floor. The housing conditions in Bath are incredible owing to the fact
that there are about 17000 people over & above usual number in the
town—this is owing to government ministries being here, including a
bit of the Admiralty. One thing is certain. I shall not be able to leave
immediately after my second operation, even if, as I hope, it goes off
normally. They will either have to keep me at the home until Tizzard
says go, or let me come back here—we cannot be turned out to sleep on
park benches. All an awful bother, but after all there is a war. My eye:
after having seen it 4 days ago (a nasty sight I thought) I had a good
look at it again this morning & for the first time I think) almost dare to
hope that there will not be any hideous distortion. The only swelling
now remaining, or at all events the only marked swelling, is a large
blackish pea in the corner by the nose. The dip in middle of lower lid
seems to have straightened out & the eyeball is clearing fast. Of course

---

3. Bristol is the major commercial city in the West of England, Avonshire. It had been
bombed heavily.
1. Mrs. Widdon's dog San.

the lid is very red rimmed & the scars still show a bit but if I escape the feared distortion after the haemorrhage I do thank God. Anyhow there was nothing disgusting looking about my eye this morning. I may tell you that it was so awful after the operation & haemorrhage that even the nurses flinched, they tell me. However, on all hands I hear Tizzard very highly spoken of and if he has saved his muttons over this very troublesome eye (that is to be decided in 2 weeks) he shall have the honour of carving R.H's right eyelid. My love to you, my dear.

Your John [John's signature]

[Bath stationery, Una's handwriting]

19. 9. 41

Darling, this answers two letters of yours. The one of yesterday: I really am both delighted and impressed by the news that the jobs you coached for Oxford passed in your subject, namely in French. I do feel that this shows that your coaching, or perhaps your method must have been first class because we English are known to be the worst linguists in the world—congratulations. Today's letter: I dont know why you did not get a letter from me yesterday unless I posted too late for the country post the evening before last. I think I did, anyhow either Una or myself have written every day. My eye was unbandaged yesterday as I expect you know by now. There is still swelling in the extreme corner, slight discolouration & redness of the lower lid & scar tissue, all of which I am assured will pass. There are times when my eye feels so well that I forget the operation, at other times it feels most disagreeable—not pain, but a kind of intensely sensitive, shriekingly nervy feeling, but on the whole I think I have cause to be very grateful that after all I look like having a sound eye in the end. The other eye is to be operated on as I told you yesterday on Sept: 30th, I go into the home the day before. Please light millions of candles and pray billions of prayers that this time I shall avoid the haemorrhage or any other complications.

The weather here was lovely yesterday but not so nice today. Our little Jane is on my lap as Una writes & sends you much love she also sends sympathy over San's illness.

By the way is he dead yet?

Your John [John's signature]

[Bath stationery, Una's handwriting]

25. 9. 41

Darling. I got your letter of 24th this morning. I don't really mind about not going to cinemas & so on as I really do want to rest up before Tuesday. By the way, send yr Monday letter to:
Church Street Nursing Home
8 Upper Church Street
Bath.
Somehow I have not once sat out in the garden at Lady de Blaquiere's[1] though she has begged me to do so, her house is rather a tiring walk from here but the garden lovely when you get there. I think I adore this muggy Bath climate but am told that it is not at all good for the chest as it is very damp in the winter. Last night we had what was called a fire drill in this hotel, two old gentlemen priests suffering from rheumatoid arthritis tried to work a stirrup pump on our landing but without success, the pump screeched like a siren & that was all that happened. I said that I thought an enema or a stomach pump would be more useful for incendiary bombs! Today we have had a call, it seems, from an infuriated inspector who complains that we cannot get at the gas meter to turn off the gas in the cellar because of the rows of live juice bottles!! It really was a ludicrous performance & I laughed so much at what I heard going on outside the door that my nurse had to stop washing my eye. My eye is making very good progress indeed,
[penciled by John] Bless you

Your John

By late autumn Souline had refused to accept John's terms concerning her residence and close supervision. She had moved to Oxford, more than sixty miles and two counties away from Lynton. Never again would she consent to live near John and Una.

Nov. 7th 1941

Evguenia. Regarding any future plans that you may have in mind I shall be willing to discuss these with you when I am feeling better, but I may

---

1. Marie Lucienne Henriette Adine, OBE, daughter of George Desbarats of Montreal. She lived at 8 The Circus, Bath.

say that your new friends and your political views are both highly objectionable to me, also I wonder whether you have fully realized the extreme beastliness of taking advantage of my operations to renew your friendship with people whom you well know I asked you to drop. But this, no doubt, is a matter of sentiment and sentiment does not enter into your calculations, it seems.

But one thing is left to me in self defense, & that you have forced me regretfully to use. This evening you quite deliberately and with full medical knowledge of the state of my heart,[1] did your utmost to make a scene, & then to force upon me your schemes for Oxford, thus causing me anxiety & worry within 48 hours of my having had an attack, and all this with the most unexpected suddeness and with an obvious wish to make me ill. This being so when your next month's allowance comes due on Dec 1st it will be less by £5. I regret having to resort to such a method.

Radclyffe Hall

[Bath stationery]

Dec. 1st 1941

Darling. Firstly I can read your letters myself & I do, but I am not supposed to write. My appointments are now made in London & I want you to come to me for the day on Tuesday Dec 9th or Wednesday Dec 10th. Catch the earliest train you can & taxie straight to the Rembrant Hotel where I am going to stay—I shall await you there. Go on receipt of this & find out trains for December, then send me a wire here to Bath as to hour your train arrives which will give me some sort of idea when you should reach my hotel, also whether you come Tuesday or Wednesday. I will pay journey & taxies. Enclosed find stamped telegraph form for reply. Also I send cheque for £5.2.0. being £3 for riding, £1–8– for December heating & 14/— for the two weeks you were in Oxford prior to Dec 1st. The usual price I have been asked in rooms for coal is 6d per scuttle. Curiously enough I was going over expenses the other day & find that Mrs Hancock charges 18/6 a month for an all day fire (coal) which works out round 4/6 per week, and coal is supposed to be

---

1. Although there is no specific evidence of heart attacks or heart problems at this time, John did have an enlarged aorta, had been ordered to moderate emotional responses, and had already begun to experience a general (and total) health breakdown.

extra expensive in Lynton because of transport. Surely as you are making a prolonged stay Mrs Dare would make a concession? 1/— a scuttle is really unusually dear <u>for rooms</u>. I have a note in my diary that the Crown Hotel of Lynton would have charged me 6^d a scuttle & that is an hotel not lodgings—am afraid you will find Oxford very dear if everything is on this scale. Here it has turned very cold but we have a gass fire with a slot meter in the bedroom—am surprised you have not the same.

I dare write no more.

Your John. [letter written in pencil]

[Hotel Rembrandt stationery—London]

Dec. 12th 1941

Darling. Thank you for your letter written on train. I saw Dawson yesterday and here is the report. 1) He made a very through examination of my lungs, (he is considered the greatest expert in England) He heard the damaged places immediately and of course the plurisy damage to both bases and consequent lack of expansion, he also says that the expansion is uneven, being more curtailed on right side, it seems. Heart: 2) He considers that I could safely take a general anaesthetic but says that the eye man is sure to want to use a local. 3) Generally: He wishes me to imploy an eye surgeon in whom he has great faith, namely Williamson Noble, but he insists that before the eye is opened up yet again, my teeth must be X Rayed. He contends that it might be dangerous if there were any infected upper teeth as this might set up sepsis in wound & I think he is very right so this morning I am going to have all teeth X Rayed, Dawson will then examine the plates & decide what must be done. I have an appointment with eye surgeon for today week but when he can begin to carve me up will, I understand, depend on the teeth. Re. my general health: he says that although my blood pressure is not too bad, it is of the kind that would almost certainly rush up under strain or long hours of intensive work such as I have done in the past. This being so I must try to save myself as much as possible, & if I work through the whole of one night I must remain in bed doing nothing during the next day and not work again even on the following day. He tells me that he fears the blood pressure not going down after work if I strain myself too much at my age, in this event it would remain at a <u>fixed</u> high level which might be dangerous. Am I merry & bright? I <u>don't</u>

think! Worried over my work and wondering whether it will ever be possible to obey rules & produce inspirational work as in the good days. Well, that's all, I will keep you posted (if you wish) re. all developements. God bless & keep you in these very grave & dangerous times.

Your John.

1942

1942 is the last year of the letters to Souline, many of them dictated by John and in Una's handwriting. The winter of 1941–42 proved disastrous for John's health. For several months she lay near death in the London Clinic, first with severe bronchitis, followed by pleurisy and then double pneumonia. Her teeth abcessed and many had to be extracted. Her eyelids continued to plague her. Finally in mid-April she was allowed to return to Lynton to complete her convalescence.

[Hotel Rembrandt stationery]

Sunday. Feb 22nd 1942

My very dear. Having had an enormous blanket bath then dressed & got up I am rather tired so only a few lines. Days ago the doctor said I might go alone to the bath room, but no sooner had he said it than he unsaid it because of the bitter cold which still persists—I am tired of the cold & of these four walls, but please observe that I am writing much better and in ink! Tomorrow I shall send off your cheque dated for March 1st. Una will have signed it as I am asking her to continue with the power of Attorney as I simply could not attend to business just yet. God bless you, and thank you for your prayers & the candles, and do not let go of my hand.

Your John

February 26th 1942.

My darling. I really am longing to see you again but next week is impossible as all appointments are waiting to be filled in like a boring jigsaw puzzle—I have decided to consult Gillies about my eye—as Duke

Ellton and Lord Dawson's Williamson Noble completely disagree, as
you know but I will remind you. Noble is anxious for me to see Gillies
who (I think) is to come & see me here in my room next Friday. From
Duke Elder, you see, I heard that there was real danger to the eye itself
if this condition goes on & an operation is neglected, but from Noble I
hear that the operation on tissues damaged by Tizzard: "Tizzard's mess"
is very dangerous & that he will not undertake it, so now for a plastic
surgeon! Then next week comes Lord D. to give an opinion as to when
four more teeth may be taken out, also as to the origin of certain sounds
that persist in left lung but which the G.P. considers in no way serious—
Lord D will also say, when he has examined me, when I can go downstairs, or at least I hope so. If he consents I shall have the teeth out next
week, all of which explains why I do not want to waste a visit from you
by these uncertainties & miseries—so I think you must come week after
next, but will arrange all later.

Meanwhile <u>please send</u> the sweets as I enjoy them so much, dear
heart, and thank you for giving me your share, but should you not keep
1/4 lb. for R.C.P? No chocolates to be had today, but some soon I hope.
Must stop as I am not very fit & feel like a limp rag today—

Your John

Excuse bad writing, spelling & general mess.

March 27th 1942

My darling R.C.P. You are quite right, of course, about my trying to do
a little more every day in prepairation for the long home-journey. I was
just saying this very thing when your letter arrived. I am now (weather
permitting) going for a drive every early afternoon, or during the morning. Yesterday I took Una to some shops but remained in the car myself.
Today I shall get out at Drews[1] myself as I want to see them about
putting a new strap to the cover of my dressing case, one of the straps
being just about to break. Every day a little progress towards normal life
again if only my damned out nurse will not keep on at me! But really
she is so good, self-sacrificing & devoted that I aught not to complain of
her, but she gets on my nerves, more shame to me! I enclose two
cutting[s] that you may not have seen & that may interest you. The wail

---

1. A fashionable luggage shop.

of the White Russians was in the Standard, the other in the Daily Sketch this morning. I am certain the Russian Colonel & Major are right up to a point,[2] but there is always England that must, at all costs, be protected and we have never pretended to having "<u>hugh</u> armies" However only the coming months or maybe even the coming weeks or days will show what is going to happen. Meanwhile I send the White Russian cutting so that you may see that you have companions in the boredom of this 10.30 curfew.

Listen though my dearest Piggie, these are very, very grave, uncertain and highly dangerous times for us all. The gravity of the moment simply <u>must be faced</u> by you as well as by every soul on this island. Anything may happen at any moment now, have you realized this? The government has spoken in very clear terms. The debate in the House of Lords has clearly set forth what will happen if the German's attempt an invasion—laws are already passed that would be brought into action immediately, & one of the first of these terrible but most necessary laws would be the virtual stopping of all transport[3]—but no doubt you have read it all for yourself. It is war and to the death so I feel that we must not grumble, but what we must do, absolutely, is to use our common sense & face up to stark facts. We cannot expect Russia to keep us safe forever & so our government expects us to be prepared for an invasion (which may never come, but which <u>may come</u>, make no mistake.)

Well, I must now stop & get up and dress & potter downstairs for one hour before lunch, then an early lunch & out for a drive.

God bless & bless you & keep you

Your John.

[Hotel Rembrandt stationery]

April 6th 1942

Evguenia. This is being written after quiet consideration, and I hope that you also have been considering the position. I tried, as much as you would let me speak, to point out certain hard truths and causes that you would have for anxiety. If you really mean to pursue this very wrong

2. The exact reference is unclear, but there had been serious complaints about military assistance to the Soviet regime.

3. England had every reason to prepare for invasion, as the intense bombing raids of 1941 and 1942, as well as intelligence reports, indicated.

course at such a time then I cannot fully contribute to what I consider to be for your ill & in no way for your good. I repeat what I said in case in the heat of the moment you may have failed to understand it. I want you to take up residence again in the <u>same county as I am in</u>. Not in the same town—I do not insist on that—but in the same county, and upon your agreeing to this perfectly correct and natural wish of mine depends your allowance. I am not prepared to give you £250 a year with which to harm yourself, that I am adamant about. But because of the great fondness I have felt for you I do not wish to feel that you are entirely deserted at such a time, even though you would have brought this on yourself.

Therefore: I am prepared as from the first of May to allow you £100 a year (supposing that nothing in the nature of a financial disaster occurs) but this allowance of £100 a year will be entirely dependant upon you always letting me know <u>honestly</u> your address—the cheque will be sent to you on the first of every month as heretofore, but only if you agree to give me immediately any change of address. The alternative to this is—no address no cheque, or 2) that you will come & domicile & find work in my county when the allowance will be paid at the old rate. I shall be glad to hear from you immediately. If you are out when this letter arrives, please send your reply by another taxi which will, of course, be paid at this end.

John

<u>Please read carefully and keep for future reference</u>. [superscript]

The Wayside. Lynton.

April 11th 1942

I have your letter of April 10th, Evguenia. In it you say that you hope that I am your friend. I am and always have been your friend, patiently and faithfully I have remained your friend though again & again you have persisted in treating me as an enemy—God only knows why. And now you have forced me once more to make a clear statement regarding my carefully considered decisions, this in case you may think that I wrote to you in haste last Monday evening in London. In fairness to you and because I am indeed your true friend who have your wellfare at heart, (and who else is there in your life who stands as close to you as I do?) I am determined to do all that I can to protect you during this time of very real danger whether you want my protection or not, the point being that you need it, & any sane person would say that I am right.

I wish you, indeed I do most earnestly beg of you, once more to become resident in Devonshire, this for your own sake and also in order to lift some of the burdon of anxiety from off of a very sick woman. When I say resident in Devon I naturally rule out Plymouth & Dartmouth[1] or any other acute danger zone. Also I in no way insist upon Lynton as I have told you already. The point is simple, Evguenia: I want you to be resident in the county where I now must perforce be. I am not going into all the reasons for this yet again because I have explained them to you already, and because you must know that they are very sound & wise.

Here then is a clear setting forth of what I consider to be my duty, for I will not be a party to your exposing yourself to any unnecessary danger, to any probably avoidable danger at a time when so much danger is unavoidable in any case. I will not contribute to your risk, to a complete seperation from you in certain events, by supplying financial assistance. Therefore, 1.) On May 1st your allowance will be paid at the present rate of £250 a year free of income tax, and this will be done where ever you may be resident, provided I have your address. 2.) On June 1st if you are resident in Devon, either in a job here in Devon or unimployed, (always excluding the afore mentioned acute danger areas,) your allowance will be paid at the present rate & will (short of some unforseen disaster) continue at the rate of £250 per ann. provided that you remain in the same county as myself and always let me know any change of address. 3.) If on June 1st you are not resident in the county of Devon, either imployed or unimployed, then your allowance will be paid at the rate of £100 a year free of income tax, again provided you keep me regularly informed of your address or of any change of address permanant or even temporary. But please note that as from the day— whenever that may be, either upon or after June 1st—as from the day you return to being a resident in Devon, your allowance will be paid at the old rate of £250 a year.

And now I want to point out that whatever work you decide to take and where ever you decide to take it, you must be very careful to know

---

1. Two port cities on the English Channel, strategically important naval centers during the war.

what obligatons you are undertaking. For your own sake be more than careful not to get into anything that means that you are bound for the duration of the war. I cannot stress this point too gravely because from such binding contracts there is no appeal & no release, and the most severe penalties are imposed for failure to keep such contracts. As a foreigner you must make any employer explain everything clearly to you—you have a right to this. Also better not say, perhaps, as I have heard you say: "I want work for the duration of the war." "For the duraton" is what is said of the binding contracts I have referred to above.

I want you to write to me please, Evguenia, and I will continue to pay postage, and naturally I shall want to know about the Red X job. But do please remember that for you good sleeping accomodation is well nigh essential, and I am hearing on all sides that some of the accomodation provided is very bad indeed, for which one cannot blame the government who are struggling to cope with an unheard of situation, all the same no good to yourself or England if you ruin your health. Remember also that most real country cottages have no inside sanitation but only earth closets in the gardens, sometimes not near the cottage either, and in any case death traps in cold or wet weather unless one is accustomed to such primitive conditions; until quite recently the only closet at Edie Craig's was an earth closet. Then again heating is going to become worse & worse as time goes on. Above all bear in mind that when you agree to a salary, although £80 a year is so far free of income tax, every farthing you earn over & above that sum will be taxed, you will also have to contribute to the health insurance[2] though I cannot speak well of the doctors judging from what I have seen with my servants, and secretaries even. The care given is not that of the American Hospital or of Radclyffe Hall. Finally this question there has just been raised of your being a foreigner. Would it not save expense, time & possible irritation if, when writing about a job, you clearly stated that you are a Russian Refugee? I think it would. You should add however, that you are the posesser of an 'Unconditional Visa' & have become 'A Permanent Resident Alian.'

Am I not proving that I am your friend?

John

---

2. A payroll tax to subsidize medical care.

The Wayside. Lynton

[no date]

My dear Evguenia. I am now enclosing the long letter I wrote to you on 11th in answer to your note of 10th to me. I have been keeping this long letter back in order to give it yet more careful consideration from every point of view, and this because nothing must be done by either of us acting upon a hasty impulse at this time when death is always near. It was indeed this conviction of the wrongness of parting in anger that prompted me to call you up that Tuesday evening to say—as I now repeat—"Senza Rancor."[1] I had another reason for keeping the enclosed letter back: I have been hoping against hope that in view of everything you were willing to reside once more in Devon, but this hoped for letter has not arrived. You see I am now, God knows for how long, a virtual prisoner in this west country, and there are moments, I do confess, when I feel that this unhappy fact rejoices you, makes you feel on your part that you have succeeded in shaking me off at last—but then I simply will not allow myself to believe such a thing of you, no, I will not. When I say that I am become a prisoner here, I mean that Devon must be my war-time home if I want to save my lungs, & you too know this. Again I am not well enough to travel to you in present conditions if you needed me, but I think I could most certainly hope to reach you if you were in this county, and you could, in case of extreme need, reach me short of an actual invasion and perhaps even then. About your very natural wish to work, surely you will be able to find secretarial work in Devon while avoiding the one or two actual danger zones—I have no doubt of this, none. And the fact that you have made up your mind to go in for a secretarial job, that you yourself tell me that your shorthand is not yet up to the required speed, & moreover, in view of the fact that I see from advertisements in the newspapers that shorthand seems to be essential in nearly every decently paid position, I am prepared to pay in addition to your allowance of £250 a year, all fees for you to continue your studies in Exeter as follows: I will pay for you to take a business course at Exeter University—the course I have in mind would include typing & shorthand, the typing and shorthand being taught on behalf of the University by Mr W.L. Shortland of "Elmside Commercial College 54. Elmisde, Exeter. At the "Elmside Commercial

---

1. Without rancor.

College" you could be prepared for all or any of the exams in connection with serious secretarial work and could take a diploma; such a diploma is, of course, very much to be desired and should prove a great help when looking for work. Indeed I really make you two offers: 1) To take the business course at the University of Exeter which course would, as I have said, include typing and shorthand & an ultimate diploma if you passed your exams, and 2) if this does not appeal to you then simply to attend the "Elmside Commercial College", leaving the University out altogether. This could be done, you to be coached, if you wish, for the obtaining of the diploma. A good commercial training would be a fine background for all & any kind of secretarial work and later for a possible position of trust. Myself I rather incline to the University of Exeter course, but you would be free to decide whether you prefer suggestion no 1, or no 2. Of course these offers are subject to your taking work in Devon, or I should say, seeking for work in Devon. The work you have put in at Oxford would not be lost, on the contrary it should be a great help to you. This is a compromise that I feel you should be willing to accept. The Principal of the Commercial College is sending me the prospectus & this I will send on to you. I expect you already know a good deal about Exeter University courses, but particulars of this special "Business Course" could easily be obtained. I shall expect to hear from you.

Your friend John

PS You may feel that you are far enough advanced & need no more training, in which case come back to Devon & look for work—

The Wayside. Lynton.

Telephone. Lynton 2159
April 28th 1942

My dear Evguenia. Enclosed find cheque for your May allowance: £22.16.8. (including heating)

For the rest, I have received your letter of April 23rd which I have carefully read, and I have little to add to my last two letters except: 1) that I cannot believe that you are serious when you suggest that I, who am scarcely convalescent from months of illness including 3 operations on my eyelids, and who am trying to get strong enough for a fourth operation which even the great Gillies is not too keen on performing on my damaged tissues; who moreover am forbidden by Dawson to go out in the wind or, indeed, do anything tiring before I have the X Ray of my lungs sometime in June—that I can get out and look for & find a suitable secretarial job for you in Devon when you are perfectly capable of looking for work yourself—well its fantastic, thats all! The more so as you will be in posession of your full allowance from the day on which you resume residence in Devonshire. But I think, all the same that your idea of Barnstaple may very well be a good one and that there must be plenty of secretarial work to be had there. 2) That in view of the two nights heavy bombing of Exeter last week, I must now (at any rate for the present) add Exeter to the acute danger zones, mentioned in my previous letter, in which I cannot contribute to your living; it is therefore a good thing that you have no wish to study at the Elmhurst [Elmside] Commercial College. And 3) I forgot to say that naturally I will pay your travelling expenses should you decide to return to Devon.

Please acknowledge the receipt of this letter with cheque by return, and do not forget to let me know even a temporary change of address. Also please let me know what you intend to do before June 1st so that I may know the amount to send you for that month's allowance.

Your John

P.S These so called: "Reprisal" Raids are becomming very grave. Captain Spinks (air force ground staff) has just told us that he is still unable to ascertain, after 48 hours, whether his wife in Bath is alive or dead—— all communications are cut.

The Wayside.

Telephone: Lynton: 2159.
June 4th 1942

My dear. I was waiting to hear from you before sending a cheque. I now enclose £10.6.8, being one month's allowance at £100 a year and the usual £2—for heating, this latter I propose to pay you even during the summer as although we are having a heat wave today it will probably be arctic tomorrow. Thank you for being so clear about your address to which you are going on the 9th.:

And now about writing to me: I want you to write to me whenever you feel inclined, and I shall want to hear how you find this work & so on. But whether you feel inclined or not I am going to ask you to write always without fail towards the end of each month & in good time before your cheque is due as I cannot send a cheque these days without being absolutely certain of your whereabouts. A lost cheque gives such infinate trouble to banks & if one goes astray one has to stop it. Therefore even if you are still at the same address you must please write & say so as I shall take nothing for granted.

And now three questions that please answer when you acknowledge this letter. 1) Did you give me as referee to the War Office or any other office—the Red X for instance? I think you will naturally have done so but I would like to know this. 2.) What steps have you taken, or are you proposing to take, to make it quite fool-proof to your employers that (apart from being your referee etc.) I stand to you as "Next of Kin." in the event of illness or mishap or accident? 3) And are you still wearing the identity disk I gave you?

For myself: My convalescence has been somewhat retarded by the fact that I have "cracked" my ankle & am in a plaster case. It happened with great simplicity: I was taking the dogs out one morning two weeks ago & must have slipped on the front door step. I did not fall but felt myself stumble & then a big pain—Mrs Handcock who was there says that my foot slipped sideways off the step. This mishap has temporarily delayed all my plans—& I shall not be able to go to London when I had arranged to do so as the plaster case will be on another month or six weeks. Well I think thats all.

Your John

PS Money for postage to me. Have you any left? If not I will send some—let me know when answering this letter.

The Wayside.
[in pencil] Telephone Lynton 2159.
June 16th [1942]

Darling. This will be an untidy letter as I am writing on my lap in bed. I have caught a chill, but naturally with such a devilish change from tropical heat to almost winter cold—naturally I have caught a chill, and me hobbling about at a snail's pace (though I am pretty cleavor they think with my sticks) and still below par from that big illness & then the cracked ankle not helping either! But, blessed be God, the chill is in my tummie[1] and not on my unhappy chest, and so I expect I shall be much better tomorrow. Thank you for the p.c.[2] Yes, a splendid old English mansion, Elizabethan I judge from the chimneys—I forget the name of the Peerage to which the estate belongs. But do you know that Bramshill was the house chosen by Lucas Malet for the setting of her really great book: "The History of Sir Richard Calmady"?[3] Well it was. I read the really inspiring & reassuring news that all army practices this summer are to be carried out all over England with <u>live</u> ammination! So if on your rambles you should chance on one or more soldiers or home guards who look like being even remotely connected with manoeuvers you had better fly to cover. No, but seriously, everyone will have to be careful from now on—if one gets in the way having failed to see say a small red flag perhaps, well one may be shot or blown up & thats that. Also I read & hear on BBC. that there are to be no more rubber boots, or rubber soles & so—I am glad that you have rubber boots bought through <u>my</u> foresight, & I take the full credit for it. I suppose also no more raincoats or mackintoshs[e]s—no more anything quite soon! I am down on my luck, down hearted & have a kind of beaten feeling, but really I am never beaten which must be thanks to my north country blood; no, I shall rise up again into the full light of my talent. Consider: "The battle of The Well" as they called it—I came out of that bitter fight wounded but not too gravely so to prevent my writing: "The Master of the House" And may I live to write one more book—yes, please, God.

Your address at the cottage & telephone number of nearby house: Only one more detail—give me the name of the people with whom you are boarding. In an emergency the name of the cottage might not be enough, I want to be able to say to the people at the Hartley Wintney 180[4]—"May I speak to Miss Souline who is billeted with Mrs . . . . . at Inholmes." I presume they would go & fetch you, but I aught to have that name. May I, please? You are, and always have been, one of those who despise details, or forget details, or suddenly feel bored in the middle of giving them & thus leave out something important. If I am

---

1. This is the first indication in the letters to Souline of the cancer that was to cause John's death sixteen months later.

2. Souline had sent a postcard from Bramshill.

3. Lucas Malet was the pen name of Mary St. Leger Harrison, who died in 1931. The novel mentioned was published in 1901.

4. The telephone exchange in Oxford where Souline had moved.

over careful you are much too careless, yes, much! The day is grey & it rains from time to time—the war drags on & I with it. To turn to a more cheerful topic: I have seen the Weeden granddaughter, a lovely & amusing infant, Mrs Weedin is crazy about it. I have a feeling that the old thing would appreciate a card or perhaps a letter from you—You need not feel awquard with her as I have done what I considered correct & paid up for your full holiday as I understood it was to be,[5] this was only fair especially as she had offers for Easter. I paid her immediately after sending you the £1—No more as I am getting tired. All the same I think I am going to get up, I have had too much bed these last months and am growing to hate it.

Your John

The Wayside. Lynton.

June 27th 1942

Darling. I was so extremely glad to get your telegram yesterday & to know that all is in order & that you will arrive at Barnstaple Junction July 3rd at 3. p.m. I am motoring over to the station to meet you—all being well. Should anything unforseen happen to prevent my coming, you will find Bentall[1] waiting outside station, and this will also apply if there is difficulty in my getting to the platform as there may be—stairs to get across to the other side for instance. In such a case I will be waiting in the car. I have but little news—Una is up & about and able to go for walks even. It was only the beginnings of lead poisoning which thanks to Nightingale[2] we nipped in the bud, but she looked & felt awful. She will stay away in hospital for a few more days, just until all painting has ceased & the smell gone off. I think there must be something extra poisonous in this war-brand of paint because a house-painter, who has been at it for years, is now in the hospital so terribly lead poisoned that he is very ill indeed & Harper, the Barnstaple heart specialist had to be sent for yesterday. To add the last straw to the confusion, Jane has come into season & Fido (so good & chased [chaste]

---

5. Souline had arranged to spend her Easter holiday in Lynton, although she did not carry out those plans.

1. A local Lynton man whom John engaged for any errands requiring motoring. Gasoline was, of course, severely rationed and hence only certain errands of an absolutely necessary nature were allowed by local authorities.

2. The doctor in Lynton.

as a rule) has developed a ranting sex complex &, as he must surely know, much too soon. My old witch of a nurse gets on my nerves until I could scream, but I aught to be ashamed of myself as she is devoted to me and marvelous with the dogs, but oh, her face! her voice! her mind!!! Anyhow I'm damned sick & tired of being a crock, though I am putting on flesh & looking better I do think. Lynton is full to bursting again— not a bed to be had anywhere, but in this little house you will have a nice airy room—I am moving the old witch down to Fido's room which I fear you would find too hot because of the pipes. No more now as they want to set the table for lunch. How much was the telegram? But I will pay all when we meet.

Your John—

The Wayside. Lynton.

Telephone Lynton: 2159
July 13th 1942

My darling. Your letter of 10th telling of your safe arrival came by the first post this morning. The address you give is certainly not all it might be but better than nothing for the moment. But surely darling, your hostel or the B.B.C itself has a telephone number that I could use to get at you in a real & grave emergency? Only then would I use it, that goes without saying, but please send me the telephone number for emergancy all in case of illness; also where do I send you a telegram? These two things I feel that I aught to know. I expect that in the fuss of your arrival you forgot about them. Presently I expect you will have rooms of your own to which I can write or wire, but meanwhile I am quite certain that in the event of a grave emergency they would understand my telephoning you, & of course we all have a perfect right to telegraph. I should think that one of your fellow workers—say Miss Roberts, (Mr Roberts sister) could tell you what I want to know. It would be a relief to me if you could find rooms in a house where there was a telephone—try to when eventually you look for rooms. I expect your next letter will be more enlightening, and I quite understand this one being a bit distracted, especially as you cannot have even begun to learn the ropes yet having just arrived—never mind. Now about your work: Whatever you do don't get stage fright (as I see you are well on the way to doing) I am sure you can hold the job down as far as the brain part goes—health is the only thing you will have to consider & carefully. Your hearing: the blocking of your ears naturally gets tiresome if you get cold—even a little cold (I have not been plagued with you for over 8 years not to notice these things!) You are now living in a bad climate generally and also particularly (the Severn Valley) therefore, Piggie, don't be a fool. Don't get wet. You 'simply must' understand that a mackintosh & umbrella are almost a uniform in England, yet you arrived down here with neither! Will you try to grasp the fact that it may be fine when you start on a journey and a deluge when you arrive at your destination— really for an intelligent woman you seem pecularly stupid about this, a perfect fool-Pig, in fact. Your rain-coat can always be strapped around your dressing case or carried over your arm—and why are you the only woman who cannot carry an umbrella? No, I am not joking, I am deadly serious. I feel that all I write is in vain having actually had blood rows with you over this dozens of times, but I know you wish to keep fit for your new work and as I shall not see the stamping as you read this, I am warning you yet again. I have sent two letters and a telegram of good wishes for your new venture, but all have gone to Bramshill as arranged. As you do not mention the telegram I presume you have not received it—or the letters? Oh, well you have certainly succeeded in cutting yourself off from me. All the same, my dear, I do ask for a telephone number and how one gets a wire to you while you are still at the hostel, & I hardly think I am unreasonable or that anyone living would consider me so. And how will my letters reach you? One usually has to collect them one's self from a P.O. Box, but surely they will not expect you to do this if you are, as you say, 8 miles from anything? May I know this also as I would not like my letters to go astray. I am sure there must be some simple explanation of all this, but that you have not yet had time to find it out. No government office can exact a complete divorce from friends & relatives in these dreadful days, I refuse to believe it. But my poor little Piggie, if you will only be reasonably careful of yourself I am sure you need not be afraid of the work. What can I say or do except to beg you to remember that you are not alone in the world, that you must always promise to let me know if you are not well. My dear I am so different from you in nearly every way that I am getting to the stage when I do not expect you to understand how I feel about anything, especially about our being cut off at such a time. To me this is so awful that I, in your place, simply must have found out about telephone & telegrams, but I don't expect that this aspect even struck you for a moment! Anyhow I wish you all the best of luck and beg you to avoid colds for the sake of those poor ears to say nothing of all the rest.

On Tuesday July 21st I go to London, arriving some time in the afternoon—I must go (ridiculously) in an ambulance because I am still very lame & must not risk the trains, crowds etc, so Nightingale says, and indeed I am sure he is right. No hotel may now keep anyone for more than one week even with a doctor's certificate, and so I am driven to going to the London Clinic as a week is too short a time for all I have to do—lung X Ray & so on. Write to me at: London Clinic. Devonshire Place. London. W.1. from July 21st and after until further notice. Meanwhile any letters sent to Wayside will be forwarded of course. God bless you.

John

Oh, Piggie—do please take care of yourself.

[London Clinic stationery]

July 30th 1942

Darling. Enclosed find your August cheque. I had a beastly time yesterday because one place would not stop bleeding, dentist had to come 3 times! But it has been plugged & seems all right this morning. Naturally—as it never rains but it pours—we had a visit from our German pests last night again—very noisy once or twice, so get on ones slacks in case one was ordered down stairs. We were not, but everyone who can puts on something warm & decent. I hear on the BBC that the principal activity was your way—Got Una to ring up and ask if you were O.K. I did not think it advisable to bother anyone to get you to come to telephone as that was not strictly necessary, moreover I gathered the other morning that you leave for work before 8. a.m. and thought that it must remind you of the old American Hospital days. I hope you get that R.C.P. umbrella all right, and I have put a spell on it so that you dare not loose it. No, seriously, dear, you simply must be careful these days because what is lost can't be replaced more often than not. I am a little late with the cheque owing to dentist, X Rays & so on—you may not get it until after the first as there is a Bank Holiday. As I have told you, Dawson's secretary rang up to say that the X Rays are all right, from which I am certain that there is no T.B. fresh outbreak, the old scars have held. When I see Dawson he will tell me any differences, if any, between the Italian pictures & these new ones—I mean re. expansion & so on. No more now as I am supposed to be resting.

God Bless you & keep you safe in these unthinkably mad and dreadful days is the constant prayer of

Your John

The Wayside.

August 25. 1942

My darling R.C.P. Your letter of 23rd has greatly relieved my mind. Of course I was worried over the night work because I know that when nursing in Paris you were not allowed to do it by Fuller, nor aught you ever to do it if it can be avoided. Yesterday I rode old Tilbits[1] up to the moor, Dawson says I must try to get the pure air into my lungs before the winter. You would have laughed at my efforts to get on & off even with the block[2] to help me, my ankle is so weak and useless as yet, but if I take every possible precaution I am told that the exercise is good for the darned thing. I shall try to ride twice a week. You do not ask me about the final medical discussions re. your poor John but I expect you will want to know them—yes? Well then Dawson. He found the X. Rays O.K. nothing has started up again owing to the illness; this I have told you. But I had a final talk with him before leaving and his regime for me is really the bloody limit—I may not go out in a cold wind, in cold rain or snow—wind plus rain is particularly bad as it puts a double strain on my lungs—cold wind & rain of course. Can you beat it? I was going to take the A R.P. telephone again[3] but this has made all war work quite out of the question. I know what it is, in the ordinary way I should have been sent off to Switzerland after the plurisy, or at least to the south of France, especially in view of my T.B. scars, but this being out of the question the poor man has to do the best for me that he can. Well, Piggie, I have been an impatient woman all my life so no doubt this little purgatory will be for the good of my soul. But oh, oh, oh!!! I have lost a dear friend of many years—our Rev. Mother Abbess[4] died

---

1. A rented horse, not the one John had bought, whose name was Tommy.
2. A raised step for mounting a horse.
3. Air Raid Patrol.
4. The Wayside, where John and Una were living, was next door to a convent of Poor Clare sisters, to whom Una left the bulk of her estate.

yesterday morning, but thank God her really fearful suffering is over and she has undoubtedly gone to the happy and peaceful meadows of heaven. Many a time she has prayed for your safety and wellfair so please say a little prayer for her. Darling, would it be possible, do you think, for you to give me some idea as to when you will get a holiday and for how long? I know not yet, of course, but about when? My dear I do so want to see your Chink face some days, Yes, I do.

Your John, and please

God bless and keep my Evguenia safe.

P.S I do envy your lovely writing paper.

The Wayside.

Oct 27th 1942

Darling. Enclosed find the November cheque plus heating—at the rate of £250 per. ann. Your letter of 23rd (the last one) has rather confused me. When you were here you thought your job would come to an end about Oct 28th or 29th. Then in your last letter but one, you said definately that your job finished on Nov. 9th, now, writing on 23rd Oct, you say that you are free in a week, which would mean on Oct 30th Please when is the BBC work ending? As for your plans, you know my opinion which is that you aught, most emphatically to have a good rest; shattered nerves are no advantage if you take new work. I would like you to come here to Lynton for the rest, and even, perhaps stay over Christmas, then start looking for work. Where from I do not know, perhaps from Evesham[1]—what do you think? But if you will consent to make a real, long stay here, you naturally cannot go on keeping your room meanwhile at Evesham—not money enough for that these days; but doubtless you could get another room when you wanted it. I would be very happy if (only until you are rested) you could park yourself at the Widdens where you would have that electric fire & be well cared for—this would immencely relieve my mind. It has now turned bitter cold & I worry about you. The day may come, oh, you of the hard and ungrateful heart, when there will be no one to worry about you, and then you are going to know the meaning of complete loneliness—yes you are, God help you. Una is well but thinner than ever, probably

---

1. A town a few miles from Stratford.

through rushing about in search of food & so on, though I will say that by comparison with most other places, we in Lynton have scarcely suffered at all—another reason for my hoping that you will come here for your rest. As for riding, we have done scarcely any as the weather has been stormy; today is perfect but I am afraid too cold for me just at the moment. I am anxiously awaiting your news re. plans. I told Mrs Hume about your deafness at times & how straining your job had been, her only comment was: that <u>she</u> could not have stood it for a day, let alone for a night. Everyone is awfully nice. As for your cussed & most unattractive **Bens,**[2] if you come you can go & sit in their laps for all I shall mind and listen to their fulsom praise of a country they have taken <u>very</u> good care never to set foot in, and of a Regime they have taken <u>very</u>, <u>very</u> good care indeed not to live under. But really, my dear, they are not worth you & I quarrelling about. As you know I will not meet them, but beyond this simple fact you need have no anxiety that I shall in any way attempt to interfere with your friendship with them these days. You must choose your own friends—as, indeed, you always have done—and why not?

By the way, what happened about that job at Taunton? It is, of course, rather unfortunate that the **Bens** keep a Gutter-Pig, also that they do not approve of crowns, unless on decapitated heads, but perhaps you will be able to wear a sponge bag over yours, or something, when you are with them. By the way, also, I am told on excellent authority that the Old Devil's baronet brother left him all this money. Oh, these communists & friends of the poor! Well, well, never mind—anyhow the old sister is nice & harmless, you tell me.

Again—God bless & keep you, and may he listen attentively, leaning out of his big, bright cloud, to your Piggie prayer.

Your John

The Wayside.

November 9th 1942.

My darling R.C.P. I got your letter of 4th, and see that you are going to stay where you are for the moment. I enclose a £1 note for postage; postage money is certainly not due yet, but no matter.

---

2. A Lynton family of socialist-leaning, pro-Soviet political views with whom Souline had spend considerable time during her stay in Lynton in 1941.

Christmas. I would much like you to spend it with me. I am not going to grovel to you about this, but you know quite well how I feel. It cannot, I think, be said that I take up very much of your time these days! Now about dates: in view of the <u>awful</u> travelling, I ask you to come 10 days before Christmas, that is on <u>Tuesday December 15th</u>. Nearer Christmas the trains will be too awful. If I can I will meet you with car at Barnstaple, but it would have to coinside with a dentist appointment. I shall leave it to you to get a room—am sure Mrs Widden will take you, if however she cannot, then please come here. I can offer you the little <u>warm</u> room, never cold in it. The upper room has no heating. I expect you would be more comfortable at the Widdens in your old, nice bright & well heated room. Another thing. The nearer we come to Christmas the more uncertain & long delayed the posts will become. I hear that the muddle is going to be awful, as they are taking any sort of Rabbit on to help. Well then, darling, it will be up to you to get in touch with Chief Constable—Major Morris of Exeter as soon as possible so as to get your permission. I would suggest that you do not take a job until after Christmas, then go ahead. Naturally, whether you are in this house or at the Widdens, it is <u>clearly understood that</u> you have Christmas dinner with us here. I am O.K. again and am taking every precaution possible. There has been some rotten wet weather, but now it is lovely again. I was down in Lynmouth[1] this morning & it was perfect— I wished you could have been there with me to see the beauty of the sea & rivers & the lovely colour of the trees on the hills. Sometimes I think that this is the most beautiful spot in all the world: up here the moors, and at Lynmouth the rivers & the sea. The war news is fine; it would seem that the British Lion & the Yankee Eagle are awake & striking hard at long last. Come to me for Christmas, darling.

God bless & keep you now and always. And do avoid dangerous places. Hitler will die with a bad sting in his tail, I am afraid. But my England—your England will never die.

Your John.

---

1. A coastal fishing village just down the hills from Lynton.

The Wayside.

Tel. Lynton 2159
Nov. 25th [1942]

My darling R.C.P. Your letter posted on 23rd came yesterday the 24th—
lord the posts do vary, and are likely to get more and more erratic as
Christmas comes nearer. Darling do please make up your Pig mind not
to take work again until after Christmas so that I may count on your
coming definately on Dec. 15. Start off again fresh after the new year,
early in January, say the first week. Yes, yes darling, so write at once to
Major Morris Chief Constable of Devon.

Chief Constable's Office

Exeter.

and get the usual permission. Also write about your room to Mrs
Widdens if you have not done so already. We—that is to say Una—has
actually managed to get a turkey and a plumb pudding, by saying that
you were coming, so you see you must come if only for the sake of that
turkey! Now do not fail to let me know 1) Where your train will come
from.

2) At which station (Barnstaple Junction—or the station you left from
last time) the train arrives—and

3) At what hour it arrives.

Oh, I knew I had a bit of news. Jeanne Reece[1] escaped from unoccu-
pied France just before the Germans broke the Armistace & swarmed
over the whole poor country. We do not yet know how she managed to
get out, but a long letter from her tells of the appalling conditions under
which she has been living; (if you can call it living!) You shall see
Jeanne's letter when you come. The unhappy Hume household is ser-
vantless and is, says Miss Bosanquet, feeling very old when it comes to
doing every single thing including lighting the kitchen range of a morning. I am sorry for them, the more so as they are being game to the end.
Mrs Widden told me that she is feeling better when I met her the other
day. One of the teachers at The Fares fell down an area, or something,
the other night because she would go out without a torch and God's
black out was very black indeed. Nightingale was with me but had to fly
to the rescue. Bad concussion I believe, nothing worse and not one of
your friends I think. Also a certain poor old man who worked at Bath

---

1. The wife of John Holroyd-Reece.

Hotel, was sent out to deliever a newspaper and instead of delivering the paper he delivered himself to his maker by plunging over something or other down onto the beach beneath—the next morning he was found dead. I think this is the extent of my news. But apropos of news—what fine war news & what particularly fine news from Russia—Courage they most certainly have to an enormous & glorious extent. I do pray that Stalingrad may be relieved & so, it would seem, it will be, though one fears to hope too much.

God bless & keep you and bring you to me on Dec. 15th. And do not immagine that I have hidden chains with which to keep you a prisoner in Lynton, because there are no chains.

Your John

The Wayside

Dec. 8th 1942

My darling. I was so anxious to catch posts with my two express letters to you yesterday in answer to yours of 6th, that I forgot something really important. It is this: I have had a talk with faithful Bentall and he says that it is absolutely necessary that he should not be seen driving through Barnstaple. The most he is legally permitted to do is to drive me to the Imperial Hotel and park his car there. I must make my own way to the dentist, & back to the Hotel for food, as I have had to do before.

This means that he cannot take the car to the station to meet you. But being Bentall, he is going to the station on foot. He will meet your train, be on platform or at entrance, (but probably on platform) and will "escort" you and your luggage back to the Imperial Hotel. If I have got finished with my dentist I shall be waiting for you in the lounge; if I am not quite through with the dentist, you will wait for me in the lounge. Then we will all drive home together. The car will have been left at the hotel.

But, and this is really urgent, it may be raining or snowing or both! The walk from Station to Imperial is long enough for you to get wet through, & then you would the drive home in wet cloths—fatal. Therefore, my dear, you simply must have your waterproof and umbrella handy—waterproof strapped round one of your bags. There is nothing else to be done, nothing. I hope you will not be stubborn about this, because in war time it is foolish to be stubborn and also it is unkind. Well thats that, and you may expect to see Bentall's face & later mine.

Interesting that you have been doing translation for the Ministry of Information. I was sorry to hear about your Russian friend's T.B. She must be very careful of our dreadful English winter, but I suppose she knows this.

God bless & keep you.

Your John

The Wayside.

December 17th 1942.

Darling. (I really cannot imitate your ridiculous and childish: "Dear John" and so I begin Darling.)

Well then, Darling, I have got your letter of the 15th written before leaving for your new job, and I have made a note of your P.O. Box address.

You will very naturally want to know about finances, and as I am most anxious that your mind should be entirely free for your work, I write to let you know where you stand as far as I am concerned. If you will refer to that paper I gave you, upon which I worked everything out, you will understand what I propose to do now, I hope.

You are receiving £3 a week, but all found.

At Mrs Widden's you paid £2.15 a week for room and board. Thus you spent £143 per ann.

Your cash salary now comes to £156. per. ann. but to this there must of course be added the room & board money which I have taken at the old rate of £143 per ann. Thus you are really receiving the equivalent of £244 per ann. (call it £300)

I shall therefore be sending you as from January 1st, monthly payments at the rate of £100 a year, plus £24 a year for heating. Total £124. The heating money should come in as a little extra tip, because your heating will, I imagine, be provided.

I am not going to deduct from the January cheque, the proportion of the last two weeks of December for which you have recieved a payment at the rate of £250 per ann, this because you were not then earning anything and had no work in prospect—you may pocket the difference.

This, I think, covers the financial situation, and I reckon that your cash salary, plus board etc, plus my allowance of £124, will bring your annual resources up to £423. Of this my £124 will be free of income tax and thus you should have very little, if any income tax to pay.

About your circumstances; there are two things that Marjorie Hatten tells me you can let me know, and I you to let me know them at once— if you are very busy a few lines will suffice:

1) Am I right in thinking that you have signed on for the duration of the war? I feel that this may well be so.

2) Are you sleeping in the place where you work, or are you potted out somewhere?

Marjorie says it may be the one or the other, but I am hoping you sleep in the house where you work, especially during the winter weather. It would please me if you would try to get a bedroom where you work, that is if you are given any say in the matter.

Of course I shall want to know how you are getting on generally and with your work in particular. I quite realize that you must not speak of the nature of your work, but you can say whether you are happy with it or not—though perhaps you aught not even to write this. Anyhow say what you think you can as I am naturally anxious about you.

It is as though a dark, thick curtain had been dropped between us, so strange after all these years. But I am glad that you should be doing serious government work for my country which I pray God may one day be your country also. I cannot now be of any use to this dear England of mine, beyond trying to keep up the standard of English literature by giving of my best to my writing, so you must do my war-work for me. It must be an R.C.P-John job!

Lynton news. The other day there was a terrific gale, several children were blown down & had cuts; Johnnie Leath's mother was blown down and fairly badly hurt, but poor old Miss Healy (who should never have ventured out) was blown over & has a broken hip, she is in the Cottage hospital here. The poor little dog frets, one wonders what will happen to him & to her—rather awful. Mrs Widden asked Marjorie Handcock if you were coming here for Christmas about 10 days ago, Marjorie said she had not heard—you might send the Widden a few lines when you get time. Nancy Sparks whom I saw this morning enquired if you were well & asked for your address—I gave her the P.O. Box address, she says she wants to send you a Christmas card.

Myself: I have not ridden since that nasty little go at lung bases, I am supposed to have caught a chill getting my feet wet on that occasion. I

<u>insisted</u> on riding through several gushing fords, fool that I was, but I am not used to taking this sort of extra special care of myself. Nightingale seems not to want to take the responsibility of saying that I may ride again this winter, so bang goes yet one more outlet, however it can't be helped. My eyes are pretty good, but the failiour operation tells on my right eye rather when I work. Seems, though, that another operation would really be too risky thanks to poor Tizzard's hacking about. But don't worry, (what a joke, Pig, because of course you would not worry at all these dark days) still, in case you did, I say <u>don't</u>. I am all right really and can work again, thank God.

Well my Trouble and my Pain and my R.C.P. God bless you & your new work and keep you safe. I send you a heart full of sincere good wishes for your success in what you have undertaken. Four wax candles are burning for you in the church at this moment.

Your John
(Such complete nonsense the way you signed your letter: "Love Evguenia.")

Can't read this three vol novel through, so if many mistakes you must excuse them, please.

<u>Kuss der hand"</u>

I have forgotten one of <u>the</u> most important questions.

Have you given me as your **Next of Kin** and given also this address and my telephone number? <u>Please</u> let me know.

Except for a very short note written the day after Christmas, this is the last letter in the long correspondence with Souline. The weariness and sadness speak for themselves.

The Wayside.

Telephone Lynton 2159
December 20th 1942.

Darling. I was so very glad to get a letter written from your place of work. It took two days to reach me; it was posted in London on 17th and got here on 19th. This may have been due to the Christmas rush, or to the method employed in sending your letters, I don't know, but one will have to judge what happens as time goes on and meanwhile bear in mind that a delay may occur. By now I hope you have had a long letter that I posted early on 17th—about finance, it was. Then on 29th, yesterday, I sent you a couple of pound notes for a Christmas box, by registered post of course, and I hope you get them safely. I am glad that you are comfortable in your surroundings. Are you in a dormitory or have you a bedroom to yourself? Do let me know this; also I hope you will answer the questions in my letter of 17th. What has happened seems like a mad kind of total blackout. On your side you know all there is to know about me & my way of life, and if you still want to know such things then I am glad that it should be so. On my side I know nothing, therefore I think you must tell me all you can, all, that is, that it is permissable to tell me. I cannot believe that I have asked any questions that you aught not to answer. About writing: in view of this complete cut off, I want you to write to me <u>once a week</u> if only one or two lines, and need I say more often if you can find a moment, but once a week for certain—yes please, darling. This is something that you can do for John and I ask you to do it. I am certain that you will soon get the hang of your new work, though it will seem strange just at first, (whatever it may be) But surely the years of severe hospital training should stand you in good stead. I say they will. I am sending you out good and hopeful and loving thoughts every minute of the day. All I ask is that you will take great care of <u>our</u> health. In this respect I don't trust you—indeed I think you the most complete Piggie-**Fool!** Even being an R.C.P. will not protect you from getting wet. I have always been given to understand that to wear **Rubber Boots** <u>and</u> a mac, or at least gaters and a mac, was a mark of the highest distinction, as such things may only be worn by Royal Pigs. And again, I have been told that the carrying of an umbrella is another mark of distinction, the umbrella standing for the Royal Sceptre. Am I wrong? I don't think so. Well, darling, I have really no mere humble human news, except that poor old Miss Heeley is going into Barnstaple Infirmary to have an operation—a pin put in her broken bone. Here we are still having very high winds but not at all cold, thank goodness. The war seems to be going in our favour at last, but the wholesale slaughter of the Jews is too fearful, the more so as one feels helpless to do anything for the poor devils—what a load of sin to have on the souls of those who conceived of this fiendish horror. As for the French who are delivering their Jews over to the Germans, as the papers say they are doing, well—I have no words. Today I read that even those French Jews who fout for France 1914–1918 are being delivered over to torture and death. Also that all Jews who are naturalized French are to be deprived of their naturalization and all civil rights. Bad Jews there certainly are and always have been, but <u>this</u>, Ah, No! I love France, but I cannot excuse her, she has sunk too low. As for French Naturalization, it is not worth the paper it is written on, and I thank God that no one I love got naturalised. If France don't find her soul double quick time, she is going to loose it forever. I keep on spelling naturalisaton with a Z, the result of my fury with France. But why is one surprised? Things were pretty vile when we were all out there. Control the bad Jews, yes, by all means, <u>and</u> punish good & strong, but a woman is a woman and a child is a child, and both should be protected.

Well, darling, (once again) I must stop now that I have let off some steam. Write to your poor Johnnie who is trying to work against odds, though "There is life in the old dog yet." And, all things considered, I am well, nothing in the least worrying to report, but then I am not a Pig-Fool, I take ordinary precautions, & believe me its pays to do so. I shall be thinking of you on Christmas day.

God bless you and help you and keep you safe, for your own sake of course, but also for mine.

Your John

In March of 1943 John was diagnosed with abdominal and colon cancer. On October 7, holding Una's hand, she died. In her will she left everything to Una, who continued Souline's allowance. After the war Souline married a Russian émigré, Victor Makaroff. She died of bowel cancer fifteen years after John. Una died in Rome on September 24, 1963.

Index